"This book presents a comprehensive, interesting, and unique approach to the important area of empathy—an area deserving of more attention. I particularly appreciate its interdisciplinary approach, its emphasis on both individuals and organizations, and the multicultural and international perspectives in the book".

—*Jerry Biberman (University of Scranton, US)*

Organizing through Empathy

Empathy dissolves the boundaries between self and others, and feelings of altruism toward others are activated. This process results in more compassionate and caring contexts, as well as helping others in times of suffering. This book provides evidence from neuroscience and quantum physics that it is empathy that connects humanity, and that this awareness can create a more just society. It extends interest in values-based management, exploring the intellectual, physical, ecological, spiritual, and aesthetic well-being of organizations and society rather than the more common management principles of maximizing profit and efficiency.

This book challenges the existing paradigm of capitalism by providing scientific evidence and empirical data that empathy is the most important organizing mechanism. The book is unique in that it provides a comprehensive review of the transformational qualities of empathy in personal, organizational, and local contexts. Integrating an understanding based upon scientific studies of why the fields of positive psychology and organizational scholarship are important, it examines the evidence from neuroscience and presents leading-edge studies from quantum physics with implications for the organizational field. Together the chapters in this book attempt to demonstrate how empathy helps in the reduction of human suffering and the creation of a more just society.

Kathryn Pavlovich is Associate Professor at the University of Waikato, New Zealand. She has a special interest in conscious capitalism, enterprise, self-leadership, ethics, and spirituality. She has authored more than 80 internationally refereed publications, including articles in LONG RANGE PLANNING, JOURNAL OF BUSINESS ETHICS, TOURISM MANAGEMENT, and BEST PAPER PROCEEDINGS OF THE ACADEMY OF MANAGEMENT. Kathryn is currently on the five-year chair track of the U.S.-based Academy of Management's Spirituality and Religion Division.

Keiko Krahnke is Associate Professor at the University of Northern Colorado. She has research interest in empathy, systems thinking, ethics, and spirituality. Keiko's recent publications include an article in JOURNAL OF BUSINESS ETHICS, and BEST PAPER PROCEEDINGS OF THE ACADEMY OF MANAGEMENT. She has served as Chair of Management, Spirituality and Religion at the Academy of Management.

Routledge Studies in Management, Organizations, and Society

This series presents innovative work grounded in new realities, addressing issues crucial to an understanding of the contemporary world. This is the world of organized societies, where boundaries between formal and informal, public and private, local and global organizations have been displaced or have vanished, along with other nineteenth-century dichotomies and oppositions. Management, apart from becoming a specialized profession for a growing number of people, is an everyday activity for most members of modern societies.

Similarly, at the level of enquiry, culture and technology, and literature and economics, can no longer be conceived as isolated intellectual fields; conventional canons and established mainstreams are contested. Management, Organization and Society addresses these contemporary dynamics of transformation in a manner that transcends disciplinary boundaries, with books that will appeal to researchers, students, and practitioners alike.

Other titles in this series:

Organizing Through Empathy

Edited by Kathryn Pavlovich and
Keiko Krahnke

Routledge
Taylor & Francis Group

NEW YORK AND LONDON

First published 2014
by Routledge
711 Third Avenue, New York, NY 10017

Simultaneously published in the UK
by Routledge
2 Park Square, Milton Park, Abingdon, Oxon OX14 4RN

First issued in paperback 2018

*Routledge is an imprint of the Taylor & Francis Group,
an informa business*

Library of Congress Cataloging-in-Publication Data

Organizing through empathy / edited by Kathryn Pavlovich and Keiko Krahnke.
    pages cm. — (Routledge studies in management, organizations, and society ; 25)
    Includes bibliographical references and index.
    1. Organizational effectiveness.   2. Empathy.   3. Interpersonal
relations.   4. Leadership—Moral and ethical aspects.   I. Pavlovich,
Kathryn.   II. Krahnke, Keiko.
    HD58.9.O746   2013
    658.4'094—dc23
    2013005593

ISBN 13: 978-1-138-33992-7 (pbk)
ISBN 13: 978-0-415-84411-6 (hbk)

Typeset in Sabon
by Apex CoVantage, LLC

Contents

PART II B
Applied Approaches to Empathy: Decision Making

PART II C
Applied Approaches to Empathy: Contextual

Figures

Table

Introduction

Kathryn Pavlovich and Keiko Krahnke

The biggest deficit that we have in our society and in the world right now is an *empathy* deficit. We are in great need of people being able to stand in somebody else's shoes and see the world through their eyes. The great power of books is the capacity to take you out of yourself and put you somewhere else. And to suddenly say, "Oh, this is what it's like"—maybe not perfectly—but it gives you some glimpse of "This is what it is like to be a woman", or "This is what it is like to be an African-American". Or, "This is what it is like to be impoverished in India". Or "This is what it's like to be in the midst of war". So much of what binds us together in society and allows it to function effectively depends on it [empathy]. And so much of what is wrong with how we interact, and so much of what is wrong with our politics has to do with the absence of that quality of empathy"

Barack Obama, 2010

United States President Barack Obama believes that empathy has the power to change our social structures, and he speaks of the role that books can play in widening people's awareness of others. Thus, this book endeavors to bring different perspectives on empathy together to challenge the way we view the world and how we currently structure society. Empathy is widely recognized as being one of the greatest influences in building social interaction through its ability to motivate individuals to cooperate, to share resources, and to help others (de Vignemont & Singer, 2006; Van Lange, 2008). Empathy is the capacity to experience and relate to the thoughts, emotions, and experience of others and involves a heightened awareness of others. Definitions of empathy are consistent in that they all refer to the sensing and sharing of feelings of one person by another. For instance, Lamm, Batson, and Decety (2007, p. 42) define empathy in three parts, as "(1) an affective response to another person, which some believe entails sharing that person's emotional state; (2) a cognitive capacity to take the perspective of the other person; and (3) some monitoring mechanisms that keep track of the origins (self vs. other) of the expected feelings". Similarly, Oberman and Ramachandran (2007, p. 316) define empathy as "a function of one individual's experiencing the same feelings as another individual through an appreciation of similarity". Both definitions note the significance of not only appreciating the experience of another, but of also feeling that experience. Thus, empathy is a passive acknowledgment and observation of the experience of another involving both affective and cognitive states. This passivity distinguishes empathy from compassion. For example, Lilius et al. (2008, p. 195) claim that compassion is empathy plus acting in a manner intended to ease suffering. The significance of the more passive empathy as an organizing mechanism will be returned to throughout this book.

EMPATHY ENHANCES PROSOCIAL BEHAVIOR

Enhanced awareness of empathy means that one is more willing to see other perspectives and to collaboratively engage with others. In more advanced stages of empathic development, individuals see themselves as part of an interconnected whole rather than as separate. This has significant implications for global capitalism as the obvious tension between individualism and self-interest becomes incompatible with the sense of oneness that is experienced through high levels of empathy. Empathy therefore allows one to see the imprecise distinction between self and other as boundaries become blurred between actions and outcomes. Nowhere is the absence of empathy more evident than in the fragile state of our environmental ecosystem where economic agendas are prioritized over ecology as habitats are destroyed and species become extinct, with examples on every continent. For instance, in India, the lion-tailed macaque continues to be threatened because of the increasing encroachment of tea plantations in the Western Ghats (Daniels, 2003); in China, the giant panda, golden monkey, and snow leopard are on the endangered species list as a result of habitat depletion; in Indonesia, orangutans face abuse, torture, and extinction driven by a palm oil industry; in Europe, bears and wolves roam villages and kill livestock as they search for a dwindling food supply; and in the Americas, cranes, bats, and sea turtles are under threat. These are just a few examples that illustrate a low awareness of empathy toward other species. This, of course, also applies to how we interact with each other as human beings, with evidence of poverty, disease, and warfare throughout the world. Our own self-interest is usually prioritized over engagement toward others in need.

Yet, these separatist notions of self are being challenged in unlikely quarters, one of which is climate change. The last decade has seen an unprecedented spate of powerful earthquakes, tsunamis, and volcanic activity (Noy, 2011), along with increases in both floods and droughts. Stories of global response efforts, community collaboration, and individual resilience abound as individuals, communities, and nations response to these crises. While we acknowledge that these altruistic actions are often short term, and communities petition that they are then neglected and forgotten over time, the initial condition elicits a strong response of prosocial action that stays strong and enduring within the communities. This example illustrates how empathy is distinct from sympathy. Sympathy is the feeling of another's pain and can result in short-term action as the affective feeling recedes (as illustrated above; Trout, 2009). However, empathy is also the capacity to grasp and understand the conditions of others (Gallese, 2007). Thus, empathy involves both affective and cognitive states and has more durable outcomes as the experience becomes our own. As the contributors in this book will show, both cognitive and affective aspects of empathy are necessary. With only cognitive aspects, the ability to feel another's experience is limited. This is apparent in a recent study by Jack et al. (2012) who confirm that when the analytical network is engaged, our ability to appreciate the human cost of our action is repressed. This study shows for the first time that we have an in-built neural constraint on our ability to be both empathic and analytical at the same time. On the other hand, when only the affective state is activated, empathy can become short-term sympathy, emotional contagion, and/or also result in excessive emotional involvement that may deplete the empathizer's own self-care. Similarly, Decety and Michalska's (2010) study found that the basis for shared meanings and understandings began first with an emotional connection, but the cognitive connection was also necessary for empathy to emerge. We therefore argue that in order to develop a sustainable and robust global environment, we not only need to develop mature levels of empathy, but we also need a deepened awareness of factors that constitute empathy to more broadly understand the effects of our actions on others—economically, environmentally, socially, and spiritually.

EMPATHY AS SHARED EXPERIENCE

We argue that empathy is more than an enabler of prosocial behavior as prosocial behavior retains the focus on self in relation to others. We argue that empathy is a mechanism for creating a shared existence and thus moves the focus from I to WE. This is why Trout (2009) describes empathy as ecocentric rather than egocentric. We agree that empathy is a precondition to prosocial behavior, but recent discoveries in neuroscience suggest that empathy does a lot more. Empathy commits us to one another through shared connection. The discovery of mirror neurons through functional magnetic imaging (fMRI) has opened a window into witnessing the shared brain circuits and coding that stem from shared experiences with others (Keysers & Fadiga, 2008). Mirror neurons suggest that the observer has the ability to acknowledge the current state and experience of the other individual (Oberman & Ramachandran, 2007), confirming that perception and action share a common code and are "two sides of the same coin" (Iacoboni, 2009). Iacoboni continues that mirror neurons embody the interdependence of ourselves and others and thus act as the glue that connects us in a mutual dependency. Empathy is the shared neural circuit that creates "the sense of similarity between the feelings one experiences and those expressed by another" (Decety & Lamm, 2006, p. 1146).

What this means is that we experience another through an appreciation of similarity, and thus the "reciprocity of our actions constitute meaningful bonds within an intersubjective shared space" (Gallese, 2007, p. 147). Like Iacoboni (2009) above, Gallese (2007, p. 148) confirms that the same neural substrates are both executed and perceived. These mirror neurons, often called empathy neurons, are "a common underlying function mechanism . . . [that] mediates our capacity to share the meaning of actions, intentions, feelings and emotions with others". Trout (2009) reiterates that the discovery of these mirror neurons confirms the role of empathy in acting as a bridge in connecting us to one another. He emphasizes that this is not a process of dissolving boundaries but of bridging boundaries to enhance shared meanings and understandings.

EMPATHY AS AN ORGANIZING MECHANISM

Thus, we claim that empathy is more than a guide for prosocial behavior. It forms a shared experience and is the glue of social cohesion that organizes a coherent society. Nascent science suggests that consciousness is not created by the brain, but it is fundamental in nature. Quantum physicists claim that the basic forces of nature are different ripples on the string of existence (Capra, 1999), and it is through being conscious that we experience this unified sense of knowing. We argue that empathy enhances that access to a unified existence, and many of our contributors have made mention of such a state. Heaton and Travis call it "The natural state of things when the world is perceived in higher states of consciousness"; Berry and Joannidès discuss enlightenment; Atkins notes shared experience as transcendence; and Gano-Overway draws upon the African ethic of humanness (*Ubuntu*), where "my humanity is inextricably bound up in yours". Such a perspective would suggest that we are hardwired for a higher form of "transcendental empathy" that can make us better than we currently are. Transcendental empathy involves bridging across, through, and beyond, and hence extends beyond the limits of normal experience.

We therefore argue that empathy is part of our hardwiring and that we have lost sight of this collaborative connection in our search for self-interest. Yet, not only does having empathy allow us to connect with others in more meaningful ways, but developing empathy assists in creating new neural pathways for enhanced brain plasticity that allow us to better adapt and respond to new situations. Similarly, Gallese (2007, p. 147) claims that "it is through a shared experience of the world, granted by the presence of other individuals, that objectivity can be constituted". Indeed, the notion of collective sharing remains imbued within many cultures. For example, in Polynesian communities there is an expectation to help others in need; in Japan the concept of *omoiyari* internalizes a powerful feeling of social exclusion and shame for not assisting others (Trout, 2009). Being hardwired to help others is also evident in the significant rise in the numbers of social entrepreneurs. In a study on conscious entrepreneurship, Pavlovich (2012) found that those who worked in economically needy communities stated that they were profoundly "touched" by those they worked with. Kerry Hilton, Freeset India, employs over 200 women in the textile industry, and the criteria for employment is the need to leave prostitution rather than the more conventional skill-based requirement (http://freesetglobal.com/). Kerry noted that, "The women teach me things too. I didn't know this when I came here, but I discovered that the rich need the poor as much as the poor need the rich". Anne Godfrey (Rose Circles) also works with many impoverished women in India who are in situations without hope. Using offcuts of fabric from large textile manufacturers, Anne helps the women, with no technical skills, to make quilts and other products that can be sold in the West (www.rosecircles.com). She stated that "pleasure seeking activities take you away from your heart. I now feel I have done something useful in my life". A final example is Bev Missing in South Africa. Her enterprise, Rain Africa, is a handmade-labor intensive bath and body range intended to provide employment in a region with high poverty, high unemployment, and high crime (http://rainafrica.com/ethics/). Bev says that "our accountants want economies of scale. But we won't sacrifice our handmade touch because that's what the company is about—education and job creation". These case studies illustrate how empathy touches us and through being hardwired, that touch has the power to change us. These examples confirm the findings in Boyatzis et al.'s (2012) recent study: That resonant memories (positive interpersonal attunement) result in a broader, "out of the box" thinking for social change rather than dissonant memories that cognitively narrowed attention capacity.

In this book we therefore argue that heightened levels of empathy are important for finding new ways of being. Empathy allows us to embrace meaning in our world, to experience being in relationship with others. This awareness is a movement from I to WE and how we form our coexistence based upon our awareness of interdependence: ecocentric rather than egocentric. Such studies highlight the importance of finding new theories that more effectively map out the territory for the development and application of empathy. Thus, we suggest that empathy includes emotional, cognitive, and transcendental qualities. It is the latter that we argue has the particular possibility to act as a passive informal organizing mechanism in changing society.

OVERVIEW OF THE BOOK

Our contributors are experts in the field of empathy, and thus we bring together a rich variety of perspectives that contribute to our understanding of the roles, conditions, and functions of empathy. Again, we highlight the importance of empathy as a passive organizing mechanism that has the power to reengineer our social structures. In this book, the presented views touch on a range of developmental practices that include different contemplative practices so as to apply empathy in organizations through leadership, decision-making techniques, and applications within different contexts.

CONTEMPLATIVE APPROACHES

Part I explores the development of empathy at an individual level through inner technologies. This section contributes by exploring contemplative approaches to developing transcendental empathy. Despite the field being in its infancy, neuroscience research has been paramount in demonstrating the power of contemplative practices in increasing empathy through changes in brain patterns. These studies are broad ranging and involve many different practices, evident in just a few examples noted below. Lazar et al.'s (2005) seminal work on mindfulness found that regular practice increases activity in the right ventro-lateral prefrontal cortex, which dampens the amygdala response (where anger is processed) and thus facilitates the development of empathy. Later studies continue to confirm the relationship between regular mindfulness practice and stress reduction (e.g., Baer, Carmody, & Hunsinger, 2012; Hölzel et al., 2011). Enhanced states of mindfulness increases cortical thickness in the right insula region where empathy resides, while also increasing the structural thickness in the middle prefrontal and right insular areas for increased brain plasticity. A further example involves Tibetan Buddhist mind training (lojong) that utilizes meditative techniques to enhance empathy and well-being towards others. This study involves cognitive-based compassion training and showed that after eight weeks of meditation training, program participants were significantly more likely to have improved "empathic accuracy" than the control subjects through increased activity in specific parts of their brains (the inferior frontal gyrus and the dorsomedialprefontal cortex) that are associated with empathy (Mascaro, Rilling, Tenzin Negi, & Raison, 2012). Finally, a rare study on yoga confirms venerable Vedic traditions through demonstrating a strong association between mindful yoga practice and improved well-being (Carmody & Baer, 2008). Surprisingly, this study found that yoga was more effective at stress reduction than meditation and mindfulness practices as self-reported by the participants.

Our book includes three chapters that contribute to this understanding by focusing on different aspects of contemplative practice that impact on our understanding of how empathy is developed. These contributions demonstrate that empathy can be consciously developed, and support calls for more effort, attention, and recognition in education systems to enhance the development of such human capacity soft skills.

We thus begin with Dennis Heaton and Fred Travis's work at the Center for Brain, Consciousness and Cognition, Maharishi University of Management. Their chapter describes how engagement with Transcendental Meditation can result in higher experiences of transcendence and self-actualization. This "harmonizing [of] the individual with the coordinating intelligence of the natural world" (p. 36) enhances feelings and behaviors of empathy and is associated with more integrated functioning in the brain, higher levels of moral development, and positive psychological health. In this research, Heaton and Travis argue that to nurture empathy in individuals, organizations, our global society, management education, and development should incorporate practices for systematically cultivating transcendental experiences.

Our second contributors, Berry and Joannidès in chapter 2, follow this contemplative theme through focusing on four key conditions for enhancing empathy that can be attained through cultivating a spiritual orientation. They integrate two theoretical constructs, one from neurobiology and one from spirituality to develop these conditions of interpersonal attunement, intrapersonal attunement, relational safety, and shared narratives. These four conditions provide an evolutionary path of personal, community, and planetary growth that involve interpersonal attunement for developing a sacred relationship with others, intrapersonal attunement to facilitate individual inner alignment, development of relational safety that frees us from fear and thus opens us to that which is sacred, and finally an acceptance of the shared narratives that make us an interdependent global community. Berry and Joannidès present a framework that integrates these four conditions with spiritual and religious traditions. Similar to the previous chapter, they argue that empathy plays a critical role in developing a more enlightened society.

The final chapter in this sequence (chapter 3), by Paul Atkins, focuses on how mindfulness training can enhance empathy within organizations. Atkins follows Decety and Lamm's definition of empathy as "the ability to experience and understand what others feel *without confusion between oneself and others*" (italics added; 2006, p. 1146). Thus he emphasizes that excessive identification with another who is suffering can lead to personal distress and avoidance rather than empathic concern. This is particularly a problem for roles involving helping or other forms of emotional labor. There is a potential paradox as empathy appears to be motivated by a felt sense of connection between self and other, and yet it can overwhelm the empathizer. This again highlights the gap in our knowledge related to cognitive and affective aspects of empathy and poses the question of whether other conditions are also involved. As noted earlier, Jack et al. (2012) found that when only the cognitive network is activated, low levels of empathy were witnessed in the form of limited understanding of the broader effect of actions. Thus, Atkins asks, how can we understand the dynamics of self-other differentiation in a way that allows us to retain our sense of balance and harmony within our broader environment? In this chapter he therefore presents a contextual, behavioral approach that explains why mindfulness programs work to improve this self-other differentiation. We can see self and other either in terms of (a) conceptualizations, (b) a flow of experiences, or (c) as awareness itself. Atkins suggests that responding to conceptualizations of self and other can be helpful but can also impair empathy. Self-other differentiation at the level of content generally creates separation and judgment rather than empathy. Through responding at the level of present-moment experience, the essence of responding to others is experienced, but it is here that differentiation of self and other is essential for mature, sustainable empathy. At the level of awareness itself, a stable sense of self beyond threat can be contacted in such a way to support empathy. Furthermore, in rare instances one can experience a sense of shared awareness that transcends difference. Like the studies noted earlier, mindfulness training appears to support the development of all three senses of perspective taking in a way that can enhance empathy.

These studies contribute to the literature on empathy by offering three contrasting approaches to contemplative practices. However, they connect in that they extend understandings of how training and education within these practices develop empathy at an individual level. Through contemplative practice, empathy is developed through systematic and multimodal attentional capacity that thereby supports wider attentional scanning that assists in the development of a more conscious meta-awareness (Schwartz, Stapp, & Beauregard, 2005).To conclude this section (chapter 4), these contemplative approaches are woven together in "A Conceptione . . .", by Joanna Beth Tweedy, in a short poem that explores the inner dimensions of empathy as the echo of celestial silence.

APPLIED EMPATHY

Part II of the book shifts from developmental approaches that focus on contemplative practice to more applied studies that involve different organizational environments. These are developed around leadership, decision making, and contextual issues and involve empirical data through case studies and conceptual approaches.

Empathy and Leadership

The first section relates to empathy and leadership. Chapter 5, by Veronika Kisfalvi, examines how personal histories impact on leadership, linking emotional intelligence and empathy. Her work departs from current research on emotional intelligence that focuses on the awareness and management of emotions in the present. Kisfalvi instead presents a psychodynamic approach that explores the potential impact of past experience on present behavior. This approach provides a way to understand emotional reactions and capacities in the here and now by appreciating the personal history in which they are rooted. Like others previously, Kisfalvi states that "cognitive understanding is not sufficient; emotional insights that take root in the body seem to be necessary in order to change such deep-seated habitual responses and to take advantage of the brain's plasticity" (Doidge, 2007). The psychodynamic framework she presents provides a useful tool for developing self-awareness, which is closely linked to the empathetic understanding of others. Using an empirical example, she goes on to explore the role of personal history in shaping leaders' emotional lives (experienced in the body), and their capacity for developing competencies such as empathy. Finally, she presents implications of this framework for developing such empathic competencies in leaders and managers. Although using a psychological lens to explore empathy, Kisfalvi has similarities with the preceding chapters in that she concludes that being self-aware and fully present is a central characteristic of empathic leadership.

The second discussion on leadership (chapter 6) is contributed by Samuel Natale, Anthony Libertella, and Coroline Doran. They suggest that empathic leaders need to foster a holistic paradigm that embraces the thinking and feeling of people through engagement that is intrapsychic, interpersonal, and encompasses a moral imperative. The authors explore the practical benefits of integrating empathy into leadership and organizations with the objective of illustrating how theoretical concepts can be realistically applied. The use of comparative case studies illustrates how empathic concepts generate positive impacts on organizational achievements. The authors anticipate that current and nascent leaders will use the lessons from the cases to enhance their own leadership development. These lessons include having a "third ear" to listen and sense the nonobvious; to acknowledge that financial returns will occur when empathic process is in place; that the morality of the organization plays an important role in its success; and finally, that empathy is more likely to be found in organic rather than dominating control structures.

While both chapters in this section examine the dynamics of leadership, they differ in their approaches. Kisfalvi presents a conceptual approach discussing the impact of an overactive affective state on leadership, whereas Natale, Liberetta, and Coran provide examples of the practical benefits of empathy for effective leadership.

Empathy and Decision Making

The second set of applied chapters relate to empathy and decision making. In chapter 7, Emmanuelle Kleinlogel and Joerg Dietz review the role of empathy in ethical decision making with examples of when empathy facilitates and when it undermines decision making. On one hand, they propose that through altruism and moral virtue using the empathy-altruism hypothesis, positive psychology, and positive organizational scholarship, empathy fosters the ethicality of decision-making processes. On the other hand, they propose that empathy can lead to poor decisions via biased decision-making processes, and they identify personal distress, favoritism, malicious empathy, and manipulation as factors that may characterize the mindless use of empathy. The development of this model is supported through a number of case examples. Kleinlogel and Dietz highlight that mindless approaches may satisfy immediate needs, but there is no consideration of long-term outcomes or consequences within a broader environment. They conclude by discussing the implications of necessitating mindful and maturely developed empathy in decision-making processes.

Larry Pate and Traci Shoblom (in chapter 8) also mention negative aspects of empathy in decision making through what they call "primitive empathy". They suggest that primitive empathy is more akin to emotional contagion, where one only connects with the emotion of the other without cognitively processing an understanding behind the emotion. Pate and Shoblom therefore present a model for developing the cognitive and emotional roots of empathy, and they suggest that the ACES Decision-Making Technique—a practical, proven tool for reframing difficult situations—can be used effectively to increase the conscientiousness and self-aware feelings of empathy. ACES stands for Assumptions, Criteria, Evoked Set and Strategy. In this chapter, they therefore argue that the individual's level of self-awareness both enables and inhibits feelings of empathy about the plight of another. Additionally, the assumptions an individual makes will influence feelings of emotional connection or indifference toward a person in distress. The ACES Decision-Making Technique enables individuals to shift their thinking from indifference to empathic. Their model includes processes for challenging assumptions through (A), clarifying values and priorities (C), identifying the solutions being considered, and (E) identifying a list of action items necessary for making an informed decision.

Both these chapters remind us that the qualities and dimensions of empathy remain underexamined, and the authors identify in different ways how immature aspects of emotion can be used in negative ways. They highlight the importance of both cognitive and affective states for the development and application of a more mature form of empathy, one that we call transcendental empathy. The contributions from these two chapters illustrate different ways that empathy can be developed for more coherent and effective decision-making outcomes within organizations.

Empathy in Context

This final selection of chapters explores empathy within two different contexts: medicine and sports. Empathy plays an important role in the medical profession, and there is much evidence suggesting that patient healing is greatly enhanced in an empathic environment (e.g., Buckman, Tulsky, & Rodin, 2011; Cox, 2011; Hojat et al., 2011). To extend this, Don Munro, David Powis, and Miles Bore in chapter 9 present a model for predicting empathy in medical students. They note that despite the intuitive appeal of emotional intelligence, there is insufficient evidence to displace empathy as the primary measure of ability to be sensitive to patient needs. Thus, they suggest that the selection of students to professional courses would be assisted through being able to identify those who have the capacity to respond empathically to patients, families, and others. This chapter contributes to this understanding by reviewing important issues concerning empathy in medicine, including the conditions that foster it and how to predict it in medical students and medical professionals. The authors review research on methods to measure those aspects of personality that have been found to be related to caring attitudes and behaviors. A particular issue that is raised is whether it is better to try to identify and select those likely to show a high degree of empathy, or to identify and reject applicants who have characteristics that are antagonistic to empathy. A tentative model is proposed that takes account of factors such as emotional stability, conscientiousness, and self-control, which tend to support the capacity for empathic behaviors in professional people, and some factors such as narcissism that may inhibit them. They conclude that their model helps identify those with low levels of empathy that may assist in the deselection of medical students rather than aiming to only select those who score highly.

The final chapter in this applied contextual approach to empathy relates to sport environments. In chapter 10, Lori Gano-Overway examines how sport environments can develop empathy in young people. She suggests that coaches play a key role in helping young people develop. However, not only is this development with physical prowess, but also life skills for personal growth and empowerment as well as learning how to live compassionately and constructively within their communities. She integrates the African ethic of *Ubuntu* in the sport environment to illustrate the development of empathy. Tutu (1999, p. 31) explains *Ubuntu* as, "my humanity is caught up, is inextricably bound up, in yours. We belong in a bundle of life. . . . I am human because I belong, I participate, and I share". Noted by Gano-Overway, *Ubuntu* represents not only a sense of communalism in which people share a way of life but also a notion that one achieves humanness and sense of self through the positive interactions with others in the community: in other words, being relational (Metz & Gaie, 2010). This sense of oneness is not dissimilar to that discussed in Part I of this book in the application of contemplative practices to achieve such a feeling of harmony and oneness. Gano-Overway develops a team-based approach for developing young people in sport based on *Ubuntu* by developing a caring community, building team-based solidarity and harmony, promoting inclusion and acceptance, and emphasizing consensus and community-based decision making.

Concluding this section of applied approaches to empathy, Joanna Beth Tweedy in chapter 11 weaves her poem . . . *ad floridam*. She ties together the threads of Part II illustrating how each of these chapters contribute to "being every part of the whole".

A SYSTEM APPROACH

This book concludes with a "big picture" perspective by Peter Senge and Keiko Krahnke (chapter 12) who explore the future role of empathy in creating social and systemic change. As noted at the beginning of the book, we seek to explore alternative paths of social organizing, and we argue that empathy is the key condition for prosocial behavior and for connecting at a nonphysical level. In this chapter, Senge and Krahnke propose empathy beyond the cognitive and affective domains in interpersonal settings. They call this "transcendent empathy", which is the ability to see the larger system. As we face complex challenges, the ability to recognize the interconnectedness and interdependencies in human organizations and society is critical. We live in a web of interdependence, and failing to recognize this often brings negative consequences from otherwise well-intentioned interventions. The term "leader" originates in the root, "leith", which means to step across the threshold or to have the courage to step ahead. In this transformative era, we are at a threshold. Crossing the threshold, every decision we make has consequences, and cultivating transcendent empathy could make all the difference in finding the wisdom to shape a future of well-being for the whole. As examples of transcendent empathy, the following notions are discussed in this chapter: empathy as recognizing that we cocreate the world, empathy as biosphere consciousness, empathy as the ability to see connections and complexities, and empathy as culture. The chapter concludes by discussing ways to cultivate transcendent empathy.

In concluding our introduction, this interdisciplinary selection of chapter contributions is intended to extend our understanding of the power of empathy to create a paradigm shift. We argue that in developing and cultivating empathy, we have the ability to change our social structures through a deeper awareness of how our actions affect each other. Empathy connects us globally at the physical, cognitive, affective, and systems levels. These chapters contribute to the development of transcendent empathy for creating and deepening our global awareness of each other.

> Power comes not from the barrel of a gun, but from one's awareness of his or her own cultural strength and the unlimited capacity to empathize with, feel for, care, and love one's brothers and sisters.
>
> Addison Gayle (n.d).

REFERENCES

Baer, R., Carmody, J., & Hunsinger, M. (2012). Weekly change in mindfulness and perceived stress in a mindfulness-based stress reduction program. *Journal of Clinical Psychology, 68*(7), 755–765.

Boyatzis, R., Passarelli, A., Koenig, K., Lowe, M., Mathew, B., Stoller, J., & Phillips, M. (2012). Examination of the neural substrates activated in memories of experiences with resonant and dissonant leaders. *The Leadership Quarterly, 23,* 259–272.

Buckman, R., Tulsky, J., & Rodin, G. (2011). Empathic responses in clinical practice: Intuition or tuition? *Canadian Medical Association Journal, 183*(5), 569–571.

Capra, F. (1999). *The tao of physics: An exploration of the parallels between modern physics and Eastern mysticism* (4th ed.). Boston: Shambhala.

Carmody, J., & Baer, R. (2008). Relationships between mindfulness practice and levels of mindfulness, medical and psychological symptoms and well-being in a mindfulness-based stress reduction program. *Journal of Behavioral Medicine, 31*(1), 23–33. doi: 10.1007/s10865–007–9130–7

Cox, J. (2011). Empathy, identity and engagement in person-centred medicine: The sociocultural context. *Journal of Evaluation in Clinical Practice, 17*(2), 350–353.

Daniels, R. (2003). Impact of tea cultivation on anurans in the Western Ghats. *Current Science, 85*(10), retrieved from http://www.iisc.ernet.in/currsci/nov252003/1415.pdf

de Vignemont, F., & Singer, T. (2006). The empathic brain: How, when and why? *Trends in Cognitive Sciences, 10*(10), pp. 435–441.

Decety, J., & Lamm, C. (2006). Human empathy through the lens of social neuroscience. *The Scientific World Journal, 6,* 1146–1163.

Decety, J., & Michalska, K.J. (2010). Neurodevelopmental changes in the circuits underlying empathy and sympathy from childhood to adulthood. *Developmental Science, 13*(6), 886–899.

Doidge, N. (2007).*The brain that changes itself.* NY: Penguin/Viking.

Gallese, V. (2007). Commentary on Toward a neuroscience of empathy: Integrating affective and cognitive perspectives. *Neuropsychoanalysis, 9*(1), 146–151.

Gaye, A. (n.d.). Retrieved from http://www.searchquotes.com/quotation/Power_comes_not_from_the_barrel_of_a_gun,_but_from_one's_awareness_of_his_or_her_own_cultural_streng/21398/

Goleman, D., Boyatzis, R., & McKee, A. (2002). *Primal leadership: Realizing the power of emotional intelligence.* Boston: Harvard University Press.

Hojat, M., Louis, D., Markham, F., Wender, R., Rabinowitz, C., & Gonnella, J. (2011). Physicians' empathy and clinical outcomes for diabetic patients. *Academic Medicine, 86*(3), 359–364.

Hölzel, B. S., Lazar, T., Gard, Z., Schuman-Olivier, D., Vago, D. & Ulrich, O. (2011). How does mindfulness meditation work? Proposing mechanisms of action from a conceptual and neural perspective. *Perspectives on Psychological Science 6*(6), 537–559.

Iacoboni, M. (2009). *Mirroring people: The science of empathy and how we connect with others.* NY: Picador.

Jack, A.I., Dawson, A., Begany, K., Leckie, R., Barry, K., Ciccia, K., & Snyder, A. (2012). fMRI reveals reciprocal inhibition between social and physical cognitive domains, NeuroImagehttp://dx.doi.org/10.1016/j.neuroimage.2012.10

Keysers, C., & Fadiga, L. (2008). The mirror neuron system: New frontiers. *Social Neuroscience, 3*(3–4), 193–198.

Lamm, C., Batson, C.D., & Decety, J. (2007). The neural substrate of human empathy: Effects of perspective taking and cognitive appraisal. *Journal of Cognitive Neuroscience, 19*(1), 42–58.

Lazar, S., Kerr, C., Wasserman, R., Gray, J., Greve, D., & Treadway, M. (2005). Meditation experience is associated with increased cortical thickness. *NeuroReport, 16*(17), 1893–1897.

Lilius, J., Worline, M., Dutton, J., Kanov, J., Frost, P., & Maitlis, S. (2008). Contours of compassion at work. *Journal of Organizational Behavior, 29*(2), 193–218.

Mascaro, J.S., Rilling, J.K., Tenzin Negi, L., & Raison, C.L. (2012). Compassion meditation enhances empathic accuracy and related neural activity. *Social

Cognitive and Affective Neuroscience, online from September 29, doi:10.1093/scan/nss095

Metz, T., & Gaie, J.B.R. (2010). The African ethic of *Ubuntu*/Botho: Implications for research on morality. *Journal of Moral Education, 39*, 273–290.

Noy, I. (2011).The macroeconomic aftermath of the earthquake/tsunami in Japan. *Econbrowser, March 15*. Retrieved from http://www.econbrowser.com/archives/2011/03/guest_contribut_8.html

Obama, B. (2010). *Empathy and literacy speech*. Retrieved from http://www.you tube.com/watch?v=LGHbbJ5xz3g

Oberman, L., & Ramachandran, V. (2007). The simulating social mind: The role of the mirror neuron system and simulation in the social and communicative deficits of autism spectrum disorders. *Psychological Bulletin, 133*(2), 310–327.

Pavlovich, K. (2012). Faith, hope and care: Integrity and poverty alleviation through enterprise. In A. Wolfgang & A. Stachowicz-Stanusch (Eds.), *Business integrity in practice—Insights from international case studies* (pp. 79–84). NY: Business Expert Press, in the first PRME Book Collection.

Schwartz, J., Stapp, H., & Beauregard, M. (2005). Quantum physics in neuroscience and psychology: A neurophysical model of mind-brain interaction. *Philosophical Transactions of the Royal Society, 360*(1458), 1309–1327.

Trout, J. (2009).*Why empathy matters*. NY: Penguin.

Tutu, D.M. (1999). *No future without forgiveness*. NY: Doubleday.

Van Lange, P. (2008). Does empathy trigger only altruistic motivation? How about selflessness or justice? *Emotion, 8*(6), 766–774.

Part I

Contemplative Approaches to Empathy

1 Consciousness, Empathy, and the Brain

Dennis P. Heaton and Fred Travis

TRANSCENDENCE AND EMPATHY

Empathy is the sensitivity to the feelings, thoughts, and experience of another. It entails an object—the other—and also a subject or knower who is acting with empathy. As the brain and consciousness of the subject changes, so also the expression of empathy will change. Thus growth of empathy and development of consciousness go hand in hand.

Models in developmental psychology depict how higher growth of the subject transforms the frame through which one constructs meaning and relates to other people. Research on ego development (Loevinger, 1976) has observed that as one matures psychologically, one becomes better able to appreciate multiple viewpoints and interact collaboratively in social situations. Although the term "ego development" might seem to suggest an attachment to one's individual identity, observers of advanced stages of development refer to transcending a conceptually constructed self-identity and to gain a more unitive sense of oneself and one's connection to others and the cosmos (Cook-Greuter, 2000; Heaton, 2011).

Maslow's research found that many self-actualizing individuals had been transformed by ego-transcending peak experiences. Maslow's (1968) *Psychology of Being* reported that self-actualizers with peak or plateau experiences of Being were not selfish but altruistic. They tend to be motivated not by self-interested deficiency needs but what he called Being-values including truth, goodness, beauty, wholeness, perfection, justice, self-sufficiency. He mentions that for self-actualizing persons, or in moments of self-actualization, it becomes possible to have "fully disinterested, desireless, objective and holistic perception of another human being" (1968, p. 36). Thus the transformative effects of experience of transcendence can enable one to behave more empathically—with more complete and selfless perception of another.

Noting what Maslow had reported about the significance of transcendental experiences for self-actualization, Alexander, Rainforth, and Gelderloos (1991) conducted a meta-analysis of 42 independent outcomes to explore the reported effects of various meditation practices on growth of self-actualization. This meta-analysis found that the Transcendental Meditation® (TM) technique, a specific meditation practice that is described as cultivating inner wakefulness that transcends thought, had three times the effect size of other meditation and relaxation practices that had been researched longitudinally using self-actualization measures.

Our Center for Brain, Consciousness and Cognition at Maharishi University has been researching the characteristics of higher stages of development, especially brain functioning. Giving the availability of a population of subjects practicing the TM technique in our community, one focus of our research has been on the phenomenological, psychological, and physiological indicators of growth of consciousness in TM practitioners. Another focus has been on examining the psychological and physiological indicators correlating with exceptional excellence of performance in leaders, athletes, and artists. Through both streams of research we aim to contribute to scientific understanding of the higher reaches of human potential.

A central theme of our research program is to examine the transformative role of experiences of transcendental pure consciousness. The experience of pure consciousness is a silent "state of inner wakefulness with no object of thought or perception, just pure consciousness aware of its own unbounded nature" (Maharishi Mahesh Yogi, 1976, p. 123). This self-referral experience is described as a state of "pure consciousness" because it is wakefulness as its essential nature, unmixed with images, thoughts, feelings, or any other objects of perception; and as "Transcendental Consciousness" because it transcends time, space, and all relative, changing experience (Travis & Pearson, 2000). This inner state has been identified with the spiritual essence of life: "eternal silence, which is pure wakefulness, absolute alertness, pure subjectivity, pure spirituality" (Maharishi Mahesh Yogi, 1995: 271 fn.). The Transcendental Meditation technique (Rosenthal, 2011) is a simple, natural practice from the Vedic tradition that is said to make the experience of Transcendental Consciousness accessible through an effortless means that is "independent of all matters of belief and affiliation" (Shear, 2006).

REVIEW OF RESEARCH ON THE TRANSCENDENTAL MEDITATION TECHNIQUE

The TM technique is a secular practice without a strong cultural context, and so people from all religions have learned and enjoy practicing TM (Rosenthal, 2011). As reported by Travis and Shear (2010), the TM technique

---

® Transcendental Meditation and TM are registered trademarks licensed to Maharishi Vedic Education Development Corporation and used under sublicense.

represents a class of meditation practices which automatically transcends its own activity to give rise to experiences of pure consciousness—which is fundamentally different in aim, procedure, experience, and brain activity than meditation practices involving focused attention or open monitoring. This specific form of meditation practice has been taught in a consistent manner around the world and thus has lent itself to scientific study of both of the effects on mind and body during meditation and on the enduring effects outside of meditation as the result of repeated practice.

The TM technique is learned through a seven-step course of instruction and is practiced 15–20 minutes twice a day, sitting comfortably with eyes closed. It is a process of automatic self-transcending and so needs guidance from a qualified teacher to lead one to the experience of self-awareness without thought (Travis & Shear, 2010). In this meditation practice, the individual begins appreciating a mantra—a sound without meaning—at "finer" levels in which the mantra becomes increasingly secondary in experience and ultimately disappears, and self-awareness becomes more primary (Maharishi, 1969; Travis & Pearson, 2000; see Travis & Shear, 2010). The TM-Sidhi program, an advanced meditation practice based on the Yoga Sutras of Patanjali, is said to accelerate the stabilization of Transcendental Consciousness during the performance of dynamic activity.

During the practice of the TM technique there are reductions in breath rate, skin conductance, and plasma lactate (Dillbeck & Orme-Johnson, 1987), and increased electroencephalographic (EEG) coherence indicative of a state of profound restful alertness, distinct from eyes-closed relaxation or sleep (Alexander, Cranson, Boyer, & Orme-Johnson, 1986; Travis & Wallace, 1999). TM practice leads to consistent changes in brain functioning, which are distinct from the effects produced by other meditation practices (Travis & Shear, 2010). Specifically, blood flow increases to frontal areas, the executive areas of the brain, and decreases to subcortical levels. This indicates increasing activation of the frontal areas. Also, frontal alpha EEG coherence is reported during TM compared to eyes-closed rest (Travis & Wallace, 1999; Travis et al., 2010). Coherence is a mathematical measure of connections between brain areas (Thatcher, Krause, & Hrybyk, 1986). If two brain areas are engaged in the same task, then electrical activity is related between these areas. Local areas are more coherent during tasks. During TM practice, alpha coherence is seen between all areas—left and right, front and back. This global coherence is an indicator of more holistic, integrated, and expanded awareness.

Because the brain adjusts to each new experience, repeated experience of increased frontal blood flow and higher frontal alpha coherence leads to increased presence of these characteristics in activity, not just during meditation practice. Regular TM practice results in greater frontal alpha coherence during tasks after 2 to 12 months of practice (Travis et al., 2010). EEG changes after TM practice are associated with decreased negative psychological traits and increased positive psychological traits (Nidich, Rainforth et al., 2010).

The state of restful alertness gained during the practice is said to dissolve the stress in the mind and the body, leading to improvements such as reduction of high blood pressure (Schneider et al., 1995), decreased anxiety (Eppley, Abrams, & Shear, 1989), reduced health insurance utilization (Orme-Johnson, 1987; Herron, Hillis, Mandarino, Orme-Johnson, & Walton, 1996), positive changes in ego development and moral reasoning (Chandler, Alexander, & Heaton, 2005), creativity (Travis, 1979), fluid intelligence, constructive thinking, self-actualization, and reaction time (Alexander, Rainforth, & Gelderloos, 1991; Cranson et al., 1991; So & Orme-Johnson, 2001). Reviews of this research and its applications to management education (Schmidt-Wilk, Heaton, & Steingard, 2000) and leadership development (Heaton & Schmidt-Wilk, 2008) have been published in the management literature.

Some TM research studies particularly demonstrate how repeated transcending to experience the self-referral state of pure consciousness leads to empathy, harmony, and coordination. Schmidt-Wilk (2003) observed that teams of meditating executives grew to function with better cross-functional collaboration; they grew beyond their self-protective identification with separate functions to become more open and flexible in considering how to satisfy customers. In another qualitative study, Gustavsson (1992) reported that a senior executive observed that meditating managers who reported to him became better coordinated by being more cognizant of a bigger, unifying vision of the organization.

Herriott (2000; Herriott, Schmidt-Wilk, & Heaton, 2009) found that entrepreneurs who were long-term practitioners of the TM and TM-Sidhi programs reported a secure feeling of being anchored to inner fullness, inner silence. These managerial subjects also described their business performance in terms of growing intuition, holistic perspective, and fortunate coincidences. Intuition was described by interviewees as a hunch or subtle impulse from within, and as a knowingness that does not require intellectual analysis. Subjects also commonly referred to a pervasive sense of being part of a larger wholeness. According to Herriott, her subjects reported "an awareness of a more holistic, all-encompassing level of truth and reality, as a sense of integration of the inner and outer dimensions of life" (Herriott, 2000, p. 168). This feeling of a deep sense of connectedness led entrepreneurs to adopt "more universal values: going beyond individual interests to the wider interests of employees, community, or environment as a whole" (Herriott, 2000, p. 172).

Other research on the effects of the TM program for business people has provided a means of empirically testing the theory that systematic transcending promotes balanced success in activity. Studies have found that business people practicing the TM technique report improved health, decreased anxiety, increased productivity, and improved relations (Alexander, DeArmond, Heaton, Stevens, & Schmidt-Wilk, 2004; Alexander et al., 1993; Frew, 1974; Schmidt-Wilk, 2000; Schmidt-Wilk, Alexander, &

Swanson, 1996). In an eight-month pretest-posttest control group study in one company (McCollum, 1999), subjects who learned the TM technique grew significantly more than controls in their expression of leadership behaviors, as measured by the *Leadership Practices Inventory* (Kouzes & Posner, 2007).

One stream of research that can be seen as evidence of the effects of the TM technique on empathy has been in the field of criminal rehabilitation. Criminal conduct can be seen as a lack of empathy, or ability to identify with the experiences of the victims of one's crime. Employing Loevinger's measure of ego development, Alexander, Walton, and Goodman (2003) reported that maximum-security prison inmates practicing the TM technique for 20 months scored a full level higher on Loevinger's measure than did non-meditating inmates interested in learning the TM technique or inmates in other treatment programs. Higher scores on this measure of ego development are associated with greater ability to take the perspective of others from multiple points of view (Loevinger, 1976). After 17 months, the initial TM group increased another level, and a new group that learned the TM technique grew one full level from Loevinger's scale. No longitudinal increases were found in other treatment groups or demographically similar controls wait-listed to learn the TM technique (Alexander & Orme-Johnson, 2003). A 59-month study of these same inmates provides evidence that reduced psychopathology and accelerated psychological development resulting from the TM program are responsible for reductions in criminal behavior (Alexander et al., 2003).

Another longitudinal study of the TM technique and ego development involved 34 alumni of Maharishi University (Chandler et al., 2005), compared to matched samples from three other universities. In this study, an unprecedented 38% of the 34 TM subjects scored at or beyond Loevinger's Autonomous level, Stage 8, which is characterized by respect for one's own and others uniqueness, while enjoying relationships as interdependent mutual support.

A recent study by Sawhney (2012) found that length of practice of the TM program was associated with higher scores on higher states of consciousness, lower scores on anxiety, and higher scores on the trait of emotional intelligence (EI) and disposition to trust (DTT). The participants were 387 business people from 26 service and manufacturing companies that were randomly selected from the Fairfield, Iowa, Area Chamber of Commerce. Lower trait anxiety enables one to more readily reason with emotions. High EI enhances interpersonal interaction in a work context and allows an individual to appraise or perceive different situations as positive and non-threatening, demonstrating a higher DTT. Sawhney's analysis supports a model in which self-reported higher states of consciousness were an intervening variable for positive emotional outcomes; this is consistent with our view that empathy, like trust, depends on the awareness and sensitivity—the consciousness—of the knower.

NEUROPHYSIOLOGY OF HIGHER STATES OF CONSCIOUSNESS

Changes in brain functioning are concrete evidence of changes in the consciousness of the knower. As consciousness changes, so also the expression of empathy will change. Empathy is structured in consciousness, and empathy is different in different states of consciousness. Maharishi described seven states of consciousness, each of which should be accompanied by a unique style of physiological functioning. The first three are the familiar states of sleep, dreaming, and waking consciousness. The next four are called higher states of consciousness: Transcendental Consciousness in which there is awareness of pure consciousness, the higher Self, but no awareness of objects; Cosmic Consciousness in which Transcendental Consciousness is stably maintained along with waking, dreaming, and sleep; Refined Cosmic Consciousness in which perception opens to finer and more charming values of the object; and Unity Consciousness in which the infinite Self is appreciated in every object. Just as there are distinct physiological markers of sleep or dreaming states of consciousness, so also, according to Maharishi, each of the higher states of consciousness should be accompanied by a unique style of physiological functioning.

In our analysis of brain-wave patterns, we have come to identify two metrics that are associated with self-reported experiences of growth of Cosmic Consciousness (Travis, 2002; Travis, Tecce, Arenander, & Wallace, 2002). As one practices the TM technique over time, the EEG patterns during TM are seen during waking, sleeping, and dreaming. The experience of Transcendental Consciousness—pure wakefulness, absolute alertness, pure subjectivity—and the associated brain patterns now underlie and support thinking and cognition during waking, dream images during dreaming, and resting during deep sleep. The first of these metrics is higher broad-band (6–40 Hz) coherence in the prefrontal cortex (F3–F4)—a measure of brain integration. The frontal cortices are connected with other cortical, subcortical, and brain-stem structures, and are important circuits for emotion regulation (Davidson, 2002), moral reasoning (Moll et al., 2002), and decision making and planning (Fuster, 2000). A higher level of brain integration is correlated positively with higher emotional stability, higher moral reasoning, higher happiness, and more openness to experience; and negatively with anxiety (Travis, Arenander, & DuBois, 2004). Such research presents initial evidence of an association between specific indicators of brain functioning and psychological traits that may enable greater expression of empathy.

A second brain-wave metric is higher alpha power, indicating being calm and alert at the same time. Higher alpha and lower gamma frontal and central EEG power indicates inner directedness (alpha EEG) and less absorption in outer boundaries (gamma EEG). Our research has also found that higher scores on these brain measures are associated with higher performance in athletes (Harung et al., 2011) and in managers (Harung, Travis, Blank, and

Heaton, 2009), suggesting that this measure of brain functioning has important practical implications. Harung and colleagues (2009) reported on research measuring brain integration along with measures of psychological development in management research in the workplace. They reported that higher brain integration scores were found to be correlated with higher scores on moral reasoning, ego development, and self-reported experiences of Transcendental Consciousness in a sample of top performing managers. As moral development is one aspect of mature ego development, it follows that more mature individuals were found to also score higher on the measure of moral reasoning. The correlation of all of these psychological measures with a physiological measure of integrated brain functioning suggests that "brain integration may be the basis of personal integrity" (Harung et al., 2009, p. 887).

CONSCIOUSNESS AND CONNECTEDNESS

As developmental psychologists have observed, how one understands one's world changes as one progresses through stages of development. The higher states of consciousness posited in the Vedic psychology of Maharishi Mahesh Yogi do entail new ways of seeing reality: knowledge is different in different states of consciousness. Higher consciousness evolves toward increasing appreciation of the unitary nature of the world as well as increasing unification of one's self-identity with the wholeness of life. Pavlovich and Krahnke (2012) cite notions by physicists Bohm (1980) and Lazslo (1995) that the universe is an unbroken whole and that information about the whole is enfolded in every part. Pavlovich and Krahnke argue that empathy is a "connectedness organizing mechanism" related to the phenomenon of connectednesss in nature.

A related understanding about consciousness and cosmology has been brought out by quantum physicist John Hagelin, our colleague at Maharishi University of Management. In Hagelin's (1987) analysis of unified field theories in physics, the unified field would be the single element that through interacting with itself gives rise to the diversity of physical phenomena. Hagelin points out parallels of this theory in physics to the insight from Vedic seers that consciousness is primordial and creates through its self-interacting flows of knowing itself. As presented by Hagelin, the pure consciousness underlying all mental phenomena and unified field underlying all physical phenomena can be seen as identical to each other. This traditional Vedic view "in which consciousness occupies an ontologically fundamental position," Hagelin explains, "contrasts with the largely mechanistic view of nature characteristic of our particular time and culture" (1987, p. 57).

The Vedic seers' experiences of higher states of consciousness provide insight how consciousness can be the coordination mechanism within nature. What accounts for the connectedness and progressive dynamism of nature is that the all-pervading field of pure consciousness, by virtue of being conscious, is awake to itself. This makes consciousness anywhere conscious of consciousness everywhere—every point of creation is conscious of the whole. Maharishi (1986) described this dynamic nature of consciousness as the basis of all creative processes in nature:

> This self-referral state of consciousness is that one element in nature on the ground of which the infinite variety of creation is continuously emerging, growing, and dissolving. The whole field of change emerges from this field of non-change, from this self-referral, immortal state of consciousness. The interaction of the different intellectually conceived components of this unified self-referral state of consciousness is that all powerful activity at the most elementary level of nature. That activity is responsible for the innumerable varieties of life in the world, the innumerable streams of intelligence in creation. (pp. 25–26)

This description refers to "different intellectually conceived components" of self-referral consciousness. When consciousness is awake to itself, it can be conceived to be the knower, the process of knowing, and the known; but these are components of one unified state. This three-in-one character of self-referral consciousness accounts for the infinite dynamism at the basis of creation:

> When we have one and three together in that self referral state of pure consciousness, there is that infinite contraction for remaining one and there is quick expansion to become three. . . . Infinity, fully awake within itself, is fully awake to its infinite value. At the same time it is awake to its point value. In this we find the dynamism of infinity converging to a point and a point expanding to infinity. (Maharishi Mahesh Yogi, 1985, pp. 64–66)

Again, our point in presenting consciousness as the unified element in a connected cosmos is to illustrate how empathy, a connecting mechanism, is the natural state of things when the world is perceived in higher states of consciousness.

An important aspect of Maharishi's Vedic approach to consciousness is that the unified, self-interacting state of pure consciousness can be accessible to human awareness when consciousness is awake only to itself, rather than identified with objects of perception, thought, or feeling. This is the experience that aligns the individual with the holistic intelligence of nature. Procedures for systematically refining the mind and body for such experience are described in the texts of the Vedic tradition (Maharishi Mahesh Yogi, 1969; Patanjali, 1978).

Here is an approach to improving management performance by harmonizing the individual with the coordinating intelligence of natural law (Maharishi Mahesh Yogi, 1995). The self-referral consciousness at the basis of creation is "that infinite organizing power which sustains existence and promotes the evolution of everything in the universe, automatically maintaining the well-coordinated relationship of everything with everything else" (Maharishi Mahesh Yogi, 1995, p. 8). The Vedic approach to management development is to cultivate the experience of pure, self-referral consciousness in the individual, which "maintains the managing intelligence of the manager in alliance with this supreme managing intelligence of the universe" so that it is ultimately possible to attain "administration as automatic, problem-free, ever-progressive, and ever-evolutionary as the administration of the universe through Natural Law" (Maharishi Mahesh Yogi, 1995, p. 8).

The notion of an organizing intelligence of natural law is certainly not unique to Maharishi. Harmon (1988, p. 119) presented the outlook of deep ecology that "goes beyond the contemporary scientific framework to a subtle awareness of the oneness of all life, the interdependence of its multiple manifestations, and the irrepressibility of its tendencies towards evolution and transformation." Wheatley (1992) reviewed new theories in science and their implications for management. These theories describe a conscious universe that is self-organizing, self-evolving, and contains an implicate order interconnecting everything in nature. Ray wrote of a new paradigm of business based on "wholeness and connectedness" and "doing business from our most profound inner awareness and in connection with the consciousness of others and the earth" (1993, pp. 4–5). Maharishi's assertion that that intelligence of nature is available deep within the consciousness of everyone can be seen as a contemporary expression what Huxley termed in his book *The Perennial Philosophy*—the recognition of "the universal immanence of the spiritual Ground of all existence" (Huxley 1945, p. 7).

Self-referral consciousness is the glue connecting everything; and this same self-referral consciousness can be experienced by every individual when the mind transcends thinking and consciousness is awake only to itself. This understanding about consciousness raises the possibility that anyone of us could feel absolute empathy for any and everyone else. As explained by Hagelin (1987, p. 59), the experience of this state of pure consciousness bridges the gap between self and other:

> The experience of the unified field of consciousness, in which the observer, the process of observation and the observed are unified, is considered to be a means of realizing the ultimate inseparability of the observer and the observed, leading to a completely unified view of self and the environment traditionally known as 'enlightenment' or 'unity consciousness'.

To recapitulate, self-referral means that consciousness is awake to itself. Self-referral consciousness is a property that pervades the universe. This same self-referral state of consciousness is open to direct experience by the individual mind in a state of awareness that transcends objects of thinking and perception, so that the object of consciousness is consciousness itself. This state of consciousness in the individual mind is identical to the connecting intelligence of nature. Such experiences are said to bridge the gap between the knower and the object of knowledge, the self, and other—which means a high degree of realization of empathy.

A vision of ultimate empathy in unity consciousness is expounded in the Vedic literature in the verse: "sees the Self in all beings and all beings in the Self" (*Bhagavad-Gita*, chap. 6, verse 29). Such an end point of development has been conjectured by development psychologist Robert Kegan:

> The ultimate state of development would have to do with some way in which the self has become entirely identified with the world. It would be the recognition essentially of the oneness of the universe, which is something we have heard over and over again in wisdom literatures of the East and West. (in Debold, 2002, p. 2)

FIELD EFFECTS OF MEDITATION ON COLLECTIVE CONSCIOUSNESS

From the perspective of the subjective tradition of Vedic knowledge we have seen the notion that consciousness is inherent in everything and therefore is the mechanism connecting everything. We reported the viewpoint of Hagelin, from his familiarity with both modern physics and the Vedic tradition, that consciousness is the unified field that theoretical physics has been seeking to understand. This notion of consciousness as a field that is present everywhere presents a theoretical ground for understanding empirical evidence that collective practice of meditation technologies has field effects in the broader society.

As explained in Davies and Alexander (2005, p. 289), Maharishi described successive levels of "collective consciousness"—the consciousness of a family, community, city, nation, or the whole world—as dynamically interacting fields that influence individual and collective behavior at each level of social organization. Davies and Alexander explain that greater coherence at any level of collective consciousness means greater integration, complementarity, and peace among diverse individuals and groups; while greater incoherence is reflected in narrower perspectives, greater conflict, and susceptibility to social problems. Maharishi argued that the coherence of any social system as a whole could be enhanced by a field effect generated from the group practice of technologies of consciousness by a small number of members within the society. Through this effect, thinking and behavior throughout the social system are affected in a positive direction by a shift toward coherence in the collective consciousness.

A number of social experiments have been conducted to test the theoretical proposition that a small proportion of the members of society, through group practice of the Transcendental Meditation and TM-Sidhi Program could measurably reduce negative indicators and increase positive indicators of quality of life in society. Notable studies have included a prospective experimental study to test the impact of these procedures in the context of political violence in the Middle East (Orme-Johnson, Alexander, Davies, Chandler & Larimore, 1988) and a demonstration project to reduce urban crime in Washington, DC (Hagelin et al., 1999). The Middle East project was a prospective experiment using data from blinded public sources, a priori predictions, and an independent project review board. During a two-month period, a group of Israeli meditators was assembled in Jerusalem to practice the TM and TM-Sidhi program together as a group (Orme-Johnson et al., 1988). The outcome variables were social indicators including crime, auto accidents, fires, war deaths, war intensity, stock market, and national mood. The independent variable was the daily number of meditators in the group, which ranged from 65 to 241. Box-Jenkins impact assessment, cross-correlation, and transfer function analyses, supported a causal relationship between changes in the size of the meditation group, and indicators of the quality of life in Jerusalem and Israel, as well as changes in the war in Lebanon.

The initial publication of the research by Orme-Johnson et al. (1988) was met with some skepticism. Brown (2005) found that scientists, politicians, and the press usually reacted emotionally rather that rationally to this research. As explained in Orme-Johnson and Oates (2009), the original study went through twice as many reviewers as usual before it was published (Russett, 1988); despite the editor's skepticism, it was published because of the compelling rigor of its statistical methods. Orme-Johnson and Oates explain that critics such as Fales and Markovsky (1997) proposed a number of alternative hypotheses, which were not supported by further empirical analyses reported by Orme-Johnson and Oates. Those critics rationalized rejecting empirical data because it was presented in terms of theories that were difficult to understand from orthodox paradigms; Orme-Johnson and Oates responded that such rejection of empirical data because of unfamiliar theory is "opposite of what the scientific endeavor means to most scholars" (p. 155).

The theory that coherence can be generated in collective consciousness has been applied in the field of management; Harung, Heaton, and Alexander (1999) presented their vision of what highly developed collective consciousness will look like in organizations. In their view, such organizations will be characterized by abundant expression of individual creativity along with a harmonious collective spirit. Organizations are evolving toward a superfluid collective consciousness that connects individual minds on a common, transcendental ground. Those working in such an organization will commonly experience fortuitous coincidences in which the work of others is found to spontaneously support what one is trying to accomplish. A highly coherent organization will have a low resistance culture, where people work together without friction or loss of energy. In the vision of Harung et al., organizations with collective coherence will manifest a seemingly automatic coordination of numerous elements, such as is continuously taking place in the distinct and yet interrelated organ systems in the body.

A Vedic expression captures this ideal of coherence of collective consciousness in organizations:

> *Saṃgachchhadhvaṃsaṃvadadhvaṃsaṃvo manāṃsi jānatām*
> *devā bhāgaṃyathā pūrve sanjānānā upāsate . . .*
> *samānī va ākūtiḥ samānā hṛdayāni vaḥ*
> *samānam astu vo mano yathā vaḥ susahāsati*
> Go together, speak together, know your minds to be functioning together from a common source . . .
> United be your purpose, harmonious be your feelings, collected be your mind, in the same way as all the various aspects of the universe exist in togetherness, wholeness
>
> (*Rk Ved*, 10.194.4)

Such a state of harmony realizes spirituality in management, which Mitroff and Denton (1999, p. 83) characterized as "the basic feeling of being connected with one's complete self, others and the entire universe".

At Maharishi University of Management (MUM) our teaching of socially and environmentally responsible management is grounded in the experience and understanding of growth toward feelings of connectedness through development of consciousness. The practice of the TM technique is built into classes so that each student and teacher is growing in experience of higher states of consciousness; and such experiences are intellectually connected to the content of business studies. For example, the concluding point of a business lesson on stakeholder management is that unity consciousness finds a natural congruence between self-interest (universal Self) and creating good for the society. In this way, the academic content of each business class conveys a theoretical perspective that one's own experience of developing consciousness leads to positive impacts for all parties, and that the lack of development to such a unified identity is the fundamental cause of life-damaging social and environmental impacts.

CONCLUSION

Pavlovich and Krahnke (2012, p. 131) associated empathy with experiences that transcend the rational ego-self "to develop a more expansive, integrated and enlightened state underlying connectedness". This chapter has elaborated their conception by exploring pure consciousness—in which consciousness itself is knower, process of knowing, and known—as the foundational level of nature's creativity. We presented the TM technique as a practice to systematically cultivate transcendental pure consciousness, and we reviewed some research studies that have provided evidence that repeated experience of pure consciousness through the TM technique has beneficial effects for the expression of empathy.

We shared the management approach of Maharishi Mahesh Yogi, which is all about harnessing the self-referral creativity at the basis of nature's functioning. Since natural law interconnects everything, management grounded in this level can promote balanced progress and fulfillment for the individual, the corporation, and the larger environment (Maharishi Mahesh Yogi, 1995, p. 11). Just as different expressions of life support each other in the ecology of nature, so also in a natural law-based ecology of business, enlightened organizations will fulfill their own interests while benefiting the greater social whole in which they operate. Through developing coherence in individual and collective consciousness, organization will come to display high degrees of empathy—understanding and sharing in what others feel. Our collective life will increasingly manifest connectedness through natural law, to be like the wholeness of the universe—a unity of diversity.

REFERENCES

Alexander, C. N., Cranson, R. W., Boyer, R., & Orme-Johnson, D. W. (1986). Transcendental consciousness: A fourth state of consciousness beyond sleep, dreaming and waking. In J. Gackenbach (Ed.), *Sourcebook on sleep and dreams* (pp. 282–315). NY: Garland.

Alexander, C. N., Davies, J. L., Dixon, C., Dillbeck, M. C., Druker, S. M., Oetzel, R.,... Orme-Johnson, D. W. (1990). Growth of higher stages of consciousness: Maharishi's Vedic psychology of human development. In C. N. Alexander & E. J. Langer (Eds.), *Higher stages of human development: Perspectives on adult growth* (pp. 286–341). NY: Oxford University Press.

Alexander, C. N., DeArmond, D. L., Heaton, D. P., Stevens M. M., & Schmidt-Wilk, J. (2004). *Does spiritual practice reduce managerial stress? A prospective study of the Transcendental Meditation Program in business.* Paper presented at the annual meeting of the Academy of Management, New Orleans.

Alexander, C. N. & Orme-Johnson, D. W. (2003). Walpole study of the Transcendental Meditation program in maximum security prisoners II: Longitudinal study of development and psychopathology. *Journal of Offender Rehabilitation, 36*, 127–160.

Alexander, C., Rainforth, M., Frank, P., Grant, J., Von Stade, C., & Walton, K. (2003). Walpole study of the Transcendental Meditation Program in maximum security prisoners III: Reduced recidivism. *Journal of Offender Rehabilitation, 36*, 161–180.

Alexander, C. N., Rainforth, M. V., & Gelderloos, P. (1991). Transcendental Meditation, self-actualization, and psychological health: A conceptual overview and statistical meta-analysis. *Journal of Social Behavior and Personality, 6*(5), 189–247.

Alexander, C. N., Swanson, G. C., Rainforth, M. V., Carlisle, T. W., Todd, C. C., & Oates, R. (1993). Effects of the Transcendental Meditation program on stress-reduction, health, and employee development: A prospective study in two occupational settings. *Anxiety, Stress, and Coping, 6*, 245–262.

Alexander, C. N., Walton, K. G., & Goodman. R. S. (2003). Walpole study of the Transcendental Meditation program in maximum security prisoners I: Cross-sectional differences in development and psychopathology. *Journal of Offender Rehabilitation, 36,* 97–125.

Bohm, D. (1980). *Wholeness and the implicate order.* London: Ark Paperbacks.

Brown, C. L. (2005). Overcoming barriers to use of promising research among elite Middle East policy groups. *Journal of Social Behavior and Personality, 17*(1), 489–546.

Chandler, H. M., Alexander, C. N., & Heaton, D. P. (2005). Transcendental Meditation and postconventional self-development: A 10-year longitudinal study. *Journal of Social Behavior and Personality, 17,* 93–121.

Cook-Greuter, S. R. (2000). Mature ego development: A gateway to ego transcendence? *Journal of Adult Development, 7,* 227–240.

Cranson, R. W., Orme-Johnson, D. W., Gackenbach, J., Dillbeck, M. C., Jones, C. H., & Alexander, C. N. (1991). Transcendental Meditation and improved performance on intelligence-related measures: A longitudinal study. *Journal of Personality and Individual Differences, 12,* 1105–1116.

Davidson, R. J. (2002). Anxiety and affective style: Role of prefrontal cortex and amygdala. *Biological Psychiatry, 51*(1), 68–80.

Davies, J. L., & Alexander, C. N. (2005). Alleviating political violence through reducing collective tension: Impact assessment analysis of the Lebanon war. *Journal of Social Behavior and Personality, 17,* 285–338.

Debold, E. (2002). Epistemology, fourth order consciousness, and the subject-object relationship, or . . . how the self evolves with Robert Kegan. *What Is Enlightenment, 22,* Fall-Winter, 2002. Retrieved March 12, 2008, from http://www.wie.org/j22/kegan.asp?page=2

Dillbeck, M. C. (1988). The self-interacting dynamics of consciousness as the source of the creative process in nature and in human life: The mechanics of individual intelligence arising from the field of cosmic intelligence—the cosmic psyche. *Modern Science and Vedic Science, 2*(3), 245–278.

Dillbeck, M. C., & Orme-Johnson, D. W. (1987). Physiological differences between Transcendental Meditation and rest. *American Psychologist, 42,* 879–881.

Eppley, K. R., Abrams, A. I., & Shear, J. (1989). Differential effects of relaxation techniques on trait anxiety: A meta-analysis. *Journal of Clinical Psychology, 45,* 957–974.

Fales, E., & Markovsky, B. (1997). Evaluating heterodox theories. *Social Forces, 76,* 511–525.

Frew, D. R. (1974). Transcendental Meditation and productivity. *Academy of Management Journal, 17,* 245–262.

Fuster, J. M. (2000). Executive frontal functions. *Experimental Brain Research, 133*(1), 66–70.

Gustavsson, B. (1992). *The transcendent organization.* Unpublished doctoral dissertation. University of Stockholm.

Hagelin, J. S. (1987). Is consciousness the unified field? A field theorist's perspective. *Modern Science and Vedic Science, 1*(1), 29–88.

Hagelin, J. S., Rainforth, M. V., Orme-Johnson, D. W., Cavanaugh, K. L., Alexander, C. N., Shatkin, S. F., . . . Ross, E. (1999). Effects of group practice of the Transcendental Meditation program on preventing violent crime in Washington DC: Results of the national demonstration project, June–July 1993. *Social Indicators Research, 47,*153–201.

Harmon, W. (1988). *Global mind change.* NY: Warner Books.

Harung, H. S., Heaton, D. P., & Alexander, C. N. (1999). Evolution of organizations in the new millennium. *Leadership and Organization Development Journal, 20*(3), 198–207.

Harung, H., Travis, F., Blank, W., & Heaton, D. (2009). Higher development, brain integration, and excellence in leadership. *Management Decision*, 47(6), 872–894.

Harung, H. S., Travis, F., Pensgaard, A. M., Boes, R., Cook-Greuter, S., & Daley, K. (2011). Higher psycho-physiological refinement in world-class Norwegian athletes: Brain measures of performance capacity. *Scandanavian Journal of Medicine and Science in Sports, 21*(1), 32–41.

Heaton, D. P. (2011). Transcendent experience and development of the post-representational self. In A. Pfaffenberger, P. Marko, & A. Combs (Eds.), *The postconventional personality: Perspectives on higher development* (pp. 175–188). Albany, NY: SUNY Press.

Heaton, D. P., & Schmidt-Wilk, J. (2008). Leadership development through development of consciousness. In G. Biberman & L. Tischler (Eds.), *Spirituality in business: Current theory and practice and future directions* (pp. 125–140). London: Palgrave Macmillan.

Heaton, D. P., Travis, F., & Subramaniam, R. (2012). A consciousness-based approach to management education for integrity. In C. Wankel & A. Stachowicz-Stanusch (Eds.), *Handbook of research on teaching ethics in business and management education* (pp. 66–79). Hershey PA: IGI Global.

Herron, R. E., Hillis, S. L., Mandarino, J. V., Orme-Johnson, D. W., & Walton, K. G. (1996). Reducing medical costs: The impact of the Transcendental Meditation Program on government payments to physicians in Quebec. *American Journal of Health Promotion, 10*(3), 206–216.

Herriott, E. M. (2000). *Elements of entrepreneurial success: The links among inner competencies, inner development and success.* Unpublished doctoral dissertation. Maharishi University of Management, Fairfield, IA.

Herriott, E. M., Schmidt-Wilk, J., & Heaton, D. P. (2009). Spiritual dimensions of entrepreneurship in Transcendental Meditation and TM-Sidhi Program practitioners. *Journal of Management, Spirituality and Religion, 6*(3), 195–208.

Huxley, A. (1945). *The perennial philosophy.* NY: Harper & Row.

Jantsch, E. (1980). *The self-organizing universe.* Oxford: Pergamon Press.

Kouzes, J. M., & Posner, B. Z. (2007). *The leadership challenge* (4th ed.). San Francisco: Jossey-Bass.

Laszlo, E. (1995). *The interconnected universe: Conceptual foundations of a trans-disciplinary unified theory.* Singapore: World Scientific.

Loevinger, J. (1976). *Ego development: Conceptions and theories.* San Francisco: Jossey-Bass.

Maharishi Mahesh Yogi (1963). *Science of being and art of living.* New York: Signet.

Maharishi Mahesh Yogi (1969). *On the Bhagavad-Gita: A new translation and commentary with Sanskrit text—Chapters 1 to 6.* Baltimore: Penguin/Arkana.

Maharishi Mahesh Yogi (1972). *The science of creative intelligence.* Videotaped course manual. Fairfield, IA: Maharishi International University Press.

Maharishi Mahesh Yogi (1976). *Creating an ideal society: A global undertaking.* Rheinweiler, Germany: MERU Press.

Maharishi Mahesh Yogi (1985). Inaugural address of His Holiness Maharishi Mahesh Yogi. In *Maharishi Vedic University Inauguration* (pp. 56–78). Washington, DC: Age of Enlightenment Press.

Maharishi Mahesh Yogi (1986). *Life supported by natural law.* Fairfield, IA: Maharishi International University Press.

Maharishi Mahesh Yogi (1994). *Vedic knowledge for everyone.* India: Age of Enlightenment Publications.

Maharishi Mahesh Yogi (1995). *Maharishi University of Management: Wholeness on the move.* Vlodrop, Holland: Maharishi Vedic University Press.

Maslow, A. H. (1968). *Towards a psychology of being.* NY: Van Nostrand Reinhold.

Maslow, A. H. (1998). *Maslow on management.* NY: John Wiley & Sons.

McCollum, B. (1999). Leadership development and self-development: An empirical study. *Career Development International, 4*, 149–154.

Mitroff, I.I., & Denton, E.A. (1999). A study of spirituality in the workplace. *Sloan Management Review* (Summer), 83–92.

Moll, J., de Oliveira-Souza, R., Eslinger, P.J., Bramati, I.E., Mouräao-Miranda, J., Andreiuolo, P.A., & Pessoa, L. (2002). The neural correlates of moral sensitivity: A functional magnetic resonance imaging investigation of basic and moral emotions. *Journal of Neuroscience: The Official Journal of the Society for Neuroscience, 22*(7), 2730–2736.

Nidich S.I., Rainforth, M.V., Haaga, D.A., Travis, F., King, C, Salerno, S., . . . Schneider, R. (2010). A randomized controlled trial on effects of the Transcendental Meditation program on blood pressure, psychological distress, and coping in young adults. *American Journal of Hypertension, 22*, 1326–1331.

Orme-Johnson, D.W. (1987). Medical care utilization and the Transcendental Meditation Program. *Psychosomatic Medicine, 49*, 493–507.

Orme-Johnson, D.W. (2000). An overview of Charles Alexander's contribution to psychology: Developing higher states of consciousness in the individual and society. *Journal of Adult Development, 7*, 199–216.

Orme-Johnson, D.W., Alexander, C.N., Davies, J.L., Chandler, H.M., & Larimore,W.E. (1988). Peace project in the Middle East: Effects of the Maharishi technology of the unified field. *Journal of Conflict Resolution, 32*, 776–812.

Orme-Johnson D.W., & Oates, R.M. (2009). A field-theoretic view of consciousness: Reply to critics. *Journal of Scientific Exploration, 23*(2): 139–166.

Patanjali (1978). *Yoga sutras.* (R. Prasada, Trans.). New Delhi: Oriental Books Reprint Corp. (Original work published 1912).

Pavlovich, K., & Krahnke, K. (2012). Empathy, connectedness, and organization. *Journal of Business Ethics, 105*(1), 131–137.

Ray, M.L. (1993). Introduction. In M.L. Ray & A. Renzler (Eds.), *The new paradigm in business: Emerging strategies for leadership and organizational change* (pp. 1–15). Los Angeles: Jeremy P. Tarcher/Perigree.

Rig Veda (1896). Translated by Ralph T. Griffith.

Rosenthal, N. (2011), *Transcendence: Healing and transformation through transcendental meditation.* NY: Tarcher.

Russett, B. (1988). Editor's comment. *Journal of Conflict Resolution, 32*, 773–775.

Sawhney, S. (2012). *Effects of the TM Technique on anxiety, emotional intelligence and trust: Implications for supply chain management.* Unpublished doctoral dissertation. Maharishi University of Management, Fairfield, IA.

Schmidt-Wilk, J. (2000). Consciousness-based management development: Case studies of international top management teams. *Journal of Transnational Management Development, 5*, 61–85.

Schmidt-Wilk, J. 2003. TQM and the Transcendental Meditation Program in a Swedish top management team. *The TQM Magazine, 15*, 219–229.

Schmidt-Wilk, J., Alexander, C.N., & Swanson, G.C. (1996). Developing consciousness in organizations: The Transcendental Meditation program in business. *Journal of Business and Psychology, 10*, 429–444.

Schmidt-Wilk, J., Heaton, D.P., & Steingard, D. (2000). Higher education for higher consciousness. *Journal of Management Education, 24*, 580–611.

Schneider, R.H., Staggers, F., Alexander, C.N., Sheppard, W., Rainforth, M., & Kondwani, K. (1995). A randomized controlled trial of stress reduction for hypertension in older African Americans. *Hypertension, 26*(5), 820–827.

Shear, J. (2006). Transcendental Meditation. In J. Shear (Ed.), *The Experience of meditation: Experts introduce the major traditions* (pp. 23–48). St. Paul, MN: Paragon House.

So, K. T., & Orme-Johnson, D. W. (2001). Three randomized experiments on the longitudinal effects of the transcendental meditation technique on cognition. *Intelligence, 29*, 419–440.

Thatcher, R. W, Krause, P., & Hrybyk, M. (1986). Cortico-cortical associations and EEG coherence: A two-compartmental model. *Electroencephalography Clinical Neurophysiology, 64*(2):123–43.

Thatcher, R. W., North, D. M., & Biver, C. J. (2008). Development of cortical connections as measured by EEG coherence and phase delays. *Human Brain Mapping, 29*(12), 1400–1415.

Travis, F. (1979). The TM Technique and creativity: A longitudinal study of Cornell University undergraduates. *The Journal of Creative Behavior, 13*, 169–180.

Travis, F. T., Arenander, A., & DuBois, D. (2004) Psychological and physiological characteristics of a proposed object-referral/self-referral continuum of self-awareness. *Consciousness and Cognition, 13*(2), 401–420.

Travis, F., Haaga, D., Hagelin, J., Arenander, A., Tanner, M., & Schneider, R. (2010). A self-referential default brain state: patterns of coherence, power, and eLORETA sources during eyes-closed rest and Transcendental Meditation practice. *Cognitive Processing, 11*(1), 21–30.

Travis, F., Harung, H. S., & Lagrosen, Y. (2011). Moral development, executive functioning, peak experiences and brain patterns in professional and amateur classical musicians: Interpreted in light of a Unified Theory of Performance. *Consciousness and Cognition, 20*(4), 1256–1264.

Travis, F., & Pearson, C. (2000). Pure consciousness: Distinct phenomenological and physiological correlates of "consciousness itself". *International Journal of Neuroscience, 100*, 1–4.

Travis, F., & Shear, J. (2010). Focused attention, open monitoring and automatic self-transcending: Categories to organize meditations from Vedic, Buddhist and Chinese traditions. *Consciousness and Cognition, 19*, 1110–1119.

Travis, F. T., Tecce, J., Arenander, A., & Wallace, R. K. (2002). Patterns of EEG coherence, power, and contingent negative variation characterize the integration of transcendental and waking states. *Biological Psychology, 61*, 293–319.

Travis, F., & Wallace, R. K. (1999). Autonomic and EEG patterns during eyes-closed rest and Transcendental Meditation (TM) practice: The basis for a neural model of TM practice. *Consciousness and Cognition, 8*(3), 302–318.

Wheatley, M. J. (1992). *Leadership and the new science: Learning about organization from an orderly universe.* San Francisco: Berrett-Koehler.

2 The Source of Empathy in our Lives

An Explanatory Journey into the Realm of Spirituality

Dunia Harajli Berry and Vassili Joannidès

INTRODUCTION

Empathy "is the capacity to think and feel oneself into the inner life of another person. It is our lifelong ability to experience what another person experiences, though usually, and appropriately, to an attenuated degree" (Kohut, 1971, p. 82). It is an "emotional response that emanates from the emotional state of another individual, and although empathy is defined as a shared emotional response, it is contingent on cognition as well as emotional factors" (Feshbach, 1997, p. 35). Empathy not only includes the cognitive ability to understand another person's perspective but also the ability for feeling and experiencing emotions.

Psychologists define empathy as "cognitive empathy" when one is aware and understands the thoughts, feelings, perceptions and intentions of others; and "emotional empathy" as "the vicarious affective response to another person" (Hoffman, 2000, p. 29). Feeling empathic, one has the "capacity to directly grasp the meanings of the action, intentions, emotions, and sensations of those we experience" (Wilson, 2011, p. 311). Thus people have an innate capacity for attunement (cognitive and emotional) that adorns personal growth by forming deep connections with others (Bennett, 2001).

Nineteenth-century estheticians used the German word *Einfuhlung* to describe "the capacity on the part of the observer to feel his [sic] way into a work of art and know it from within" (Bennett, 2001, p. 10). *Einfuhlung* literally means *"feeling into"*. Through observation, the person is projecting his or her feelings and body sensations (Gauss, 1973–1974). It was the English translation by psychologist Edward B. Titchener that transformed the German word into empathy: Responding to something exterior, empathy is the interior activity in the mind. Empathy makes it possible for us to transcend the boundaries that separate us. Empathy illuminates the fact that beneath human differences lies a "reservoir made of common developmental themes" that people have in common (Bennett, 2001, p. 31).

The purpose of this chapter is first to identify, explore, and understand the key conditions needed for empathy to emerge; and second, to show how these conditions form an interesting link between spirituality, religion, and empathic behavior. The chapter integrates two frameworks to link the preconditions of empathy with the spiritual activity of living in the present that characterizes most spiritual and religious texts. The four preconditions of empathy identified by Hollingsworth (2008) are extracted from research in Interpersonal Neurobiology (IPNB) and include *Interpersonal Attunement, Intrapersonal Attunement, Relational Safety, and Shared Narratives*. We argue that these four conditions assist in the development of conditions that form the basic components of any spiritual or religious experience, typically referring "to a more structured form or practice of spirituality" (Morrison & Borgen, 2010, p. 36). Weaving empathy with spirituality, this chapter draws heavily on Eckert Tolle's (2004, 2005) Power of Now, embedded in most religious traditions. Being in the Now is about becoming deeply conscious of this present moment. The ideas presented in this chapter are summarized in Table 2.1.

Table 2.1   Conditions of Possibility for Empathy through Components of Spirituality and Religion

Conditions of possibility for Empathy	Explanation	Components of Spirituality	Components of Religion	Chapter Highlights
Interpersonal Attunement	Sense of emotional resonance	The encounter with the other is experienced as a mediator of the Sacred	Reflection of God's creations; behaviour guided by religious morals	Being present; Awareness of all creation
Intrapersonal Attunement	Mindfulness Self-awareness	Experiencing the conscious 'I'	Prayer; reflection in the present	Meditative practices
Relational Safety	To become free from fear; to have safety and trust	Safe environments of spiritual practices; evoking of deep existential vulnerabilities	God as the Saviour; religious worship as a form of protection	Being mode Surrendering to the present
Shared Narratives	Story telling: a tool for emotional and neural integration	Speaking, reading and listening to Sacred narratives make us experience the Divine	Religious stories; Holy books (Koran, Bible, Torah)	Listening and healing

INTERPERSONAL ATTUNEMENT

In this section, the first condition for empathy is described and applied. Interpersonal Attunement is the caring relationship and experience of emotional connections with another attentive individual (Hollingsworth, 2008). When human beings feel *felt* and understood by others, they experience a form of emotional attunement with another attentive person that enables higher levels of well-being to become possible. This "includes increased capacities to share in the states of others while maintaining secure, regulated states of self-awareness" (*op. cit.* p. 850). The secure and attuned attachments over time enable an individual to love more and fear less; this makes one more capable of sharing the feelings and sufferings of others and increases the chances that action to alleviate misery will be taken.

Interpersonal Attunement from a Spiritual Perspective

Interpersonal Attunement is suggested to be a component of spirituality that Hollingsworth defines as "a way of relating to the Sacred that fosters empathic connectedness with others in their suffering and promotes action to ease their distress" (2008, p. 850). It makes our interaction with others a transcendence of the "ordinary". "When our manner of relating to the Sacred becomes integrated with nonthreatening, face to face, voice to voice, body to body interactions between others and ourselves, possibilities for qualitative holistic transformation toward more compassionate ways of being in the world may open up before us" (*op. cit.* p. 850).

From a spiritual stand, Interpersonal Attunement translates into an encounter with another as a mediator of that which is sacred. Once one has a glimpse of awareness or presence, one can make a "conscious choice to be present rather than to indulge in useless thinking" (Tolle, 2005, p. 261). As one becomes present, every action and every deed can be charged with spiritual power. You become "aware, meaning you are not only conscious of things (objects), but you are also conscious of being conscious" (*op. cit.* p. 228). So when you meet people at work or other places, you give them your full attention and "you are no longer there primarily as a person, but as a field of awareness, of alert presence" (*op. cit.* p. 269). This field of awareness between one and others becomes the primary purpose for the interaction. The space of awareness becomes more important than what may be said or done. Although one does not avoid doing things on a practical level, "the doing unfolds not only more easily, but more powerfully when the dimension of Being is acknowledged and so becomes primary" (*op. cit.* p. 270). The connectedness felt between human beings arises from that unifying field of awareness that Tolle argues is the most essential factor in our relationships.

The Power of Being Present

Tolle (2004) suggests that the power of being Present liberates humans from the chains of blurred boundaries; one begins to feel empathy toward others as the boundaries between self and others dissolve. Being, which cannot be grasped by our minds, is felt when our attention is fully and intensely in the Now.

Caruso and Salovey (2004) state that when we attend to our own emotions in the Now, we are more able to tap into the emotional data before consciously thinking of it, and thus we gain the ability to empathically connect with others. Gaining an intuitive insight from our feelings in the present makes us feel things deeply, and we can begin to acquire a strong emotional imagination and major emotional empathy (Caruso & Salovey, 2004). Cognitive empathy is also strengthened when we have a wiser understanding of emotions and their causes. The opportunity for empathy eventuates when we try to imagine what may happen next in terms of how people feel. The emotional "what-if" analyses are generated when we are more able to reason about feelings and understand why a person feels the way they do and how these feelings may change over time (Caruso & Salovey, 2004). Thus, "empathy is more than feeling love; it is a universal connection, a conduit for carrying experience that goes beyond time and space as we conventionally know them" (Pavlovich & Krahnke, 2012, p. 135). This attention in the Now gives us the capacity to empathize as empathy can only take place in the immediacy of Now (Forsyth, 1980).This is developed when we become "conscious of the unmanifested directly through the radiance and power of our conscious presence and indirectly through the sensuous realm . . . in every creature, every flower, every life-form in the universe" (Molisa, 2011, p. 465). Even nature can positively affect feelings of transcendence of the self, giving opportunities to connect with nature, with creation, with one's concept of God, or simply with others (Reese & Myers, 2012).

Interpersonal Attunement from a Religious Perspective

Turning to religion as a solid form of spiritual practice, we see that most religions also cultivate feelings of transcendence of self. They address humans in the present tense, telling us to reflect, listen, see, serve, give, forgive, and worship in the present. In Interpersonal Attunement, people are awakening and becoming enlightened to a renewed spiritual human interaction. Reflecting on the Now, we see that religions share deep commonalities and point to Now as the key to spiritual egoless state of enlightenment (Tolle, 2004, 2005). To this end, Interpersonal Attunement with its connecting power, emotional sensations, and consciousness of being fully Present makes humans more aware, less egocentric (Sanders, Hopkins & Geroy, 2003), and therefore more empathic (Hollingsworth, 2008).

INTRAPERSONAL ATTUNEMENT

The second condition of possibility for empathy is Intrapersonal Attunement. The first practice discussed is to achieve intrapersonal attunement through mindfulness. Hollingsworth (2008, p. 850) describes mindful awareness as "intentional, nonjudgmental attentiveness to our own thoughts, feelings, and bodily states in the present moment . . ." through noticing, respecting, and loving oneself. Such practices have been shown to change previous patterns of fear, inflexibility, and defensiveness into new patterns of "calm, adaptability, and balance" (*op. cit.* p. 851). One's ability to be mindful is likely to be directly related to one's ability to experience connectedness with others. As in interpersonal relationships or secure attachment relationships, "repeated experiences of internal resonance via mindfulness practices may expand our capacities for connection with others, guide us toward increased abilities to regulate our emotions, cause us to 'feel into' the pain of others with greater depth and lead us to desire and work towards alleviation of others suffering" (*op. cit.* p. 851).

Intrapersonal Attunement from a Spiritual Perspective

Intrapersonal Attunement is another component of spirituality. Many argue that humans are not complete without a spiritual dimension, and "transcendence is the most inclusive level of consciousness" (Sanders et al., 2003, p. 27). Such people believe that becoming aware of one's own state of consciousness is a deep spiritual experience. Hollingsworth (2008, p. 851) again confers that "Experiencing the conscious 'I' as an observer of our own mental representations and bodily sensations can lead us to affirm ourselves as Sacred in some sense". He continues that this condition requires us to relate intrapersonally with care, respect, curiosity, and love, which become vital aspects of relating to the sacred to foster empathy. Bestowing self-kindness, recognizing and honoring the sacredness of others, feeling connected and taking action to better lives are central to spirituality.

The bond connecting everything (self-referral consciousness) is the awakened consciousness to self and can be experienced by every individual when the mind transcends thinking and consciousness is awake only to itself. This understanding of consciousness raises the possibility that any one of us could feel empathy for anyone and everyone. Similar to the connecting intelligence of nature, this state of pure consciousness closes the gap between self and others so that the object of consciousness is consciousness itself. This self-referral experience of state of "pure consciousness" as an inner state is said to be the spiritual essence of life, the eternal silence, which is pure wakefulness, absolute alertness, pure subjectivity, pure spirituality (Hollingsworth, 2008). The experience of a unified field of consciousness with the unification of the observer, the process of observation, and the observed displays an ultimate inseparability of the observer and observed, leading to a unified outlook of self and the surroundings, known as enlightenment and unity consciousness (Hagelin, 1987; Tolle, 2004). Bridging the gap between the knower and the object of knowledge (self and other) can result in a high degree of empathy.

People with a high degree of empathy will tend to help others without regard for any personal gain. Transcending the needs of the self and experiencing empathy will lead to connectedness and loving kindness. This requires "some degree of suspension of self-engagement" (Kristeller & Johnson, 2005, p. 394), which can be achieved through meditative practices.

Meditative Practices

Meditative practices all share a common conscious "attempt to focus attention in a non-analytical way and an attempt not to dwell on discursive, ruminating thought" (Kristeller & Johnson, 2005, p. 394). Three types are most common. The first is concentrative meditation where attention is focused on an object; the second is mindfulness meditation where attention "is purposely kept open, attending to whatever enters the field of awareness . . . the object of awareness can be an emotion, an image or an external object" (op. cit. p. 394). A third type is a directed meditation where the content is important and is there to engage a certain part of the self but in a mindful rather than judgmental way. For example, concentrating on interpersonal connectedness, pain, or even physical sensations such as hunger or stress can be used first to increase awareness and second to modify the nature of the "cognitive or emotional response to these experiences" (Kristeller & Johnson, 2005, p. 395).

Most meditative traditions contain the elements of all three types. But regardless of what type of meditation practice is used, the goal is to "train the mind to disengage from usual modes of thinking, attention, and reaction to the objects of consciousness" (Kristeller & Johnson, 2005, p. 396). Meditative practices can cultivate mindfulness, by "focusing attention on the experience of thoughts, emotions, and body sensations, simply observing them as they arise and pass away" (Hölzel et al., 2012, p. 538). Our ability to notice bodily sensations or what is called body awareness will not only be enhanced but will also lead to greater awareness of one's emotional life, especially in regulating emotions. Thus, developing this internal awareness of one's own experience through meditation can be an important precondition for empathic response (Hölzel et al., 2012). "Empathy, like trust, depends on the awareness and sensitivity—the consciousness—of the knower". The expression of empathy will change as consciousness changes as empathy is structured in consciousness.

Meditative practices can also to lead to consistent changes in the functions of the brain (Hölzel et al., 2012). Brain patterns during the experience of meditation show an increase of blood flow to the attention regulating parts of the brain (the frontal areas) and the executive parts of the brain (the anterior cingulated cortex) that enable people to take the others' perspectives from multiple viewpoints. Mindfulness practices on the brain were found to be similar to those of attuned relationships. That is, "the same areas in the prefrontal cortex appear to be strengthened whether one is experiencing empathic connection with oneself or with another human being others" (Hollingsworth, 2008, p. 846). Employing conscious control of one's attention with the goal of resonating with distinct aspects of the self may stimulate areas of the brain to become active in ways that encourage integration with others. Interestingly, the "empathic forms of communication are one of the hallmarks of the healthy human brain" (Bennett, 2001, p. 120). When certain regions of the prefrontal cortice are damaged, a patient's empathy is impaired (Shamay-Tsoory, Tomer, Goldsher, Berger, & Aharon-Peretz, 2004). This suggests that a subset of brain regions can impact both one's awareness of body sensations and one's social cognition and empathic responses (Hölzel et al., 2012).

Meditative training can therefore be seen as "a powerful means of engaging a universal psychological process—that of shifting one's preoccupation with self to a sense of connectedness with others" (Kristeller & Johnson, 2005, p. 404). Mindful meditation is not merely relaxation but rather an attunement (empathy) with the others' needs. The detached self evolves and starts to cast away "superficial levels of identity in favor of a more integrated self" (Kristeller & Johnson, 2005, p. 397). The next section will examine such practices through a religious lens.

Intrapersonal Attunement from a Religious Perspective

Central to Intrapersonal Attunement is religious prayer, a form of transcendental meditation practice within all religions that helps Being in the world. "All meditative spiritual traditions emphasize that the extended goal of contemplative prayer practice is an opening of the heart, a heightening of compassion, a preparation for loving and caring more deeply for others" (Kristeller & Johnson, 2005, p. 399). Repetitive contemplative prayer is a means that requests attentiveness and submission to Now. It is the power within ritual and worships that "powerfully shapes us and connects us to each other" (Hogue, 2003, p. 37), a means by which empathy can be fostered (Kristeller & Johnson, 2005). For example, research has found that Tibetan monks with over 10,000 hours of meditation showed greater activation in subset brain regions linked to empathic response as they listened to people suffering (Hölzel et al., 2012).

One may wonder how it is possible for the most self-focused of practices to cultivate the opposite (Kristeller & Johnson, 2005). Released from the tight grip of the egocentric "I", empathy development is stimulated. The universal capacity for connectedness cultivated through prayer facilitates a transcendence of self by exposing our innate ability to experience the feelings and needs of others. By "turning one's will over to a

Higher power and taking a moral inventory" (Kristeller & Johnson, 2005, p. 403), by switching one's reality status to a Being mode (Fromm, 1976), and by reflecting upon the Present (Tolle, 2004), these traditions suggest that one can be "paid back in fruits of the spirit" (Kristeller & Johnson, 2005, p. 403).

As discussed, Intrapersonal Attunement, a condition of possibility for empathy can be developed through diverse meditative practices. Such practices, while challenging and requiring self-discipline, are replaced by a sense of safety and well-being that gives one the strength to meet fear, sadness, and anger by turning toward them (connecting) rather than away from them (separating) (Hölzel et al., 2012). This leads us to relational safety, the next condition of possibility for empathy to emerge.

RELATIONAL SAFETY

Relational Safety, the sense of security that people feel within themselves, encourages empathy and is the third condition of possibility for empathy to emerge. As Maslow (1943) noted, feeling safe and secure is a fundamental physiological condition for human survival. The absence of economic and social safety can result in a separation of self that can close off empathic connections with others. For example, interpersonal relationships replete with conflict, distrust, and insecurity can cause people to feel threatened, emotionally deregulated, and cut off from empathic ties. On the other hand, interpersonal relationships marked by mutual security and fidelity can help people regulate fear responses and become more open to empathically caring for others. Relational safety therefore refers to freeing individuals from fear in order to enhance empathy (Hollingsworth, 2008). In this section, we argue that relational safety is more able to be achieved through living in the Now, which releases one from fear.

Relational Safety from a Spiritual Perspective

Being aware of Relational Safety allows people to seek answers to deeply embedded existential fears and vulnerabilities. This process provides a niche of security by "creating safe relational spaces for communal experiences of the divine" (Hollingsworth, 2008, p .852). Most faith traditions have practices that involve face-to-face communications with others such as instruction, confession, group rituals, and community building. Safe, relational environments provide a platform for people to open up to each other, themselves, and the sacred.

Being in the moment and feeling connected is a basis for Relational Safety. The present moment is a reality where the ego incessantly tries to pull people from into a space occupied with human drama. This process pushes us into fear and away from enlightenment. Tolle (2004, p. 12) describes enlightenment as, "A state of connectedness with something immeasurable and indestructible, something that, almost paradoxically, is essentially you and also much greater than you. It is finding your true nature beyond name and form . . . [it is] the natural state of felt oneness with Being". The enlightened state brings about "the transcendence of the sense of fear, incompleteness and lack that is the suffering that serves as the experiential basis of egoic consciousness" (op. cit. p. 12). To be spiritually enlightened is to be "conscious of who you are—not just your thoughts and emotions and everything else that happens in the world, but of yourself as the inner space, the alert and intensely alive stillness in which it happens, that connects you to the Source, the One life of which we are all part of" (Molisa, 2012, p. 464).

To feel a sense of security, Tolle (2004) speaks of an "awakening" that makes us rise above our individual ego that seeks to perpetuate itself in the world of materialism. The ego seeks to drain us by dwelling over the past or worrying about the future. Our ego never allows the Now to shine. Thus we lose the moment and therefore the sight of beauty that prevails around us. Engrossed in self-pity, regret, anger, and fear, we become a prisoner of our own doing. Being fully present is central to spirituality and as already noted, empathy is experienced in the Present. Empathy is only possible "if the context which exists in one's own experience and has been encountered in innumerable ways is always—and with all the potentialities contained in it—present and ready" (Dilthey, 1976, p. 226).

The great Sufi poet Al Rumi once wrote "past and future veil God from our sight; burn up both of them with fire" (Tolle, 2004, pp. 51–52). To be in the present moment demands complete awareness: Past and future are but illusions. To feel connected and to have empathy is when one knows "that every life form cannot pass away because of their everlasting eternal oneness with the Source" (op. cit. p. 140).

The spiritual dimension of relational safety also draws on Fromm's (1976) "Being and having mode". When living in the "having mode", we seek possessions, not because we are afraid of dying, but afraid of losing what we have whether it be ego, possessions or identity. Such people look for sources outside of self to feel safe. Fromm (1976, p. 89) asked "If I am what I have and if what I have is lost, who then am I?" He provided the following answer: "Nobody but a defeated, deflated, pathetic testimony to a wrong way of living." In looking outside of ourselves, we can become defensive, hard, paranoid, angry, and lonely. Ongoing mental activity (about the past and future) is what prevents consciousness from becoming aware of oneself and our empathic relations with others.

Without relational safety, it is possible to end up with severe addictions in an unconscious endeavor to remove inner turmoil (Tolle, 2004). Yet these are but brief gratifications as people do not relinquish their pain. It remains within the unconscious and keeps guiding feelings and behavior. On the other hand, the "Being mode" exists only in the here and now. Fromm (1976, p. 103) suggests that "the more we rid ourselves of the craving for possession in all its forms, particularly our ego-boundness, the less is the fear of dying, since there is nothing to lose". Feeling secure and surrendering to the present is also a way of Being that makes us feel empathy by "letting go of mental-emotional resistance to what is" (Tolle, 2004, p. 134). Inner resistance is said to cut people off from themselves, from each other, and the world at large. It is a "state of inner or spiritual alienation as it strengthens the feeling of separateness on which the ego depends for its survival" (Molisa, 2011, p. 466). This absence of relational safety reduces the ability to feel empathy with others. Rather, people who feel relationally safe are more likely to live in the "Being mode" and surrender to the present moment of being in a relationship. This awareness of the sacred realm allows empathic people to share a purpose with others. They "see each stone, each leaf, each frog, each human face, for what it truly is, in all its distinctiveness and intensity of its specific being" (McDaniel, 2006, p. 50). They observe, listen, and feel all that surrounds them (including nature and animals), feeling a connection common to all humanity (McDaniel, 2006).

A false sense of relational safety is seen where the ego wants to hold on to the material world, property, land, wealth as any sort of mundane security. Rather, relational safety involves developing a sense of awareness and empathy of "the Sacredness of life and its divine beauty" . . . one where life "without fear is grounded in an unshakeable inner peace" (Molisa, 2011, p. 464).

Relational Safety from a Religious Perspective

Relational safety is also a component of many religions. It is suggested that people who see God as their saviour are usually not as afraid. Their deep existential vulnerabilities are more in control (Bennett, 2001), and their openness to the sacred in a "collective worship" context is seen as a way to becoming a more empathic person (Hollingsworth, 2008).Feeling secure and free from harm comes from experiencing interpersonal and intrapersonal attunement. These conditions along with relational safety make empathic responses more likely to emerge.

SHARED NARRATIVES

Shared Narratives is the fourth and final condition of possibility for empathy to emerge. Narratives require participation of people's conscious memory, knowledge, sensations, feelings, and behaviors. In combining multiple functions, narratives provide the context with a resource for emotional integration. Narrations enable us to share others experiences while still holding onto our own perspectives (Hollingsworth, 2008). Emerging from such connectedness, "empathy enables people to suspend judgment and to comprehend paradigmatic differences to foster more enlightened relationships. This in return creates more humanitarian, interactive and creative environments" (Pavlovich & Krahnke, 2012, p. 133). Through dissolving the boundary between self and others, through sharing and listening to experiences, empathy emerges as a universal connection enabling people to feel and access coherent harmony (Pavlovich & Krahnke, 2012).

Constituting a component of spirituality, Shared Narratives are at the core of human spirituality where "speaking, reading, and/or hearing Sacred narratives from our traditions are at the heart of many experiences of the divine" (Hollingsworth, 2008, p. 852). People therefore get a sense of participating in something greater than themselves when listening to or reciting narratives. Empathic connections between self and others and the "deep personal meaning and transcendent participation", means that shared narratives can raise one to greater levels of concern with the pain of others, and motivate one to "stand in solidarity with those who are suffering by weaving their stories into the fabric of our own" (op. cit., p. 853).

Shared Narratives from a Religious Perspective

We suggest that Shared Narratives are embraced by all religions. Religion causes empathic behavior in social settings to emerge (Alma, 2008). Training one's empathic abilities and the development of religion as a language of "personal resonance that stimulates mutual understanding" is one of the big challenges faced in our world (op. cit. p. 63). When we are listening to a narrative, a recitation of the *Koran* or a sermon, our brains are mimicking not only the actions of the preacher but also the character's actions in the stories being told. "Either seeing or hearing an event prompts the brain to imagine its own body performing an action" (Hogue, 2003, p. 36). These shared narratives enhance the development of empathy. Almost all philosophical and religious traditions have been associated with listening and healing. "Listening has occupied a central place in religion, where the belief in a God that listens to our prayers, and knows our innermost thoughts, has been a core feather of many religions" (Bennett, 2001, p. 52). A listener is one who understands and makes way for empathic communication where the "enduring wish for understanding as a prelude to healing is by its nature, spiritual" (p. 55). When the listener is engaged in a caring way, when he or she is listening responsively, and intervening in corrective ways, empathy prevails (Bennett, 2001).

As a vehicle for healing (Kohut, 1971), empathy at its deepest level makes people feel the peace emanated by another, whether conscious or not. Thus empathy is corrective for both the speaker and the listener. It comes into "play for the most part to fill in the blanks: to bridge a gap, understand an inconsistency, pursue and clarify an implicit motive" (Bennett, 2001, p. 232).On another note, one can see that all religions in the end share 'deep commonalities' (Tolle, 2004, 2005), evident in these narratives. What matters is not the distinction but rather how the differences "carry the universal that happens to them like a grace" (Badiou, 2003, p. 106). What is important is trying to overlook differences in customs, opinions, and ideologies and stressing what unites us, the worship of One God as "an indifference that tolerates differences" (op. cit. p. 99).

EMPATHY AND SPIRITUALITY

Finally, to strengthen the points described above, we would like to provide a brief description of a study that shows a positive correlation between religion and empathy. The study shows a positive link between spiritual well-being and empathy in Christian students in a graduate counseling program.Morrison and Borgen (2010, p. 27) asked the question: "How do Christian spiritual and religious beliefs help and hinder counsellors' empathy for clients?" They identified 242 out of 267 incidents where religion helped participants' empathy toward clients. The research asked participants who self-identified with spirituality based on Christianity to give their own definitions of religion and spirituality; these were later used to categorize and interpret the incidents reported. Specifically, participating counselors were asked to recall both positive and negative incidents (such as an event, a counseling session, or a client) where their religion helped develop their empathy (or hindered it). A majority of categories confirmed that a spiritual connection helped the counselor understand the client in a more empathic way. Significantly, more than two-thirds of the participants endorsed the category "relationship to faith leading directly/naturally to an empathic relationship with the client". The findings of the study illustrated the many ways Christian spirituality enhanced their felt empathy. Recommendations made from the study included increased awareness of spirituality and religion as a cultural variable that promotes empathy. While the authors acknowledged the limitations of the findings, this study provides a baseline for the relationship between empathy and other religious traditions. As shown in the previous section, Shared Narratives as a condition of possibility for empathy to emerge brings different people into the same stories, emotions, and feelings.

As discussed in this chapter, the conditions for empathy to emerge resonate with spiritual components. A spiritually nourished life is one that may witness empathic behavior toward others. To have empathy, we argue that people need to embrace their inner spiritual selves, be present and aware, and awaken to their purpose in life. We argue that this is possible through these four conditions of Interpersonal Attunement, Intrapersonal Attunement, Relational Safety, and Shared Narratives. Together, the four conditions of possibility form an interrelated thread of insights that weave both our empathic potential with our spirituality. Significantly, Hollingsworth (2008) suggests that there are strong links between mental health, emotional regulation, secure attachments, and coherent narratives. Understanding oneself and others, diving deep into self-reflection and meditation, letting go of insecurities and fears, learning to listen to one self and to others, and accepting human vulnerabilities not only regulate and control emotions but also help build empathy. The table below summarizes these four conditions of possibility for empathy from our understanding of Hollingsworth's (2008) definitions.

CONCLUDING THOUGHTS

The human soul and consciousness appear like a philosophy where subjectivity, feeling, experience, and creativity are alive. Living in a "disenchanted universe where we are nothing more than the predictable next step in a biophysical algorithm" (Duffy, 2009, p. 1), our spirit, the life force that keeps us alive and breathing is gasping for fulfillment (Garcia-Zamor, 2003).

Spirituality has been defined as our inner consciousness, a process of enlightenment (Dehler & Welsh, 1994), and "the basic feeling of being connected with one's complete self, others and the entire universe" (Mitroff & Denton, 1999, p. 83). Common to spirituality and religion is an overriding concern for "transcending a material existence" (Probst & Strand, 2010, p. 142). The freedom to be in touch with our souls gives rise to empathy, which in turn leads to altruistic behavior (Chin-Fang Yang & Chin-Yi Chen, 2012; Pavlovich & Krahnke, 2012).

This chapter set out to show that when taken together, the four conditions for empathy to emerge make up the basic components of spirituality. We argue that human beings are naturally hardwired toward empathy through spirituality. The thoughts presented have been the nesting grounds of common teachings of mystical, spiritual, and religious prophets throughout time. The people who are able to transcend their ego and their "having mode" will not only have inner security, but also better interpersonal and intrapersonal relationships. When empathy is embedded within a spiritual framework, it frees the ego from self-serving purposes.

Spiritual Growth————) Empathy————) Increased Connectedness & Altruism

We conclude that those who foster a culture of spirituality, respect for others, and freedom of faith and belief are more likely to reveal the very conditions needed for empathy to develop. In a broader context, "enlightened managers and entrepreneurs strive to transcend divisions around the globe, and reach the balance between social good and self-interest, trust-based and legal relationships, teamwork and individual stars" (Chen, 2010). Through developing coherence in individual and collective consciousness, organizations will come to display high levels of empathy—understanding and sharing in what others feel. Our collective life will increasingly manifest connectedness through natural law, so that the collective life, like the wholeness of the universe, is a unity of diversity. Finally, to "find the Life we have lost in living and the wisdom we have lost in knowledge" (T. S. Eliot, 1934), and to do everything possible at work to feel and help others (empathy) will stem from being accepted, understood, and respected (spirituality). Spirituality gives us a direction to the path of empathy, which makes us who we are.

REFERENCES

Alma, H. A. (2008). Self-development as a spiritual process: The role of empathy and imagination in finding spiritual orientation. *Pastoral Psychology, 57*, 59–63.

Badiou, A. (2003). *Saint Paul: The foundation of universalism.* Palo Alto, CA: Stanford University Press.

Bennet, J. M. (2001). *The empathic healer: An endangered species.* London: Academic Press.

Caruso, D. R., & Salovey, P. (2004). *The emotionally intelligent manager.* San Francisco: Jossey-Bass.

Chen, M. J. (2010). *West meets east: Enlightening, balancing and transcending.* In the Academy of Management Conference, San Antonio, August 8–12, 2011.

Chin-Fang Yang, & Chin-Yi Chen. (2012). The impact of spiritual leadership on organizational behavior: A multi-sample analysis. *Journal of Business Ethics, 105*(1), 107–114.

Dehler, G. E., & Welsh, M. A. (2003).The experience of work: Spirituality and the new workplace. In R. A. Giacalone & C. L. Jurkiewicz (Eds.), *Handbook of Workplace Spirituality and Organizational Performance* (pp. 108–122). NY: M. E. Sharpe.

Dilthey, W. (1976). *Selective writings.* Ed. H. P. Richman. England: Cambridge University Press.

Duffy, D. J. (2009). Mirror neurons and the re-enchantment of bioethics. *The American Journal of Bioethics, 9*(9), 2–4.

Eliot, T. S. (1934). *The rock: The complete poems and plays.* Orlando, FL: Harcourt Press.

Feshbach, N. D. (1997). Empathy: The formative years—Implications for clinical practice. In A. C. Bohart & L. S. Greenberg (Eds.), *Empathy reconsidered: New directions in psychotherapy* (pp. 33–39). Washington, DC: American Psychological Association.

Forsyth, G. (1980). Analysis of the concept of empathy-illustrations of one approach. *Advances in Nursing Science 2*, 33–42.

Fromm, E. (1976). *To have or to be?* NY: Harper & Row.

Garcia-Zamor, J. C. (2003). Workplace spirituality and organizational performance. *Public Administration Review, 63*, 355–363.

Gauss, C. E. (1973–1974). Empathy. In P. P. Wiener (Ed.), *Dictionary of the history of ideas: Studies of selected pivotal ideas* (Vol. 2, pp. 85–89). NY: Scribner.

Hagelin, J. S. (1987). Is consciousness the unified field? A field theorist's perspective. *Modern Science and Vedic Science, 1*(1), 29–88.

Hoffman, M. (2000). *Empathy and moral development: Implications for caring and justice.* England: Cambridge University Press.

Hogue, D. A. (2003).Sensing the other in worship: Mirror neurons and the empathizing brain. *Liturgy, 21*(3), 31–39.

Hollingsworth, A. (2008). Neuroscience and spirituality: Implications of interpersonal neurobiology for a spirituality of compassion. *Zygon, 43* (4), 837–860.

Hölzel, B. K., Lazar, S. W., Gard, T., Schuman-Olivier, Z., Vago, D. R., Ott, U., & Schuman-Olivier, Z. (2012). Perspectives on psychological science: Conceptual and neural perspective. *Perspectives on Psychological Science.* doi:10.1177/1745691611419671

Kohut, H. (1971). *The analysis of the self.* NY: International Universities Press.

Kristeller, L. J., & Johnson, T. (2005). Science looks at spirituality. Cultivating loving kindness of meditation on empathy, compassion, and altruism. *Zygon, 40*(2), 391–407.

Maslow, A. H. (1943). A theory of human motivation. *Psychological Review 50*(4), 370–396.

McDaniel, J. (2006). All animals matter: Marc Bekoff's contribution to constructive Christian theology. *Journal of Religion and Spirituality, 41*(1), 32–52.

Mitroff, I., & Denton, E. (1999). *A spiritual audit of corporate America: A hard look at spirituality, religion, and values in the workplace.* San Francisco: Jossey-Bass.

Molisa, P. (2011). A spiritual reflection on emancipation and accounting. *Critical Perspectives on Accounting, 22*, 453–484.

Morrison, M., & Borgen, W. A. (2010). How Christian spiritual and religious beliefs help and hinder counselors' empathy toward clients. *Counseling and Values, 55*, 25–45.

Pavlovich, K., & Krahnke, K. (2012). Empathy, connectedness and organization. *Journal of Business Ethics, 105*, 131–137.

Probst T. M., & Strand, P. (2010). Perceiving and responding to job insecurity: A workplace spirituality perspective. *Journal of Management, Spirituality & Religion, 7*(2), 135–156.

Reese, F. R., & Myers, E. J. (2012). EcoWellness: The missing factor in holistic wellness models. *Journaling of Counseling & Development, 90*, 400–407.

Sanders, E. J., Hopkins, E. W., & Geroy, D. G. (2003). From transactional to transcendental: Towards an integrated theory of leadership. *Journal of Leadership & Organizational Studies, 9*(4), 21–31.

Shamay-Tsoory, S. R., Tomer, R., Goldsher, D., Berger, B. D., & Aharon-Peretz, J. (2004). Impairment in cognitive and affective empathy in patients with brain lesions: Anatomical and cognitive correlates. *Journal of Clinical and Experimental Neuropsychology, 28*(8), 1113–1127.

Tolle, E. (2005). *A new earth: Create a better life.* London: Penguin.

Tolle, E. (2004). *The power of now.* Adelaide, South Australia: Hachette.

Wilson C. B. (2011). Mirroring processes, religious perception and ecological adaptation: Toward an empathic theory of religion. *Journal for the Study of Religion, Nature & Culture, 5*(3), 307–326.

3 Empathy, Self-Other Differentiation, and Mindfulness Training

Paul W. B. Atkins

INTRODUCTION

If organizations are to become more empathic, then simple and effective, interventions are required to improve individual empathy. Historically, efforts to increase empathic responding in organizations have relied mainly upon either communication skills training or emotional intelligence training. Both of these approaches tacitly assume that improving empathy is a matter of improving skills. While both approaches can be effective in organizations, in this chapter I argue that both ignore a deeper aspect of sustainable empathy: the capacity to balance a felt sense of connection with ongoing differentiation from another. Empathizing with others in the absence of a well-differentiated sense of self can lead to secondary stress and burnout—particularly in roles involving helping or other forms of emotional labor.

This chapter presents an approach to understanding the basic psychological processes underpinning the construction of a sense of self and the capacity to take the perspective of others. I describe the interplay between thinking about the self and other that results in empathic concern, personal distress, or a range of other more or less helpful affective responses in the presence of another person (Atkins & Parker, 2012). In brief, I describe how we can see self and other either at the level of (a) conceptualizations, (b) a flow of experiences, or (c) as awareness itself; and how the nature and extent of differentiation needed at each of these three levels to support empathy is distinct. The chapter then reviews evidence that mindfulness training demonstrably improves empathy and suggests that this positive effect is at least in part the result of a changed relationship to the self and improved perspective taking.

Empathy can be understood in its broadest sense as simply the responses of one person to the observed experiences of another (Davis, 1983). In the West at least, empathic responses are generally understood to consist of both cognitive and affective elements. Empathy involves understanding the perspective of the other, as well as caring: a bodily or emotional response to the other. For Davis (1983), perspective taking is the "tendency to spontaneously adopt the psychological point of view of others" (Davis, 1983, p. 114). Having understood another's perspective, a range of possible affective responses are possible, including empathic concern and personal distress. Empathic concern refers to the "other-oriented emotional response elicited by and congruent with the perceived welfare of a person in need" (Batson & Ahmad, 2009, p. 6). By contrast, personal distress is a "self-focused, aversive reaction to the vicarious experience of another's emotion" (e.g., as discomfort or anxiety; Eisenberg, 2010, p. 130). Perspective taking is the primary process associated with noticing and appraising the experience of another, while empathic concern or personal distress are secondary processes that are the products of that noticing and appraising (Atkins & Parker, 2012).

Perspective taking can also lead to other emotions. Atkins and Parker (2012) argued that a person may take the perspective of another in the sense that he or she understands the other is suffering but fails to respond if he or she appraises the person as irrelevant to his or her goals or selves in some way. This corresponds to a kind of "cold" perspective taking of understanding the other without really caring about them. Similarly, if an appraisal is made that the other is deserving of her suffering, then other emotions such as anger or disgust may occur. And if a person appraises that he or she does not have the capacity to cope with a secondary experience of suffering, he or she is likely to act defensively to avoid exposure to that suffering. This is what the literature refers to as a personal distress response.

A key determinant of whether perspective taking is followed by personal distress and avoidance, or empathic concern and compassion, appears to be the degree of self-other differentiation. Indeed Decety and Lamm argued that empathy is "the ability to experience and understand what others feel without confusion between oneself and others" (italics added; 2006, p. 1146). Empathizing with another can lead to personal distress when a person is unable to differentiate herself adequately from the other. Professional helpers can experience secondary traumatic stress or "compassion fatigue" (Figley, 2002) if they do not have sufficient self-other differentiation or emotional separation from others (Badger, Royse, & Craig, 2008; Decety & Lamm, 2006). Thomas and Otis demonstrated that emotional separation was negatively associated with burnout and compassion fatigue and concluded that risks arose when practitioners cared for clients "without the ability to keep themselves separate" (2010, p. 93). Carl Rogers, the psychologist most closely associated with empathic approaches to psychotherapy, saw empathy as sensing *"the client's private world as if it were your own, but without ever losing the 'as if' quality"* (Rogers, 1992, p. 829; emphasis added).

This latter quote beautifully illustrates the paradox of empathy. On the one hand, true empathy calls for a sense of the person's situation "from the inside"—a sense of oneness and connection. But effective helping requires a capacity to differentiate one's own responding from the responding of the other. How can we think about the nature of "self-other differentiation" in a way that allows us to develop helpful interventions? And is it possible to foster self-other differentiation? These questions represent both a gap in the literature and a practical concern. Without addressing how a person defines herself and takes the perspective of others, interventions to enhance empathy are simply dealing with the expression rather than the causes of empathy. To answer these questions we need to understand how a sense of self and other develops across the lifespan.

I now address these questions using a contextual behavioral account of language and cognition known as Relational Frame Theory (Hayes, Barnes-Holmes, & Roche, 2001). This will require some exposition of basic learning processes. The reader may be more familiar with attempts to understand perspective taking as "theory of mind" (Baron-Cohen & Wheelwright, 2004) and/or stages of epistemological development (Kegan, 1994; Piaget, 1969). I hope to provide enough of a technical framework to understand the core ideas of Relational Frame Theory, and thereby provide a more precise understanding of the nature of perspective taking and relationships.

THE DEVELOPMENT OF A SENSE OF SELF AND OTHER AND ITS IMPLICATIONS FOR EMPATHY

From a behavioral perspective, self is a verb—not a noun. The construction of sense of self is a process of self-discrimination. A prototypical form of this behavior can be found in pigeons who are able to "report" on their previous behavior by differentially pecking one key if they have previously responded to a stimulus and another if they have not. With the advent of verbal capabilities, human self-discrimination becomes vastly more complex. As children we all receive multiple exemplar training in reporting our own behavior. We are continually reinforced for being able to appropriately report "I want . . .", "I am . . .", "I know . . .", "you are", "you want", and so on. From this perspective, the self is a "repertoire of behavior imparted by an organized set of contingencies" (Skinner, 1974, p. 149). As a behavior, we might more appropriately use the word "selfing" to indicate the activity of creating and re-creating the self through verbal interaction with others in a community, however here I use the noun form as it is more widely understood.

We construct a sense of self in response to the functional demands of social interactions. This process is inherently social and linguistic—our 'knowing' is a function of environmental contingencies rather than any internal "force" or "drive". According to Skinner: "In arranging conditions under which a person describes the public or private world in which he lives, a community generates that very special form of behavior called knowing . . . Self-knowledge is of social origin. It is only when a person's private world becomes important to others that it is made important to him" (Skinner, 1974, pp. 30–31).

The development of self and cognition begins in interactions with others. The acquisition of human language begins with learning simple name-object pairings. Through exposure to many, many examples, the child learns to relate symbols to events and symbols to symbols. Initially a child might be reinforced by a smiling parent for looking toward the cat in the presence of the parent saying "where is the cat?" Gradually they are also reinforced for saying the word "cat" in the presence of an actual cat or a picture. With enough practice, they eventually learn to derive the reverse relationship automatically so that, for example, having seen a boat in a picture book and being told it is called a "boat" (object → name), the child is subsequently able to point to a boat when asked "where is the boat?" (name → object). This pattern of exposure to relational responding continues over thousands of examples of increasingly complex relations, including spatial, oppositional, hierarchical, temporal, evaluative, and comparative. Such relational responding is called relational framing. Relational framing has three defining features.

Mutual entailment refers to the fact that a relation in one direction always corresponds to a second relation in the opposite direction. For example, if a child learns that coin A is worth more than coin B, he will derive that B is worth less than A.

Combinational entailment refers to derivation of combined relationships. For example, if the child now learns that coin B is worth more than coin C, he will derive that A is also worth more than C (as well as C < A and C < B).

Transformation of stimulus functions refers to the way in which words and symbols become meaningful. From a relational frame theory perspective, to change the meaning of an object or event is to change the way the organism responds to that object or event. For example, imagine a child has previously experienced buying sweets using coin B such that coin B is seen as desirable. If the child is now introduced to two new coins, A and C, and is told that A is "worth more" than B, she will choose A over both B and C even though only B has previously been directly reinforced. In other words, A acquires new stimulus functions through relating based upon arbitrary symbols rather than formal properties or direct exposure.

The notion of transformation of stimulus functions is particularly important for understanding the difference between behavioral approaches to selfing and cognitive approaches. As we will see, self is not a thing or even a representation inside the person influencing behavior; it is a response of the whole person to a context that calls for particular forms of behavior. Similarly, from this perspective, cognition and emotion, including perspective taking and empathy, are not hypothetical mental causes but a form of behavior—namely, private relational responding. Next we describe how this capacity to relationally frame events both leads to the formation of a sense of self at the same time as making it possible for a person to take the perspective of others and experience empathy.

The capacity to differentiate self from others, and therefore to empathize, takes years to develop in children (Kegan, 1994). Relational Frame

Theory suggests this is because it involves repeated exposure to a language community making skilled use of a particular form of relational responding known as deictic framing (McHugh, Stewart, & Hooper, 2012). Deictic framing involves three main relational frames: I-YOU, *HERE-THERE* and *NOW-THEN*. Children struggle with learning these distinctions. For example, when asked "What did YOU have for breakfast?" a young child may respond with what the speaker had for breakfast. Or she may mistakenly believe an absent observer would know where a hidden doll is located because the child knows where the doll is located. In cognitive psychology, this "false belief task" (Wimmer & Perner, 1983) demonstrates whether or not a child is able to represent another's perspective internally. In relational frame theory terms, the child's behavior indicates whether or not the child has developed an appropriately complex repertoire of relational responding, specifically to contextual stimuli representing self and other.

Deictic framing takes years to learn because it requires abstraction. Most forms of relating have physical analogues in the world. For example, the comparative relational frame "more than" can be taught by comparing actual physical amounts of a liquid. But deictic relational frames have no physical analogue and depend entirely upon the point of view for experience. HERE is only HERE relative to my current point of view. If I move over THERE it becomes a new HERE, and what was previously HERE becomes THERE. The quality of "HERE" only exists relative to my perspective, not as a physical property of the world. Skillfully using deictic framing relies upon the child abstracting a point of view from which experience is witnessed.

In summary, I have argued self is a behavior based upon a form of verbal relating that allows us to abstract a point of view upon the world, a sense of knowing distinct from others. From this perspective, self can only exist in reciprocal interaction with other. Self is born from interaction with a linguistic community. But there can be no "I" without a "YOU". Thus it is also this process of deictic relational framing that allows us to take the perspective of others. McHugh, Barnes-Holmes, and Barnes-Holmes (2004) demonstrated that older children were increasingly effective at answering questions ranging from "I have a red brick and you have a green brick. Which brick do you have?" through to such complex deictic framing as "Yesterday you were sitting there on the blue chair, today you are sitting here on the black chair. If here was there and there was here; and if now was then and then was now. Where would you be sitting now?" Over time children learn to correctly use increasingly complex deictic frames to take the perspective of others.

If self and perspective taking is verbal relational behavior, then there are three functionally distinct senses of self: self as the content of verbal relations (the conceptualized self), self as the process of verbal relations (the knowing self), and self as the context of verbal relations (the transcendent self; Hayes, 1984). And since I-YOU is one distinction, not two, the establishment of these senses of self also establishes other-as-content, other-as-process, and other-as-context. These distinctions will allow a more precise specification of the particular form of self-other differentiation required to experience empathic concern rather than personal distress.

SELF-AS-CONTENT AND OTHER-AS-CONTENT: THE CONCEPTUALIZED SELF AND THE CONCEPTUALIZED OTHER

As children, we learn very quickly that it is helpful to be able to describe ourselves to others. The social environment provides numerous reinforcers for being able to consistently describe characteristic preferences, capabilities, and experiences. For example, if at one meal a child says she liked broccoli and at the next she says she doesn't, a parent will be quick to point out that the child's descriptions of herself is inconsistent and will reinforce more consistent self-descriptions.

Self-as-content is our capacity to relate one thing to another applied to conceptualizing (i.e., abstracting) qualities of our own behavior. Such descriptions allow others to predict our behavior, and provide a concise and greatly simplified summary of our history of experience (e.g., "I am a psychologist"). Over time we learn to internalize our conceptualized self and form stable but covert beliefs about our identity. In the workplace, self-as-content might refer to our job attitudes, the things we characteristically like and dislike, our perceived roles and responsibilities, and our place in a network of social relationships.

Other-as-content refers to such verbal relating regarding the stable features of others in the service of understanding and predicting others. A wide range of theories, social perception, and cognition describe how we continually evaluate and conceptualize others in terms of stable characteristics, histories, and roles in order to predict their behavior (Dweck, Hong, & Chiu, 1993; Fiske & Taylor, 1991; Hogg, 2001). These theories demonstrate that conceptualizing about self and other is an essential aspect of social interaction.

But verbal relating regarding self-as-content and other-as-content are a double edged sword in terms of empathic responding. On the one hand, self/other-as-content can provide useful summaries of learning histories that inform understanding of how the self and other might respond to a given situation. For example, the statement "I am a psychologist, you are an engineer and, as such, we are likely to have very different views of the world" might aid understanding. Similarly, characterizing one's own stable personal values (e.g., "I value close relationship with my colleagues") can also motivate more empathic responding (Atkins & Parker, 2012). Other-as-content can also be helpful. Imagining the other's learning history, their personality, preferences, goals, and values can inform appropriately targeted empathic responding.

However, conceptualizations of self and other can also interfere with empathy because of the rigidity and context insensitivity of such conceptualizations. Atkins and Parker (2012) described in detail how appraisals of self and others can interfere with compassionate responding. For example, if we make an appraisal that a person is personally responsible for the situation in which he finds himself, we are less likely to experience empathic concern and more likely to experience other emotions such as anger. Similarly, appraisals that the other is in some way irrelevant to our lives and goals are likely to lead to apathy rather than empathic engagement. Finally, in appraisals that we are unable to cope with the aversive emotions likely to result from engagement with another who is suffering, we are more likely to avoid the situation than respond compassionately (Atkins & Parker, 2012). One can easily imagine how such self-as-content beliefs such as "I am not a good listener", "I am supposed to be an expert with the answers", or "I am tougher than you are" can interfere with empathic responding.

At the same time, judgments and projections regarding the other can also interfere with empathy. Imagining another's learning history, personality, preferences, and goals and values is a fallible process. For example, even after years of marriage, partners can seriously misjudge how a person is likely to respond to a given situation. Thus empathic responding from other-as-content must also be tempered by paying attention to the dynamic cues available in each moment from other-as-process.

SELF-AS-PROCESS: THE KNOWING SELF

Self-as-process refers to the reporting of an experience of self in the present moment. It is the behavior of overtly and covertly describing thoughts, feelings, sensa-tions, memories and images occurring HERE-NOW.[1] Self-as-process behavior also receives a great deal of social reinforcement. Statements like "I am happy", "My stomach is hurting", or "I don't understand what I am meant to do" provide useful and predictive information to others. Over time, such statements about the self also serve useful private functions. To say "I am happy" may be highly predictive of what will happen in the next instance or in a very similar context in the future whereas self-as-content descriptions such as "I am generally a happy person" provide broad predictability across contexts. Self-as-process descriptions are more flexible, dynamic, and context sensitive than self-as-content descriptions. Being able to flexibly monitor our own state is the basis of successful self-regulation.

Other-as-process refers to one's overt and covert description of the immediate, ongoing experience of the other. Other-as-process is a central component of perspective taking and empathic responding: It is "based on a moment-to-moment construction of reactions of the other" (Barnes-Holmes, Hayes, & Dymond, 2001, p. 134). Batson (2009) distinguished between an "imag-ine-other" per-spective that involves imagining how the other sees his or her situation and feels as a result, and an "imagine-self" perspective that involves imagining how you would see the situation were you in the other person's position. Verbal relating regarding other-as-process could involve either of these forms of constructing another's experience, but only an "imagine-other" perspective would be likely to be experienced as empathic in the sense of "standing in the shoes of another". Accurate other-as-process is the basis of a psychotherapist effectively engaging with a client, or a speaker successfully reading their audience.

Self-other differentiation at the level of process appears to be particularly important for experiencing empathy without unhealthy personal distress. The verbal relating described here as self-as-process and other-as-process is the fundamental self-regulatory process associated with empathy. Decety and Lamm (2006) reviewed studies of the neural processes underpinning empathy and described how such verbal, self-regulatory processes are essential for self-other differentiation:

> one critical question debated among social psychologists is whether perspective-taking instructions induce empathic concern and/or personal distress, and to what extent prosocial motivation springs from self-other overlap . . . The recent work reviewed here demonstrates that adopting a self-perspective when observing others in pain results in stronger feelings of personal distress and activates the pain matrix to a larger extent, as well as the amygdala [involved in threat detection]. Such a complete self-other merging seems to be detrimental to empathic concern . . . Conversely, when participants take the other's perspective, there is less overlap between the neural circuits involved in the processing of first-hand experience of pain, and they indeed report more feelings of empathic concern. From these studies, it can be concluded that empathy relies both on bottomup information processing (shared neural systems between first-hand emotional experience and the perception or imagination of the other's experience), as well as top-down information processing that allows modulation and self-regulation." (Decety & Lamm, 2006, p. 1160)

In other words, we must notice our own experience, the other's experience and the difference between the two. From a relational frame theory perspective, to notice is to respond, and specifically to make meaning of the cues provided by the other. That is, to "notice" is to verbally relate; to construct a relational network regarding the state of the other (other-as-process). The neural and behavioral evidence indicates that, unless one is also able to construct a discrete relational network regarding our own experience (self-as-process) and hold both relational networks in a frame of distinction, our experience will mirror the other's, and we will experience personal distress rather than empathic concern. Knowing one's own self-as-process allows one to self-regulate to avoid the detrimental effects of shared neural systems that do not differentiate between self and other.

We are now in a position to better understand the precise nature of self-other differentiation required for empathic responding rather than personal distress. I have argued that self-other differentiation at the level of content can be helpful, but can also easily create disconnection from the other if one is not conscious of automatic appraisals and judgments regarding the other. By contrast, differentiation at the level of process is a key component of mature empathy. To illustrate, the sort of verbal relating I have in mind could be expressed covertly or overtly as follows: "There is my process occurring here and now and there is your process occurring here and now. I can acknowledge your process and indeed care about it without having to have the same process myself. Conversely there is no reason why your process must be the same as my process. I can acknowledge your process, even deeply care about your process and want something that is more satisfying or enjoyable for you, without experiencing the distress you are experiencing." One can easily recognize mature self-other differentiation in this statement and appreciate why such complex relational framing can take a lifetime to acquire.

SELF-AS-CONTEXT: THE TRANSCENDENT SELF

Self-as-context refers to the context within which verbal relational framing is occurring. In relational frame theory, self-as-context is understood as the point of view or locus from which events are experienced. Self-as-context is awareness, but it is awareness conditioned by the prior acquisition of deictic framing that allows a distinction between the I-HERE-NOW that perceives psychological content THERE-THEN (Hayes, 1984). That is, there is a sense of an I or ME that is doing the observing. Self-as-context is transcendent in the sense that we can never observe our point of view from outside our point of view. Torneke provides a vivid description of this aspect of self-as-context:

> We cannot observe this perspective in itself . . . We can talk or write about it, just as I am doing now, and we can observe the consequences of being able to take this perspective. We can make observations from a specific perspective or locus, but we can never observe this locus or perspective as such. Of course, this is rather obvious, because from which perspective would we observe it? All we have is I-here-now. And whatever we observe, it simply cannot be this locus, as that is the vantage from which we observe it". (Torneke, 2010, p. 107)

Other-as-context appears to be a relatively infrequent (and difficult to describe) form of verbal relating. Barnes-Holmes et al. describe other-as-context as:

when the speaker is psychologically connected to the listener as a purely conscious person. In this aspect, the speaker and the listener are one, since 'HERE and NOW' is imputed to be a singular event (i.e., one cannot be HERE and NOW, simultaneously, at different times and places). Perhaps for this reason, the level of self-as-context is associated with a sense of the transcendent other-the two go hand in hand". (Barnes-Holmes et al., 2001, p. 135)

To experience other-as-context is perhaps to experience the other as beyond time, location and, in a sense at least, separation. In this sense, self-as-context experience seems to foster a sense of oneness between self and other rather than differentiation.

In summary, I have described three forms of "selfing" behavior. Verbal relating allows us to describe to ourselves and others (a) our abstracted qualities and experiences as content, (b) our current here-and-now experience as process, and (c) the continuity of a point of view from which we experience the world. From a contextual, behavioral perspective, such "selfing" behavior is a functional response to social contingencies. We learn to report our preferences, history, and characteristics because the social world values predictability and coherence. Similarly, we learn to report on our current experience because it allows social communication and cooperation. And while most verbal environments (with the exception of meditation retreats and philosophy seminars) do not explicitly reinforce talking about ourselves as bare awareness or perspective, we are continuously reinforced for correctly discriminating our "own" experience (I/HERE) from that of others (YOU/THERE) and for having a stable perspective from which we view experience.

Furthermore, the very same verbal relating that gives rise to these three senses of self also gives rise to three senses of other. We can relate to the other in terms of (a) our conceptualizations of their stable characteristics over time, (b) their ongoing process of knowing, or (c) (perhaps, rarely) at the level of bare awareness itself. From this perspective, deictic relating is perspective taking, and perspective taking can be developed throughout the lifespan through multiple exemplar training in shifting perspectives. In the remainder of this chapter I explore how these ideas can be used to shape thinking about interventions to improve empathy in organizations.

INTERVENTIONS TO ENHANCE EMPATHY

By far the oldest approach to improving empathy in organizations is through training in communication skills, most notably active listening (e.g., Jentz, 2007) and dialogue (Isaacs, 1999; Mazutis & Slawinski, 2008). This practical approach has been widely used in organizations for generations, and yet there appears to have been no systematic research regarding the impacts of such training upon emotional self-regulation or empathic responding. In a sense, this is an "outside-in" approach to increasing empathy. If done well, teaching a person how to behave more empathically can enhance her willingness and capacity to take the perspective of others (Coulehan et al., 2001). Although such training is widely used and effective for improving relationships, it is usually framed simply as a technique rather than as an opportunity for self-development. The reasons why such approaches might lead to changes in epistemology (Kegan, 1994) and identity have not been articulated.

Another approach to developing empathy is through improving individual skills in emotional identification, emotional understanding, and emotional management. Emotional intelligence (Goleman, 2006) has been variously defined, and there is a correspondingly wide array of approaches to improving emotional intelligence (Ciarrochi & Mayer, 2007). While research on emotional intelligence in organizations has been much more extensive than that on active listening, most of it has been directed toward measuring emotional intelligence as a capability, and research on improving emotional intelligence is still in its infancy.

Both of these approaches tacitly assume that improving empathy is a matter of improving skills. While both approaches can be extremely effective in organizations, the account of perspective taking provided above makes it clear that both of these approaches ignore a deeper aspect of sustainable empathy, the capacity to balance a felt sense of connection with ongoing differentiation from another.

More recently, many organizations have implemented mindfulness training to improve staff well-being, work engagement, and performance (Glomb, Duffy, Bono, & Yang, 2011). Mindfulness is defined by Kabat-Zinn as "paying attention on purpose, in the present moment, and non-judgmentally" (2003, p. 145). Almost all definitions of mindfulness include at least an awareness component–attending to the present moment; and an attitudinal component—acceptance of experience whether it be positive, negative, or neutral (Bishop et al., 2004). From a behavioral perspective, attending to present moment experience is functionally equivalent to self-as-process (Foody, Barnes-Holmes, & Barnes-Holmes, 2012) and amounts to responding under the control of stimuli available HERE-NOW rather than responding under the control of verbal relating regarding the past or future. Acceptance is behaviorally defined as "allowing of thoughts and feelings to be as they are without trying to change their content, form or frequency" (Fletcher, Schoendorff, & Hayes, 2010, p. 43). Acceptance and Commitment Therapy (Hayes, Strosahl, & Wilson, 2011) also adds two further concepts helpful for understanding the nature of awareness described as mindfulness: defusion and self-as-context. Defusion is recognizing thoughts and feelings as passing mental events not literal truths while self-as-context has been described at length earlier and is the sense of self as an observer or perspective from which experience is observed (Hayes & Plumb, 2007).

Defusion and self-as-context are two sides of the same coin with defusion referring to that which I am not ("I am not my thoughts and feelings") and self-as-context referring to that which I am ("I am an observer of my experience").

The four processes of self-as-process, defusion, acceptance, and self-as-context work interactively to undermine the dominance of verbal relating, thereby supporting behavior that is more sensitive and responsive to the environment, allowing a larger set of contingencies to be noticed and a broader behavioral repertoire to be available (Vilardaga, Estevez, Levin, & Hayes, 2012). Changing the way individuals relate to their own verbal relating provides them with the capability to respond more adaptively in a wider range of contexts. In the next section I review evidence indicating that mindfulness training is associated with increases in perspective taking and empathic responding, and reductions in personal distress. I then discuss why these effects might occur using the theory of perspective taking presented above.

MINDFULNESS AND MEDITATION ARE ASSOCIATED WITH ENHANCED EMPATHY

There is now considerable evidence that mindfulness and meditation training are associated with increased levels of empathy. Since mindfulness programs are now being increasingly adopted in workplaces around the world (Glomb et al., 2011), it is timely to explore their likely impacts upon empathy and relationships in the workplace. In this section, I review the evidence from cross-sectional, intervention, qualitative, and neurological studies in turn.

Mindfulness has been positively associated with empathy in a series of cross-sectional studies. Tipsord (2009) explored the relationships between different facets of mindfulness as measured by the Five Facet Mindfulness Questionnaire (FFMQ; Baer, Smith, Hopkins, Krietemeyer, & Toney, 2006) and the Interpersonal Reactivity Index (IRI; Davis, 1983). Mindfulness was positively related to perspective taking and negatively related to personal distress. At the subscale level, higher observing scores were associated with increased perspective taking and empathic concern while higher nonreactivity scores were associated with less personal distress. Thomas and Otis (2010) found a similar pattern of results with mindfulness (FFMQ) being positively correlated with perspective taking, negatively correlated with personal distress, and unrelated to empathic concern. Greason and Cashwell (2009) also showed that mindfulness (FFMQ) correlated positively with empathy (IRI) although they did not report relationships at the subscale level for either measure. Overall, these cross-sectional studies suggest that mindfulness improves perspective taking and self-regulation to reduce personal distress.

Mindfulness training has also been linked to increases in empathy. Lesh (1970) showed that practicing Zazen meditation for 4 weeks, 30 minutes per day, increased empathic accuracy relative to control participants. The empathic accuracy task involved watching a video of a counseling client and then choosing which feeling the participant believed the client was experiencing in the video. Shapiro, Schwartz, and Bonner (1998) showed increased empathy, measured using an adapted version of the self-report Empathy Construct Rating Scale (Monica, 1981) for medical and premedical students who completed an eight-week Mindfulness Based Stress Reduction (MBSR) program. Just as in Lesh's (1970) study, improvement in empathy was mediated by reduction in anxiety. Shapiro et al. speculated that "the intervention may have helped students cultivate listening skills and develop new, more compassionate perspectives and paradigms to approach their own lives as well as their future patients' lives" (1998, p. 594). Krasner et al. (2009) also showed significant improvements in empathy among medical students as measured by the Jefferson Scale of Physician Empathy and that changes in mindfulness were correlated with changes in the perspective taking subscale of physician empathy. More recently, Shapiro, Brown, Thoresen, and Plante (2011) showed significant increases in self-reported empathy 2 and 12 months after an MBSR course. Finally, to the extent that meditators engaged in a 3-month retreat improved in self-regulatory capability, they also improved in a measure of adaptive functioning that included empathy (Sahdra et al., 2011).

However, the pattern of relationships between mindfulness training and empathy appears to be complex, and sensitive to the specific design of studies. For example, in a second study comparing an 8-week mindfulness intervention with a wait-list control group, Tipsord (2009) used a modified empathic accuracy task and showed that those trained in mindfulness (a) made more inferences regarding the mental states of others in a video and (b) were more likely to make inferences at times that corresponded to times when the subject of the video actually reported having a thought or feeling. However, those trained in mindfulness were no more accurate than the control group in their inferences regarding the mental states of others. This pattern of results suggests that mindfulness training enhanced noticing of another but did not improve the quality of inferences regarding the experience of the other.

There are also studies that have *not* shown a link between mindfulness, meditation, and empathy. For example, Beddoe and Murphy (2004) conducted an uncontrolled pretest-posttest study with only 16 participants and failed to find any effects of an MBSR course on empathy in nurses. They conclude this effect may have arisen because the nurses were very high in empathy initially. Other studies using eight-week meditation courses have also not found impacts upon measures of empathy (Galantino, Baime, Maguire, Szapary, & Farrar, 2005; Pearl & Carlozzi, 1994) but have made use of relatively weak designs. Finally, Plummer (2008) collected data from therapists and their clients and found that those who meditated were less likely to be perceived as empathic by their clients, and this effect was larger for those who spent more time meditating.

Another study used an innovative qualitative approach to show that even very brief mindfulness interventions may increase the degree to which people take the perspective of others. Block-Lerner, Adair, Plumb, Rhatigan, and Orsillo (2007) reported a study in which randomly assigned participants received either a brief mindfulness intervention, a positive thinking intervention, or a relaxation control condition. The mindfulness intervention involved instructions to be aware of, and accepting toward, whatever thoughts and feeling arose. The positive thinking intervention involved instructions encouraging the evaluation and control of thoughts and feelings. Participants watched an emotionally evocative film clip and wrote about their reactions, which were then coded using the Linguistic Inquiry Word Count program (Pennebaker, Booth, & Francis, 2007). Participants in the mindful awareness condition wrote more about other people, and used the first-person singular tense less than participants in the positive thinking group. Overall, these results suggest that even a brief mindfulness intervention can increase the degree to which participants consider others.

This pattern of results was also obtained in a qualitative study of trainee therapists. McCollum and Gehart (2010) reported that daily meditation increased the degree to which students felt compassion and acceptance toward both themselves and their clients. Most of the quotes they reported in their paper emphasized the importance of being less judgmental toward self and others. For example, one participant reported: "At my fieldwork site, the clients are struggling to function on a very basic level. What they don't need are heavy judgments about material wealth and success. The meditation is helping to guide me toward a non-judgmental acceptance of them and myself" (McCollum & Gehart, 2010, p. 356). While another stated: ". . . to be an effective therapist, one must be comfortable with the positive and negative traits that encompass oneself. How else can we convey to clients that their tears, anger and feelings are OK to have in session, if we don't accept these qualities in ourselves?" (McCollum & Gehart, 2010, p. 356). In a similar vein, Aiken (2006) reported that therapists who were also experienced meditators believed that their practices enhanced their capacity to achieve a felt sense of the client's inner experience and be more present to any pain and suffering of the client. Mindfulness training enhances empathy in part because it helps people take judgments of others (self-as-content) less seriously and instead attend more closely to their moment-to-moment process (self-as-process).

Finally, studies of brain function and structure have also suggested links between meditation practice and empathy or perspective taking. For example, Leung et al. (2012) conducted a study of long-term practitioners of loving-kindness meditation and reported increases in the grey-matter volume of the right angular gyrus, an area previously associated with empathy and perspective taking (Decety & Lamm, 2007). This finding appears to confirm earlier research showing experts in loving-kindness meditation had more activity than novices in the right angular gyrus when listening to emotional vocalizations during loving-kindness meditation (Lutz, Brefczynski-Lewis, Johnstone, & Davidson, 2008).

In summary, the weight of evidence suggests that mindfulness and meditation training are associated with increased empathy. In particular, there is consistent evidence that mindfulness is associated with lower levels of personal distress and higher levels of perspective taking. There appears to be little evidence that mindfulness increases empathic concern, at least as measured by the Interpersonal Reactivity Index (Davis, 1983). This result makes sense when one examines the items in the IRI associated with empathic concern, all of which refer to changes in the frequency or intensity of feelings. Changing the frequency or intensity of feelings is not an explicit aim of mindfulness training; rather such training is directed toward reducing automatic reactivity to unhelpful feelings.

WHY DOES MINDFULNESS TRAINING IMPROVE EMPATHY?

Mindfulness training might increase empathic responding via many pathways including improvements in emotional self-regulation and changes in relationship goals and values (see Atkins & Parker, 2012). Here I wish to focus on the effects of mindfulness training on self-other differentiation. I argue that mindfulness and meditation training have effects at the levels of content, process, and context. Specifically, mindfulness training helps create a more flexible relationship to verbal content, enhances noticing of process, and creates a stable sense of self as an awareness that is beyond threat, and these effects all support more empathic responding rather than personal distress.

MINDFULNESS CREATES A MORE FLEXIBLE RELATIONSHIP TO CONTENT

One key facet of mindfulness training is learning to see thoughts and emotions as passing mental events rather than as literal truths regulating behavior. Typically participants are instructed to witness their thoughts without judgment or elaboration. Contrast the statements "I am angry" with "I notice I am angry". In the former statement, "I" is in a frame of coordination with the experience whereas in the latter it is in a frame of distinction. This process of discriminating between self and private content is referred to as "defusion", and it is a particularly important part of mindfulness based therapies such as Acceptance and Commitment Therapy. If a thought is perceived to be "bad" and if the client is fused with that negative thought, then the functions of the self are transformed to also be "bad". Mindfulness training in therapy teaches clients to discover a place from which they can "have" rather than "be" their thoughts and feelings. It "temporarily puts the literal, temporal, and evaluative functions of language on extinction" (Hayes & Shenk, 2004, p. 252).

Defusion enables redirecting attention away from labeling of self and other, toward more flexibly engaging with one's own and the other's processes. To give some feel for how this might work in the workplace, imagine a manager who is fused with the belief that she is an expert who is supposed to provide solutions (self-as-content) or that her subordinate is incapable of finding solutions for himself (other-as-content). Faced with the subordinate expressing a difficulty, she is unlikely to empathize with the subordinate, and instead will seek to provide solutions in line with her perception of what is going on for the other. By contrast, empathically listening to the other would be engaging at the level of process.

There is evidence to suggest that promoting defusion from thoughts and feelings reduces reactivity to automatic evaluations regarding ourselves and others. Hayes, Bissett et al. (2004) showed that, relative to a control group that received multicultural training, a mindfulness-based intervention for a group of alcohol and drug counselors reduced stigmatizing attitudes toward clients and burnout at three-month follow-up. Thus, the intervention appeared to work to assist in both self-care and also caring for others. Masuda et al. (2007) reported similar results but also showed their intervention was most effective in reducing stigmatization for those participants who were experientially avoidant or fused with their judgmental thoughts. Such a process appears to be implicated in the lack of empathic responding arising from stereotyping. To the extent that a person is fused with his or her categorizations and evaluations of other human beings (other-as-content), they lose contact with the individual, unique, and dynamic qualities of the other available in the present moment and see them instead in terms of generalizations. This process appears to be similar to the depersonalization of others described by self-categorization theory (Hogg, 2001).

Empathy doesn't require defusion from all thoughts and beliefs regarding self and others. For example, behaving in response to personal preferences and capacities might provide a basis for authentic expression in the presence of another and helpful self-other differentiation. For example, Lesh (1970) found that empathy was supported by a high self-regard and self-awareness of personal characteristics.

MINDFULNESS ENHANCES NOTICING
AND SELF-REGULATION OF PROCESS

One pathway whereby mindfulness seems likely to improve empathy, and particularly perspective taking, is simply through responding to more cues provided by others. Mindfulness training courses create a context for learning to bring behavior more under the control of internal or environmental cues available in the present moment, and less under the control of verbal stimuli (thoughts and feelings) regarding the past or possible futures. Atkins and Parker (2012) reviewed evidence regarding the effects of mindfulness training and proposed that this aspect of mindfulness training improves noticing of another's emotional state by directing attention to the immediate social and emotional cues regarding that state. In other words, self-as-process and other-as-process are privileged in mindfulness training over experience at the level of content. Over time, this can lead to enhanced awareness of one's own and other's emotions, and thus can aid empathic responding in the workplace. According to Glomb et al., "a growing body of social neurobiology research indicates that our capacity to be attuned to others depends, in part, on our knowledge of our own mind and internal state" (2011, p. 132). Of course, mindfulness training does not necessarily result in long-term increases in noticing of others. To be sustainable, responding to the socio-emotional cues of others must then be reinforced by the experience of improving relationships in this way.

A key aspect of self-as-process and other-as-process is developing a willingness to be in the presence of thoughts, feelings, and sensations without seeking to change their form or frequency. This is particularly important if one is empathizing with someone who is experiencing aversive emotion because of the potential effects of secondary stress upon burnout and professional impairment (Badger et al., 2008; Figley, 2002). To the extent that a person is able to accept his unpleasant thoughts and feelings arising in the present moment, he is more able to be empathic toward others. McCracken and Yang (2008) found that rehabilitation workers with higher levels of acceptance were less likely to avoid situations in which they might encounter the suffering of their clients. Vilardaga et al. (2012) similarly found that mindfulness predicted levels of burnout among addiction counselors. When fused with negative appraisals concerning their clients, and when unable to accept difficult thoughts and feelings, counselors believed they were less able to cope, less sensitive toward their clients, and less able to effectively help them (Vilardaga et al., 2012).

MINDFULNESS CREATES A SENSE OF SELF BEYOND THREAT

The effects of mindfulness training in terms of the context of verbal relations can be understood at both a mundane level and a transcendent level. At the mundane level, self-as-context is unaffected by psychological content, and mindfulness training may therefore enhance a sense of self as relatively beyond threat. Self-as-context is constant despite changing experiential content: Although the content of experience changes, the point of view from which experience is witnessed is the same at 60 as it was at age 5. Even when experiencing distress, the practitioner realizes that some part of them (namely awareness itself) remains unchanged, is not distressed, and is beyond threat (Hayes et al., 2011). This awareness of a stable sense of self beyond threat can support responding with empathic concern rather than personal distress (Atkins & Parker, 2012). At a more transcendent level, mindfulness and intensive meditation training can provide experiences of oneness that appear to be beyond psychological content. Such states may embody the very deepest forms of empathy.

CONCLUSION

Decety and Lamm argued that empathy is "the ability to experience and understand what others feel *without confusion between oneself and others*" (italics added; 2006, p. 1146). In this chapter, I have explored what it means to be without confusion between oneself and others. One reason why a technical account of self and perspective taking is important is because it helps bridge the gap between bottom-up, automatic, and top-down, self-regulatory aspects of empathy (Decety & Lamm, 2006). I have argued that verbal relational responding is the process whereby bottom-up affective signals are interpreted, evaluated, and potentially regulated. Excessive identification with another who is suffering appears to lead to personal distress and avoidance rather than empathic concern. This is particularly a problem for roles involving helping or other forms of emotional labor.

And yet there is a potential paradox here as empathy appears to be motivated by a felt sense of connection between self and other. How can we understand self-other differentiation in a way that allows us to improve it in organizations? I have argued that responding to conceptualizations of self and other can be helpful but can also impair empathy. Self-other differentiation at the level of content generally creates separation and judgment rather than empathy. Responding at the level of present-moment experience is the essence of responding to the others experience, but it is here that differentiation of self and other is essential to avoid personal distress. At the level of awareness itself, a stable sense of self beyond threat can be contacted in such a way to support empathy. Furthermore, in rare instances one can experience a sense of shared awareness that transcends difference. Mindfulness training appears to support the development of all three senses of perspective taking in a way that can enhance empathy.

To this point, my analysis has been focused upon verbal relating from the perspective of one person. But this analysis might also be applied to understanding empathy in dyads. Many, perhaps most, social relationships in the workplace might be characterized by both parties perceiving the other in terms of verbal content. Such relationships will be somewhat disconnected as each relies upon their conceptualizations regarding the other rather than their observations of what the other might actually be experiencing in the present moment. The most effective dialogue arises when all parties operate at the level of other-as-process. And a relationship where both parties are operating at the level of other-as-context might conceivably characterize the deepest form of unconditional love.

Of course, other combinations, such as where one person attempts to engage with another's process while the other is engaging with them at the level of content might lead to a range of different outcomes. Unfortunately there is insufficient space here to pursue this line of theorizing.

This analysis has a number of broader implications for organizations. First, it provides a way of understanding why skills-based programs such as listening and dialogue training might work. Second, the issue of self-other differentiation is not just important in the context of empathy. The analysis provided above could equally have been applied to the development of authentic leadership. Understanding how we construct a sense of self and others pervades every aspect of our social experience.

NOTE

1. Kahneman and Ris (2005) refer to self-as-process as the "experiencing self" and note that it has hardly been studied in psychology because almost all instruments call for retrospective report and thus invoke remembered abstractions regarding the self.

REFERENCES

Aiken, G. A. (2006). *The potential effect of mindfulness meditation on the cultivation of empathy in psychotherapy: A qualitative inquiry.* Ph.D. 3217528, Saybrook Graduate School and Research Center, United States—California. OxResearch; ProQuest Central; ProQuest Dissertations & Theses A&I database.

Atkins, P. W., & Parker, S. K. (2012). Understanding individual compassion in organizations: The role of appraisals and psychological flexibility. *Academy of Management Review, 37*(4), 524–546.

Badger, K., Royse, D., & Craig, C. (2008). Hospital social workers and indirect trauma exposure: An exploratory study of contributing factors. *Health & Social Work, 33*(1), 63–71. doi: 10.1093/hsw/33.1.63

Baer, R. A., Smith, G. T., Hopkins, J., Krietemeyer, J., & Toney, L. (2006). Using self-report assessment methods to explore facets of mindfulness. *Assessment, 13*(1), 27–45.

Barnes-Holmes, D., Hayes, S. C., & Dymond, S. (2001). Self and self-directed rules. In S. C. Hayes, D. Barnes-Holmes, & B. Roche (Eds.), *Relational frame theory: A post-Skinnerian account of human language and cognition* (pp. 119–139). NY: Kluwer Academic/Plenum.

Baron-Cohen, S., & Wheelwright, S. (2004). The empathy quotient: An investigation of adults with Asperger syndrome or high functioning autism, and normal sex differences. *Journal of Autism and Developmental Disorders, 34*(2), 163–175. doi: 10.1023/B:JADD.0000022607.19833.00

Batson, C. D. (2009). Two forms of perspective taking: Imagining how another feels and imagining how you would feel. In K. D. Markman, W.M.P. Klein & J. A. Suhr (Eds.), *Handbook of imagination and mental simulation* (pp. 267–279). NY: Psychology Press.

68   *Paul W. B. Atkins*

Batson, C. D., & Ahmad, N. Y. (2009). *Empathy-induced altruism: A threat to the collective good altruism and prosocial behavior in groups* (Vol. 26, pp. 1–23): Emerald Group. A. E. Beddoe & S. Murphy (2004). Does mindfulness decrease stress and foster empathy among nursing students? *The Journal of Nursing Education, 43*(7), 305–312.

Bishop, S. R., Lau, M., Shapiro, S., Carlson, L., Anderson, N. D., Carmody, J., . . . Devins, G. (2004). Mindfulness: A proposed operational definition. *Clinical Psychology: Science and Practice, 11*(3), 230–241.

Block-Lerner, J., Adair, C., Plumb, J. C., Rhatigan, D. L., & Orsillo, S. M. (2007). The case for mindfulness-based approaches in the cultivation of empathy: Does nonjudgmental, present-moment awareness increase capacity for perspective-taking and empathic concern? *Journal of Marital and Family Therapy, 33*(4), 501.

Ciarrochi, J., & Mayer, J. D. (2007). *Applying emotional intelligence: A practitioner's guide xiv*, p. 169. NY: Psychology Press.

Coulehan, J. L., Platt, F. W., Egener, B., Frankel, R., Lin, C. T., Lown, B., & Salazar, W. H. (2001). "Let me see if i have this right . . .": Words that help build empathy. *Annals of Internal Medicine, 135*(3), 221–227.

Davis, M. H. (1983). Measuring individual-differences in empathy: Evidence for a multidimensional approach. *Journal of Personality and Social Psychology, 44*(1), 113–126.

Decety, J., & Lamm, C. (2006). Human empathy through the lens of social neuroscience. *The Scientific World Journal, 6,* 1146–1163. doi: 10.1100/tsw.2006.221

Decety, J., & Lamm, C. (2007). The role of the right temporoparietal junction in social interaction: How low-level computational processes contribute to meta-cognition. *The Neuroscientist, 13*(6), 580–593. doi: 10.1177/1073858407304654

Dweck, C. S., Hong, Y.-y., & Chiu, C.-y. (1993). Implicit theories: Individual differences in the likelihood and meaning of dispositional inference. *Personality and Social Psychology Bulletin, 19*(5), 644–656. doi: 10.1177/0146167293195015

Eisenberg, N. (2010). Empathy-related responding: Links with self-regulation, moral judgment, and moral behavior. In M. Mikulincer (Ed.), *Prosocial motives, emotions, and behavior: The better angels of our nature* (pp. 129–148). Washington, DC: American Psychological Association.

Figley, C. R. (2002). *Treating compassion fatigue* (pp. viii, 227). NY: Brunner-Routledge.

Fiske, S. T., & Taylor, S. E. (1991). *Social cognition* (2nd ed.). NY: McGraw-Hill.

Fletcher, L., Schoendorff, B., & Hayes, S. (2010). Searching for mindfulness in the brain: A process-oriented approach to examining the neural correlates of mindfulness. *Mindfulness, 1*(1), 41–63. doi: 10.1007/s12671–010–0006-5

Foody, M., Barnes-Holmes, Y., & Barnes-Holmes, D. (2012). The role of self in acceptance and commitment therapy. In L. McHugh & I. Stewart (Eds.), *The self and perspective taking: Contributions and applications from modern behavioral science* (pp. 125–142). Oakland, CA: Context Press.

Galantino, M. L., Baime, M., Maguire, M., Szapary, P. O., & Farrar, J. T. (2005). Short communication: Association of psychological and physiological measures of stress in health-care professionals during an 8-week mindfulness meditation program: mindfulness in practice. *Stress and Health, 21*(4), 255–261.

Glomb, T. M., Duffy, M. K., Bono, J. E., & Yang, T. (2011). Mindfulness at work. *Research in personnel and human resources management, 30,* 115–157. doi: 10.1108/S0742-7301(2011)0000030005

Goleman, D. (2006). *Working with emotional intelligence.* NY: Bantam Dell.

Greason, P. B., & Cashwell, C. S. (2009). Mindfulness and counseling self-efficacy: The mediating role of attention and empathy. *Counselor Education and Supervision, 49*(1), 2–19.

Hayes, S. C. (1984). Making sense of spirituality. *Behaviorism, 12*(2), 99–110.

Hayes, S. C., Barnes-Holmes, D., & Roche, B. (2001). *Relational frame theory: A post-Skinnerian account of human language and cognition.* NY: Kluwer Academic/Plenum.

Hayes, S. C., Bissett, R., Roget, N., Padilla, M., Kohlenberg, B. S., Fisher, G., & Niccolls, R. (2004). The Impact of acceptance and commitment training and multicultural training on the stigmatizing attitudes and professional burnout of substance *abuse counselors. Behavior Therapy, 35*(4), 821–835.

Hayes, S. C., & Plumb, J. C. (2007). Mindfulness from the bottom up: Providing an inductive framework for understanding mindfulness processes and their application to human suffering. *Psychological Inquiry, 18*(4), 242–248.

Hayes, S. C., & Shenk, C. (2004). Operationalizing mindfulness without unnecessary attachments. *Clinical Psychology: Science and Practice, 11*(3), 249.

Hayes, S. C., Strosahl, K. D., & Wilson, K. G. (2011). *Acceptance and commitment therapy: The process and practice of mindful change* (2nd ed.). NY: The Guilford Press.

Hogg, M. A. (2001). A social identity theory of leadership. *Personality and Social Psychology Review, 5*(3), 184–200. doi: 10.1207/s15327957pspr0503_1

Isaacs, W. (1999). *Dialogue and the art of thinking together.* NY: Doubleday.

Jentz, B. (2007). *Talk sense: Communicating to lead and learn.* Acton, MA: Research for Better Teaching.

Kabat-Zinn, J. (2003). Mindfulness-based interventions in context: Past, present, and future. *Clinical Psychology: Science and Practice, 10*(2), 144.

Kahneman, D., & Riis, J. (2005). Living, and thinking about it: Two perspectives on life. F. A. Huppert, N. Baylis & B. Keverne. *The science of well-being* (pp. 285–304). Oxford University Press: New York.

Kegan, R. (1994). *In over our heads: The mental demands of modern life.* Cambridge, MA: Harvard University Press.

Krasner, M. S., Epstein, R. M., Beckman, H., Suchman, A. L., Chapman, B., Mooney, C. J., & Quill, T. E. (2009). Association of an educational program in mindful communication with burnout, empathy, and attitudes among primary care physicians. *Journal of the American Medical Association, 302*(12), 1284–1293.

Lesh, T. V. (1970). Zen meditation and the development of empathy in counselors. *Journal of Humanistic Psychology, 10*(1), 39–74. doi: 10.1177/002216787001000105

Leung, M.-K. K., Chan, C. C. H., Yin, J., Lee, C.-F. F., So, K.-F. F., & Lee, T. M. C. (2012). *Increased gray-matter volume in the right angular and posterior parahippocampal gyri in loving-kindness meditators. Social cognitive and affective neuroscience.* doi: 10.1093/scan/nss076

Lutz, A., Brefczynski-Lewis, J., Johnstone, T., & Davidson, R. J. (2008). Regulation of the neural circuitry of emotion by compassion meditation: Effects of meditative expertise. *PLoS ONE, 3*(3), e1897.

Masuda, A., Hayes, S. C., Fletcher, L. B., Seignourel, P. J., Bunting, K., Herbst, S. A., . . . Lillis, J. (2007). Impact of acceptance and commitment therapy versus education on stigma toward people with psychological disorders. *Behavior Research and Therapy, 45*(11), 2764–2772.

Mazutis, D., & Slawinski, N. (2008). Leading organizational learning through authentic dialogue. *Management Learning, 39*(4), 437–456.

McCollum, E. E., & Gehart, D. R. (2010). Using mindfulness meditation to teach beginning therapists therapeutic presence: A qualitative study. *Journal of Marital and Family Therapy, 36*(3), 347–360.

McCracken, L. M., & Yang, S.-Y. (2008). A contextual cognitive-behavioral analysis of rehabilitation workers' health and well-being: Influences of acceptance, mindfulness, and values-based action. [Journal; Peer Reviewed Journal]. *Rehabilitation Psychology, 53*(4), 479–485.

McHugh, L., Barnes-Holmes, Y., & Barnes-Holmes, D. (2004). Perspective-taking as relational responding: A developmental profile. *Psychological Record, 54*(1), 115–144.

McHugh, L., Stewart, I., & Hooper, N. (2012). A contemporary functional analytic account of perspective taking. In L. McHugh & I. Stewart (Eds.), *The self and*

perspective taking: contributions and applications from modern behavioral science (pp. 55–72). Oakland, CA: Context Press.
Monica, E.L.L. (1981). Construct validity of an empathy instrument. *Research in Nursing & Health, 4*(4), 389–400. doi: 10.1002/nur.4770040406
Pearl, J. H., & Carlozzi, A. F. (1994). Effect of meditation on empathy and anxiety. *Perceptual and Motor Skills, 78*(1), 297–298.
Pennebaker, J. W., Booth, R. J., & Francis, M. E. (2007). *Operator's manual linguistic inquiry and word count:* LIWC2007. Retrieved from http://homepage.psy.utexas.edu/homepage/faculty/pennebaker/reprints/LIWC2007_OperatorManual.pdf
Piaget, J. (1969). *The psychology of the child.* NY: Harper Torch Books.
Plummer, M. P. (2008). *The impact of therapists' personal practice of mindfulness meditation on clients' experience of received empathy.* Psy.D. 3322265, Massachusetts School of Professional Psychology, United States—Massachusetts. ProQuest Dissertations & Theses A&I database.
Rogers, C. R. (1992). The necessary and sufficient conditions of therapeutic personality change. *Journal of Consulting and Clinical Psychology, 60*(6), 827–832. doi: 10.1037/0022-006x.60.6.827
Sahdra, B. K., MacLean, K. A., Ferrer, E., Shaver, P. R., Rosenberg, E. L., Jacobs, T. L., . . . Saron, C. D. (2011). Enhanced response inhibition during intensive meditation training predicts improvements in self-reported adaptive socioemotional functioning. *Emotion, 11*(2), 299–312.
Shapiro, S. L., Brown, K. W., Thoresen, C., & Plante, T. G. (2011). The moderation of mindfulness-based stress reduction effects by trait mindfulness: Results from a randomized controlled trial. *Journal of Clinical Psychology, 67*(3), 267–277. doi: 10.1002/jclp.20761
Shapiro, S. L., Schwartz, G. E., & Bonner, G. (1998). Effects of mindfulness-based stress reduction on medical and premedical students. *Journal of Behavioral Medicine, 21*(6), 581–599.
Skinner, B. F. (1974). *About behaviorism.* NY: Knopf.
Thomas, J. T., & Otis, M. D. (2010). Intrapsychic predictors of professional quality of life: mindfulness, empathy, and emotional separation. *Journal of the Society for Social Work and Research, 1*(2), 83–98.
Tipsord, J. M. (2009). The effects of mindfulness training and individual differences in mindfulness on social perception and empathy. [Dissertation]. Dissertation Abstracts International: Section B: *The Sciences and Engineering, 70*(11-B), 7273.
Torneke, N. (2010). Learning RFT. Oakland, CA: New Harbinger Publications.
Vilardaga, R., Estévez, A., Levin, M. E., & Hayes, S. C. (2012). Deictic relational responding, empathy and experiential avoidance as predictors of social anhedonia: Further contributions from relational frame theory. *The Psychological Record, 62*(3), 409–432.
Wimmer, H., & Perner, J. (1983). Beliefs about beliefs: Representation and constraining function of wrong beliefs in young children's understanding of deception. *Cognition, 13*(1), 103–128. doi: 10.1016/0010-0277(83)90004-5

4 A Conceptione . . .

Joanna Beth Tweedy

Amid the echo of celestial silence, a ripple
of bliss whispers the language
of incandescence: you are not
alone, but among; you are not
 you, but we—ours is the wild
and gracious heart of stars,
born of dust and dust of bone,
like marrow of nebulae, you are
a primordial nursery of souls, you are
 the whole in every part.

Part II

Applied Approaches to Empathy

A: Leadership

5 Working through the Past

How Personal History Influences Leaders' Emotions and Capacity for Empathy

Veronika Kisfalvi

INTRODUCTION

For well over a decade now, there has been mounting interest among organizational researchers in the role of emotions at work (Fineman, 2004; Walter, Cole, & Humphrey, 2011), with the concepts of emotional intelligence (EI), social intelligence, and their components—and how to develop these—attracting considerable attention (Goleman, 1995; Goleman & Boyatzis, 2008). Understanding and developing the components that make up EI holds particular interest for management scholars and practitioners looking for tools that can help managers enhance their interpersonal relationships with their collaborators. The capacity for empathy is one of these components, since it is integral to understanding others and thus to the social competencies associated with EI. In fact, Goleman, Boyatzis, and McKee (2002, p. 50) consider empathy to be "the fundamental competence of social awareness".

Empathy is what allows us to connect with each other. It is thought to fortify working relationships in teams (Stein, Papadogiannis, Yin, & Sitarenios, 2009), allow team members to better understand the links between emotions and behaviors (Polychroniou, 2009), and help resolve interpersonal conflicts (Humphrey, 2006). Importantly, a capacity for empathy can provide access to different perspectives, which can allow a leader or manager to reality test his or her perceptions and ideas and to thereby form a richer and more complete understanding of issues and situations. This is considered to be particularly critical at the executive level, as it can allow organizational leaders to benefit from the input of their teams, to hold up different mirrors to a given situation in order to make better decisions, and to develop strategies based on broader and more comprehensive knowledge (Simons, Pelled, & Smith, 1999). Further, empathy and self-awareness (another key component of EI), are intrinsically linked. Greater awareness of one's own emotional reactions facilitates access to others' reactions and makes for better empathic understanding. On the other hand, individuals' blind spots and emotional rigidities can make them defensive, interfering with their reality testing and empathic capabilities.

This chapter explores the influence of the past on leader's emotional reactions in the present. In it, we offer a deeper look at the temporal nature of emotions, EI, and of the capacity for empathy that has been suggested in most research approaches up to now. We propose than emotions are more than merely fleeting events; they can be deeply rooted in personal history and early formative experiences, and through the phenomenon of overdetermination (Moore & Fine, 1990), can shape leaders' key activities such as reality testing, priority setting, decision making, and strategy formation in the here and now. This perspective has practical implications for better understanding the nature of EI and the forces that might inhibit or enhance important emotional competencies such as empathy in leaders and managers.

We begin with a brief look at research on leadership effectiveness, emotions, and the more general construct of EI. We then go on to address the biological and evolutionary foundations of emotions, present some recent research on emotions in the emerging brain sciences, and discuss the way that emotions function as signals, alerting us to significant events in our environment. Our work departs from the current research on EI, which has tended to be synchronic: that is, focused on the awareness and management of emotions in the present. We present instead a psychodynamic approach, which is diachronic, focusing on the potential impact of past experience on present behavior; this approach provides a way to understand emotional reactions and capacities in the here and now by appreciating the personal history in which they are rooted. The psychodynamic framework can provide particularly useful tools for developing self-awareness, which as we have seen is closely linked to the empathic understanding of others. Using empirical examples from case study research, we go on to explore the role of personal history in shaping leaders' emotional lives (experienced in the body) and their capacity for developing competencies such as empathy and reality testing. Finally, we explore the implications of this alternative framework for developing such competencies in leaders and managers.

RESEARCH ON LEADERSHIP EFFECTIVENESS, EMOTIONS, AND EI IN ORGANIZATIONS

Until the mid-1990s, the focus of research into leadership effectiveness was almost entirely cognitively based (Fineman, 2004), a reflection of Descartes's mind-body split (Damasio, 1994; Heaphy, 2007; Kisfalvi, 1995). Exceptions to this dominant stream of work came mainly from a comparatively small body of psychodynamically oriented work (Kets de Vries & Miller, 1984; Zaleznik, 1977; Zaleznik & Kets de Vries, 1975) and from the work on vision and charisma (Schneider & Shrivastava, 1988; Westley & Mintzberg, 1989), which addressed to some extent the emotional aspects of leader-follower relationships. Interest in emotions in the workplace was given a boost by Gardner's (1993) work on multiple intelligences and by emerging findings in the neurosciences on the role of emotions in decision making (Damasio, 1994; LeDoux, 1996), particularly in social contexts, where managing and leading take place. The seminal work defining EI as a discrete concept was carried out by Mayer and his collaborators; they defined it as "an ability to recognize the meanings of emotions and their relationships, and to reason and problem-solve on the basis of them." (Mayer et al., 1999, cited in Fineman, 2004, p. 726). Mayer, Salovey, & Caruso (2002) subsequently developed a measure (the MSCEIT) based on a set of abilities that they considered to constitute EI: identifying emotions in oneself and others, using emotions to facilitate thinking, understanding emotions, and managing emotions. But it was with Goleman's (1995) book *Emotional Intelligence* that the concept firmly took hold. Since then, interest in EI as a construct, in its components, in how to measure it, in EI's role in leadership effectiveness and in how to develop EI has been intense and has spawned hundreds of journal articles (Goleman, 2006) and a highly lucrative consultancy stream (Fineman, 2004; Muyia, 2009). The literature on EI and leadership has spotlighted the role that EI and empathy play in leader effectiveness (George, 2000; Riggio & Reichard, 2008), in fostering productive leader-follower relationships, and in transformational leadership (Skinner & Spurgeon, 2005; Walter et al., 2011).

In what follows, we explore how leaders' emotions, rooted in past history, can direct their attention and solidify (even rigidify) their strategic choices, as well as enable or constrain their capacity for empathy in certain contexts, thereby shaping the content and emotional tone that marks executive team interactions. We address the important and complex role of introspection or self-awareness in this process, introspection being the one component of EI that even the harshest of critics have accepted as valid (see, for example, Locke, 2005). We also add a temporal dimension to the existing research, which has focused almost exclusively on the awareness and management of emotions (in self and others) in the moment. Current research approaches have tended to study the management of fleeting emotion states and to ignore the more deep-seated characteristics or traits that can influence emotional competencies and emotional reactions in the here and now. Our preoccupation, however, is not with the debate about whether leaders are "born or made" or the innate trait theories of emotion that have been criticized in the leadership (Bennis & Thomas, 2007) and EI literature (Goleman, 1995), but rather about the role of formative experience in molding leaders' habitual ways of reacting to certain emotionally charged situations. Our approach thus looks at personality formation which is similar to Boyatzis and Akrivou's (2006) concept of a person's "core identity. This is [a] relatively stable, and likely unconscious set of enduring individual characteristics, like his/her unconscious motives and traits, as well as roles adopted consistently in social settings" (p. 627). Our conceptual framework is based on psychodynamic concepts of emotional development, enriched by recent findings from the field of neuroscience and from the newly emerging field of neuropsychoanalysis.[1] Our approach generates what Fineman (2004) has called " 'broad band' data, representing feeling and expressed emotion in dynamic, socially situated, form. [It contrasts] to the measurer's inclination to pre-box, or freeze, emotion" (p. 723), which "tends to privilege one form of emotion knowledge (e.g., statistical trends, numerical profiles) and silences others (e.g., personal meanings, interpersonal dynamics)" (p. 724).

EMOTIONS AND THEIR ROOTS

The fact that emotions play a role in managing organizations (Fineman, 2003, 2004; George, 2000) and decision making (Damasio, 1994) including strategic decision making (Amason, 1996; Kisfalvi, 2000; Kong-Hee, 2012), is now well established. This should come as no surprise, since emotions are such a fundamental part of our experience, related to survival (Damasio, 1994); in addition, emotions are experienced—felt—in the body, sometimes intensely. Although various words are used to describe the phenomenon (emotion, affect, feeling), they all have an element of viscerality, a somatic component (see, for example, Cannon, 1927, on Jamesian views; Damasio, 1994). At times, this is the only component; a "primary emotion" (Damasio, 1984, p. 131) may be conceived of as a bodily sensation (or excitation) that is experienced as either pleasurable or not. Primary emotions[2] seem to have a cross-cultural component (Izard, 1991; Mesquita, 2003). Some have argued that their expression is innate; for example, even those blind from birth demonstrate the same facial expressions as sighted people when experiencing them (Matsumo & Williamson, 2009). In psychodynamic theory, primary emotions are thought of as somatic states of tension brought about by the workings of instinctual impulses or drives that strive for satisfaction (Westen, 1990). These bodily sensations can be motivational, in that the organism seeks relief from the tension, experienced as discomfort. Primary emotions can thus be conceived of as innate phylogenetic adaptive mechanisms; they signal a need as well as point to a means of its satisfaction. In addition, they provide the underpinnings of early cognition, when linkages begin to form between a need or desire, experienced as a sensation, and the sources of its satisfaction in the real world: "thinking evolves in the gap between the experience of the need and its satisfaction" (Segal, 1981, p. 221).

The interplay between behavior, cognition, and affect is permanent and pervasive, endemic to our species and necessary for its survival. People rarely base their actions on an exclusively cognitive or rational analysis of a situation; they also do what feels right to them, given who they are as individuals (Kisfalvi & Pitcher, 2003). Beginning with psychoanalysis (Erikson, 1985; Freud, 1975; Klein, 1948; Winnicott, 1965), itself based on Darwin's work (1827), these interrelationships have been explored in sociobiology (Bowlby, 1969; Izard, 1991), in psychology (Bower, 1981; Isen, 1982; Isen & Daubman, 1984; Lazarus, 1982, 1984; Mano, 1994; Wright and Bower,

1992; Zajonc, 1980, 1984), more recently in neuroscience (Damasio, 1995, 1999; LeDoux, 1996), neuropsychoanalysis (Solms, 2000) and in organizational studies in the form of EI (Goleman, 1995).

These studies provide a picture of an individual who comes into the world with certain innate predispositions and potentials (emotional and otherwise) laid down in neural circuitry (Damasio, 1994; Fineman, 2003; Goleman, 1995). From birth on, "these 'hard-wired' predispositions interact with [a social] environment of pleasure and pain and in so doing new neural circuitry is laid down" such that "emotions and their attendant cognitions and behaviors which form over time" establish "the contours of what we, from the outside, come to call 'character'" (Kisfalvi & Pitcher, 2003, p. 44). In other words, these continuous interactions give rise to a set of specific, identifiable, and enduring personal characteristics as well as enduring patterns of individual responses to environmental stimuli (Edelson, 1988; Erikson, 1985; Klein, 1948). The psychodynamic framework is particularly suited to studying these developmental processes, since it addresses how biological predispositions and personal history shape individuals, integrating biological predisposition, emotion, cognition, and behavior; as such, it remains "the most coherent and intellectually satisfying view of the mind" (Kandel, 1999, p. 505, in Turnbull & Solms, 2007). It respects and is able to embrace the complex nature of personal experience in a way that much other research on EI does not (Fineman, 2004, 2006).

Psychodynamic theory states that a person's stable character patterns "develop . . . as a consequence of the interaction of a broad but finite range of instinctual needs of the person and the environment's ability or inability to respond appropriately to them" (Johnson, 1994, p. 7). This environment is at first represented by the parents, and then gradually widens to include a greater range of relationships and interactions as an individual matures and moves through different experiences and developmental stages (Erikson, 1985). Some of these interactions are articulated around issues or dilemmas that are never fully resolved; each such life issue "is fundamental . . . [and] requires a constant resolution over the life span . . ." (Johnson, 1994, p. 4). This constant working through calls on defensive, adaptive, and coping strategies (Edelson, 1988). Such strategies, which help manage the often intense emotional reactions associated with the (re)activation of these life issues, slowly become anchored in an individual, forming and reinforcing connections; over time, each person develops an individual set of such strategies, or habitual reactions that he can call upon (Edelson, 1988) and which form a part of his/her character (Baudry, 1989; Johnson, 1994; Reich, 1933). This process is intimately linked to neural development, as Goleman and Boyatzis (2008, p. 81) point out: "As we explore the discoveries of neuroscience, we are struck by how closely the best psychological theories of development map to the newly charted hardwiring of the brain."

Thus, from a psychodynamic perspective, an individual's character, current interests, and behaviors are the visible tip of an iceberg with its base plunging deeply into previous life experience (Boyatzis & Akrivou, 2006; Fineman, 2003; Goleman, 2006; Kisfalvi, 2002; Schwartz & Malach-Pines, 2007). Further, the intensity of the emotional response that a particular situation or issue elicits in the present reflects its degree of historical meaningfulness for an individual, as immediate experience is unconsciously connected, through bodily reactions, to past history (Boyatzis et al., 2012; Damasio, 1994). Emotions, felt in the body, play the role of "signalling" to the person (through a sense of anxiety or excitement, for example) that the situation requires attention (Damasio, 1994; Fineman, 2003; Hochschild, 1983).

Thus, certain issues "out there" and in the here and now resonate deeply with a set of emotionally charged life issues particularly meaningful for an individual, and become highlighted for his or her attention and action. These life issues "inside" the person are themselves the outcomes of highly significant formative experiences during that person's particular life trajectory (Johnson, 1994). In addition, engagement with an issue "out there" may become multiply determined (Kisfalvi, 2000) as internal elements (such as conscious or unconscious memories) and strong emotional reactions converge to make the specific issue a stimulus for strong arousal; it becomes an almost irresistible magnet calling for the individual's attention. Edelson (1988) describes "multiple determination" (or overdetermination: see Moore & Fine, 1990) as the process of choosing a coping strategy or behavior "that eventuates in the gratification of the greatest number of wishes" (p. 112) at the same time. Wälder, in his seminal article on multiple determination, refers to "specific methods of solution in typical situations, which methods the person retains permanently" (1936, pp. 53–55). Because such reactions are multiply determined (representing a single strategy for effectively dealing with a range of emotionally charged life issues), they tend to remain quite constant, and even rigid, over a lifetime. The emotional charge that clings to such strategies can clearly have an impact (positive or negative) on the person's capacity for empathy and connectedness in situations that bring such life issues to the fore. In what follows, we present a detailed empirical example from our research that illustrates the impact of past experience and overdetermination on one leader's strategic orientations. We then go on to discuss the implications for leaders' capacity to manage their emotions and to reality test, as well as their capacity for empathy.

BEN LEVITSKY, "CAREFUL GAMBLER"[3]

Ben Levitsky was in his mid-seventies at the time we met. He was still actively running his chemical company, which he had founded forty years before; annual sales were about $35 million, and Ben considered himself to be quite a successful businessman. Over the course of the research, his particular set of consistent business priorities was identified. He considered these priorities to be essential for the continued success of his company, and he faithfully adhered to them despite his management team's frequent suggestions of alternative options. Ben's priorities consisted of *developing new products, seizing business opportunities and optimizing partnerships,* combined with *centralized financial control and decision making, hands-on involvement in the business,* and *keeping fully informed.* He termed this approach to growing his business "careful gambling"—boldly seizing opportunities, but also knowing exactly how much he was willing and able to lay on the table in order to pursue them.

It soon became clear that these priorities were not merely the result of Ben's rational appraisal of the industry or the market, or the outgrowths of his extensive business experience. They were also obviously highly emotionally charged. The emotions that Ben displayed at work were often volatile and were closely linked to his set of business priorities. He tended to display intense emotion (excitement and pleasure, or anxiety and anger) over situations that touched upon them. For example, he would proudly and excitedly describe acquiring some new products or production equipment "for peanuts!" His animation was palpable whenever anyone brought a potentially interesting business opportunity to his attention; if it involved a new product, so much the better. He was invigorated by these challenges, especially those that provided him with occasions to "wheel and deal", bringing people, products and financing together. At these times, he seemed younger, happier, and highly energized.

Conversely, he would get very angry and frustrated in situations that conflicted with his need to exert tight financial control, for example: "I like it the least when people are negligent . . . I can't accept around me laziness and carelessness and things like this". An unauthorized credit note, however small, would make him want "to explode"; with his anger barely under control, he would endlessly berate the clerk responsible for the error. Not surprisingly, his managers would try to avoid him when he was on such a rampage, until it all blew over. Ben's displays of emotion unmistakably indicated the areas in which positive action on his part could be reasonably expected, as well as what "pushed his buttons".

Ben had recently hired a number of new outside managers for his executive team on the basis of their professionalism and diverse experience. He wanted "to move his company into the twentieth century", and considering his age, he was also concerned about leaving a well-managed company to his sons. However, when these new managers came up with suggestions about changing any of [his] business priorities (such as streamlining his product line or setting up regular executive meetings to hammer out strategic orientations and decisions), they either fell upon deaf ears or triggered strong resistance. This, in turn, greatly frustrated the managers, and they could become quite impatient with Ben. This state of affairs was clearly not conducive to feelings of empathy and connectedness on the team; in fact, just the reverse. Ironically, it seemed that Ben's own intense emotional attachment to his set of business priorities was short-circuiting his "rational" analysis of what his company required and his own efforts to provide it. This attachment rendered him unable to benefit from the input of the highly competent executive team he himself had so carefully formed; it was causing impatience and friction within the team as well.

As Ben progressively revealed his life history, the deeper significance of his business priorities became apparent and his reactions more intelligible. Ben had been born in the early 1920s to an Orthodox Jewish farming family in a small village in Eastern Europe. A highly intelligent and curious child growing up in trying circumstances, Ben learned early about survival under duress, both physical and psychological. His childhood was spent doing grueling work in order to help ensure his family's survival. By the mid-1930s, when Ben was barely a teenager, Nazism's effects were already being felt; he remembered walking the streets of his village in fear. When war finally broke out, ensuring the family's survival, in all senses, became even more difficult.

In 1944, his family was deported, its members sent to various concentration camps. His parents and three siblings perished in Auschwitz. Ben, young and strong, was sent to another forced labor-concentration camp, where he had ample occasion to put his survival skills to work. He managed to survive through energy, willpower, and an ability to work the system of barter that had sprung up in the camp. To this day, he considers his camp experiences to have been his "business school". Upon his liberation, Ben returned to his village, married, and continued to run his family's farm until the new Communist government nationalized it. Ben moved to Warsaw, found work in a chemical company, and was soon made a manager. He distinguished himself by becoming an indispensable part of the planning team. When he created a number of innovative products, he was touted as a "proletarian hero", earning a countrywide reputation for his ingenuity and cost-cutting measures. A plaque to this effect was still proudly displayed in his Winnipeg office at the time of the research.

Ben and his family immigrated to North America in the late 1950s. He found a job in a chemical company, but soon tired of working for others and actively began to look for alternatives. He ran into a fellow concentration camp survivor, and the two began to distribute samples of the products Ben had developed back in Europe; and within a year of his arrival, Ben was in business with a partner. However, the partnership was short lived, due to a falling out. Ben subsequently struck out on his own, looking for different products he could manufacture while remaining in chemicals. He finally settled on the family of products his company manufactures today. He founded Benco, his first venture into business alone, setting up operations in an 800 square-foot rented garage, where he and his wife began full-scale production. She remained his loyal business partner until her death in 1995, by which time the company had greatly expanded both in size and in product mix.

Through the story of Ben's life, a consistent set of life issues (Johnson, 1994) emerged. Ben's early life on the family farm coupled with the persecution and extermination of European Jews had led to an enduring and intense preoccupation with *survival*. These experiences, reinforced by the loss of the farm to the postwar Communists, left him with a strong desire to control his own destiny and a fierce need for *autonomy*. In the camps especially, it could easily have turned lethal to look out for anyone's welfare but one's own. While the inmates may have had feelings of empathy and connectedness toward one another, in these extreme conditions, acting on such feelings could pose a very real threat to their own survival. Given the very real risks, feelings of empathy for the plight of those less able than he to work the system were not only a luxury but could have actually turned deadly for Ben. Further, his survival and autonomy could only be guaranteed by *action* (especially in the camps, remaining passive would have meant certain death), and successful action in turn led to a sense of *agency*, *achievement*, and *success* and attracted reassuring *recognition*,[4] a confirmation from the outside world that he was *making it*, in all senses.

This set of life issues had become deeply rooted in Ben's character; often forged in trauma and highly emotionally charged, they influenced all of his business activities. Each of the business issues to which he consistently gave his attention resonated deeply with many if not all of them; attending to the organizational issue allowed him to attend to a number of associated life issues simultaneously. One striking example concerned the way in which Ben had financed the growth of his business. Whereas some entrepreneurs might see borrowing from the bank as leverage and opportunity for growth, Ben saw it almost exclusively as a threat that compromised his autonomy and threatened his firm's survival, and therefore insisted on using internal financing for almost all of his expansion projects. In financial dealings, Ben was known as a hard negotiator who showed little consideration or empathy for his adversaries. The strict financial controls that he insisted on in his firm were directly linked to this need for autonomy, in that they allowed him to operate more profitably and to internally generate working capital and the funds needed for expansion. Conversely, whereas some entrepreneurs might see threat in a strategy of diversification in that it can represent a scattering of energies and loss of control, Ben saw it as an opportunity to reduce his risks and to ensure his company's survival: "so that if I have to run again, I should have somewhere to run", he explained, an explicit reference to the persecution he had survived back in Europe. His constant concern with finding and developing new products was also linked to his preoccupation with survival. In the camps, his ability to "diversify", to acquire a range of items to be used for barter ("bread was my working capital"), had literally assured his survival and allowed him to act as a free agent; in this context, it had also made him into a "rich guy" and provided him with the recognition he craved. After his liberation from the camps, he established his reputation as a leader by developing new products for his employer, for which he was publicly honored. Later, in his adopted country, manufacturing and selling his own products had ensured his autonomy and success; he had even dreamt of owning retail outlets, "to produce my product and to be able to sell it, too." Ben was convinced that the attention he devoted to these priorities was at the core of his business success.

A close look at Ben's personal history and business life reveals that his business priorities and strategies were deeply anchored in his past experiences. In fact, the more deeply a particular strategy had become enmeshed in the web of forces that had shaped him—the more it was overdetermined by these—the more consistently he acted on it, and the less likely he was to respond when his managers urged him to change it. By attending to these business priorities, he was simultaneously and unconsciously dealing with his recurrent life issues as well; the personal and the professional, the past and the present, had become inextricably entwined. These complex interrelationships and attendant emotions were what ultimately short circuited his ability to capitalize on the potential contributions of the team he had built, and his impatience with their proposals. In turn, his managers eventually became highly frustrated and impatient with Ben; they became resigned and passive, or greatly reduced their expectations, or simply left the firm. Neither side could truly hear the other, since neither side had a real understanding of or capacity to take into account the underlying emotions guiding the other. We could say that there was a clear failure of empathy on both sides.

While it can be argued that given the traumatic life history of our protagonist, this example is extreme[5] and therefore cannot be generalized, we would argue that no leader (or individual) is without a history. While the specifics may change and the phenomena may be less intense in those with a less tumultuous past, the processes of overdetermination through which personal history shapes business priorities and ultimately strategies (especially, but not only, in small entrepreneurial firms) as well as professional relationships can be generalized to other individuals and domains. To illustrate, other cases with which we are familiar—the first Henry Ford, Sam Steinberg (head of the now-defunct Steinberg empire in Quebec), Rachel Carson (whose book *Silent Spring* led to the creation of the Environmental Protection Agency in the United States and the founding of the current environmental movement) and Agnès Grossmann (one of the few internationally renowned female orchestra conductors in the world)—all had overdetermined characteristics.

Henry Ford I's need to succeed, to be powerful and perfect, coupled with his guilt over disappointing his father by leaving the family farm, all came to be symbolized by the Model-T (which he called the farmers' car), to which he adamantly refused any changes even after sales plummeted in favor of competitors' new designs. When presented with an "improved" prototype by his managers, he literally tore it apart with his bare hands (Jardim, 1970), showing a spectacular lack of empathy. Sam Steinberg's "chosen" status in his mother's (the company founder's) eyes, his promise to her to always put family first and his internalization of her business values overdetermined his hiring decisions and his unwavering commitment to a strategy of low pricing and diversification; such business decisions ultimately discouraged the best of his managers, destroyed his management team, and proved impossible to maintain (Kets de Vries, Carlock, & Florent-Treacy, 2007). Being in nature and writing about it were the strategies that Rachel Carson developed in order to cope with the challenges created by the special, often problematic relationship she had with her intrusive mother and by a particularly difficult family situation (Kisfalvi & Maguire, 2011). While clearly attuned to her natural surroundings throughout her life, Carson found close relationships to be much more challenging. On a more positive note, there is Agnès Grossmann, former conductor of Montreal's *Orchestre Métropolitain* as well as the Vienna Boys' Choir. The pervasive role that music had played in her life growing up, the shared talent and passion for music that were the hallmarks of her intense and positive childhood relationship with her father, and a network of past and present supportive relatives and teachers, combined with her own personal determination, allowed her to overcome an irreversible finger injury that ended her career as a world-class pianist and could have ended her musical career entirely. Instead, she became a successful and highly empathic orchestra conductor in a field where dictatorial approaches to conducting were much more common (Richer et al., 2003).

IMPLICATIONS FOR DEVELOPING EMOTIONAL COMPETENCIES

How would one go about developing the capacity for empathy and similar emotional competencies in someone like Ben Levitsky or some of the others leaders mentioned above? Not only was Ben a highly intelligent, capable and quite successful entrepreneur, he was also reasonably self-aware—at least in certain areas. He could clearly articulate what excited, upset, or angered him. He recognized that his company was suffering in certain areas from his own shortcomings, and that change was needed. On the cognitive or rational level, Ben realized that his company needed new ideas other than his own to prepare it for the future, and for the succession challenges that were quickly approaching. Yet he himself short circuited the very measures he had taken to deal with these issues. As Fineman points out, "Thinking and feeling interpenetrate; that is, they cannot easily be separated. Applying our intelligence, our thinking, to our emotions is not nearly as straightforward as some emotional theorists imply . . ." (2003, p. 53). Ben's personal history had left him with a legacy of unresolved and unconscious emotionally charged issues that were being regularly played out on the stage of his firm. These issues gave rise to a set of rather rigid business priorities and a constellation of strategies that he would consistently pursue. In addition, these were the very priorities and strategies that his managers would advise him to change, because they were insensitive to their true emotional significance for Ben. Ben, too, was insensitive to the emotions of his managers. Their professional opinions and advice, genuinely intended to help the business, mostly distressed and frustrated Ben because (for reasons we have seen) the thought of changing these strategies caused him too much anxiety. This was certainly not what he had expected or hoped for when he hired the new managers. And so the advice almost always went unheeded—despite his own avowed desires, and much to the chagrin of his managers. This reciprocal failure of empathy and connection set up a cycle of frustration and disappointment, creating a sense of impotence all around and a negative emotional climate in the team.

However, it should be pointed out as well that empathy is a complex phenomenon that can also have its downside for leaders. As Antonakis (2004) has said, "leaders should not be too sensitive to and unduly influenced by the emotional states of others, especially at top leader levels", since they sometimes must act in ways that go against the desires of their followers and must make difficult decisions regarding contentious issues. Leaders at the top need to trust at least some of their own emotional reactions; these reactions form the basis of their intuitions and ability to seize and create opportunities. In Ben's case, "careful gambling", fuelled by his life experiences, had enabled him to seize the opportunities that would allow his company to grow without compromising its financial health. The successes, and not only the failures or shortcomings, of the other leaders mentioned above were driven by a similarly strong inner sense of direction and (over)determination that made them impervious to more measured advice. But while these can sometimes serve them, leaders must also be able to reality test and to recognize the situations in which their overdetermined emotional reactions can lead them astray (when emotions hijack cognition: Goleman, 2006). In certain instances, Ben's emotions trumped cognition (Kisfalvi & Pitcher, 2003) and made reciprocal empathy with his managers very difficult; this, in turn, diminished his ability to benefit from his team's input. Ironically, his strong emotional reactions held him in their sway and thwarted his own desires to make positive changes in his organization. Based on Ben's case and the dynamics in his team, we propose that it is the capacity to deeply understand (not only to be aware of a current emotion, but also to understand its source), to discern (to reality test in order to see which emotions are appropriate in the current situation and which ones might be simply reactive or dysfunctional remnants of the past (Kisfalvi, 1995)) and to moderate emotions (to use this understanding and discernment to talk ourselves through our immediate visceral reactions) that underlies emotional competencies, including a capacity for empathy.

To sum up, as Fineman has said, "What we do, think and feel can be regarded as interpenetrative, context-bound and fluid . . . Emotion, in these terms, is a panoply of voices and representations—of the self, the brain, the body, upbringing and culture . . ." (Fineman, 2004, p. 720). The psychodynamic approach that we have proposed here enriches the study of emotions in organizations in this sense. It provides a temporal grounding for our understanding by addressing the role of personal history and developmental processes and stages (and their impact on both personality and brain structure) in our emotional development. It links these to the somatic reactions that are the hallmarks of our here-and-now emotional reactions. As such, it has important implications for developing emotional competencies such as empathy, by recognizing that these emotional reactions are hard to change; since emotions are so deeply "rooted in early life experiences, significant changes would not normally be expected" (Fineman, 2003, p. 51), at least not easily.

Thus, no quick fix or short-term training session is adequate for the development of greater emotional competencies in problematic areas that are deeply entrenched in personal history. Yet these are often the very areas that most need changing. In effect, EI training programs of short duration have not proven to be up to the task of bringing about lasting change; their impact seems to erode, with participants tending to revert to habitual modes of functioning relatively quickly (Boyatzis, 2006; Lord & Hall, 2005). Self-awareness of one's current emotional states and reactions is necessary but not sufficient for the lasting development of emotional competencies such as empathy. Psychodynamic approaches give us an inkling of why this might be so: they make us aware that the past never totally leaves us. Developing leaders' emotional competencies means not only acquiring the ability to gauge the emotional aspects of situations and relationships in the here-and-now, but to see the repetitive patterns—to better understand why certain situations consistently pose emotional challenges for a particular leader and to develop ways to surmount them. Cognitive understanding is not sufficient; emotional insights that take root in the body seem to be necessary in order to change such deep-seated habitual responses and to take advantage of the brain's plasticity (Doidge, 2007) in order to lay down new neural pathways that alter how we feel, think, and act. The limits of an exclusively cognitive understanding are a well-known fact in various psychotherapies (which, in fact, do change neural pathways over time—see Liggan & Kay, 1999), and well illustrated in many of Woody Allen's movies.

Psychotherapy is, happily, not the only way to gain such insight. Boyatzis (2006), for example, has designed a course for developing EI in MBA students that is focused on long-term intentional change and built on the concept of the ideal self as positive motivator (Boyatzis & Akrivou, 2006). While we agree that in order for a change process to be successful, people need to want to change, and that lasting change comes with time and effort, we believe, like Fineman (2006), that attention to personal strengths and positive motivations is not sufficient. As such, our focus here has been chiefly on what can engender emotional rigidities and therefore stand in the way of change in important areas, such as the capacity for empathy. We thus propose a complementary alternative, based on individual effort and introspection into individuals' potentially dysfunctional behavior patterns and areas of rigidity. It consists of regular, structured self-reflection around the patterns of behavior both past and present that have consistently led them into problematic situations, that have prevented them from fully expressing their leadership potential, or that have consistently been brought to their attention as problematic by others. Because the human capacity for defensive reactions such as denial and rationalization is immense (Fineman, 2003), this is a difficult proposition.

A useful method for helping individuals relax their defenses somewhat is to ask them to study the lives of others, as these can act as self-reflective mirrors. Critically reading biographies of leaders and entrepreneurs (in case study or book form[6]), thinking about their possible motivations, the repeating patterns in their lives, the problematic issues that they may or may not have overcome, and becoming aware of what in these lives strikes a particularly deep emotional cord within us, are some ways in which to practice deeper self-awareness. Regular journal writing over an extended period of time is also a useful method, as is writing in story form about our own lives and formative or challenging experiences, and our own leadership trajectories. These journal entries and narratives can then be re-read and examined more deeply for the patterns they reveal about our emotional lives and about the conversations that go on in our heads, as well as for the deep, sometimes buried sources of our reactions and behaviors. This process is similar to the insights that can be gained in a therapeutic setting, ones that are necessary for deeper levels of personal change. Such tools have in fact already been incorporated into a number of regular and executive MBA programs, and we believe they would be a useful complement to the approaches developed by Boyatzis and collaborators described above. Executive coaching could also benefit from these types of approaches.

Finally, while emotion can trump cognition, the reverse is also true. Effort spent in understanding what "pushes our buttons", what makes us, as leaders, turn a blind eye and a deaf ear to our collaborators, and why (considering the deeper roots in our personal history), can help us overcome our instantaneous, automatic, or habitual reactions to such situations—to take an emotional step back. In so doing, we can become more aware of others' experiences and perspectives and increase both our effectiveness as leaders and managers and our capacity for empathy and connectedness. The emotions may persist, but we can learn to better master the way we respond to, express, and manage them. In this sense, while we cannot alter our history or who we have become, we can alter how we interact with the world in the here and now—that is, we can better connect to those around us by reacting in a more insightful, emotionally measured, constructive, and empathic way. As Pavlovich & Krahnke (2012) have pointed out, this capacity for connectedness is crucial if we are to meet the many challenges facing us both on an organizational and on a global scale today.

NOTES

1. Neuropsychoanalysis is interested in the interface between neuroscience and psychoanalysis; its aim is to explore the ways in which these two areas of research into the mind might inform each other, with psychoanalysis providing the "what" questions and neuroscience providing the tools with which these might be explored in terms of brain functioning (Solms, 2000). According to researchers in this emerging area, Freud was first and foremost a neurologist with acute insights into the mind but without the tools to test them. As such, neuropsychoanalysis provides a way not only to validate psychoanalytic concepts through more modern tools of neuroscience, but to further develop the psychoanalytic work of Freud and others by studying the mind with the tools of brain science.
2. Anger, contempt, disgust, distress, fear, guilt, interest, joy, shame, surprise (Izard, 1991).
3. For a detailed account of the methodology used for obtaining and analyzing the data and for a more complete version of this case, see Kisfalvi (2000) and Kisfalvi and Pitcher (2003).
4. This was so even in the camps; Ben recounts that he was considered to be a "*big shot*" by the other inmates.
5. It was deliberately chosen to illustrate the concepts explored (purposeful sampling; see Eisenhardt, 1989).
6. Acting as sorts of "transitional objects" (Winnicott, 1953), these can be indirect but powerful tools for triggering self-reflection.

REFERENCES

Amason, A.C. (1996). Distinguishing the effects of functional and dysfunctional conflict on strategic decision making: Resolving a paradox for top management teams. *Academy of Management Journal, 39*(1), 123–148.

Antonakis, J. (2004). On why 'EI' will not predict leadership effectiveness beyond IQ or the 'Big Five': An extension and rejoinder. *Organizational Analysis, 12*(2), 171–182.

Baudry, F. (1989). Character, character type, and character organization. *Journal of the American Psychoanalytic Association, 37*, 655–686.

Bennis, W., & Thomas, R. (2007). *Leading for a lifetime*. Boston: HBR.

Bowlby, J. (1969). *Attachment and loss: Vol. 1. Attachment*. NY: Basic.

Boyatzis, R.E. (2006). An overview of intentional change from a complexity perspective. *Journal of Management Development, 25*(7), 607–623.

Boyatzis, R.E., & Akrivou, K. (2006). The ideal self as the driver of intentional change. *Journal of Management Development, 25*(7), 624–642.

Boyatzis, R.E., Passarelli, A.M., Koenig, K., Lowe, M., Mathew, B., Stoller, J.K., & Phillips, M. (2012). Examination of the neural substrates activated in memories of experiences with resonant and dissonant leaders. *Leadership Quarterly, 23*(2), 259–272.

Damasio, A.R. (1994). *Descartes' error: Emotion, reason and the human brain*. NY: G.P. Putnam.

Darwin, C. (1872). *The expression of emotions in man and animals*. London: Murray.

Doidge, N. (2007). *The brain that changes itself*. NY: Viking.

Eisenhardt, K.M. (1989). Building theories from case study research. *Academy of Management Review, 14*(4), 532–550.

Edelson, M. (1988). *Psychoanalysis: A theory in crisis.* Chicago: University of Chicago Press.

Erikson, E. H. (1985). *Childhood and Society.* NY: Norton.

Fineman, S. (2003). *Understanding emotions at work.* Thousand Oaks, CA: Sage.

Fineman, S. (2004). Getting the measure of emotion—and the cautionary tale of EI. *Human Relations, 57*(6), 719–740.

Fineman, S. (2006). On being positive: Concerns and counterpoints. *Academy of Management Review,* 31(2), 270–291.

Freud, S. (1975). Beyond the pleasure principle. I. J. Strachey (Ed. & Trans.), *The standard edition of the complete psychological works of Sigmund Freud* (vol. 18, pp. 7–64). London: Hogarth. (Original work published 1920.)

Gardner, H. (1993). *Frames of mind: The theory of multiple intelligences.* NY: Basic.

George, J. M. (2000). Emotions and leadership: The role of EI. *Human relations, 53*(8), 1027–1055.

Goleman, D. (1995). *Emotional intelligence.* NY: Bantam.

Goleman, D. (2006). *Emotional intelligence.* 10th Anniversary Edition. NY: Bantam.

Goleman, D., & Boyatzis, R. (2008). Social intelligence and the biology of leadership. *Harvard Business Review,* September, 74–81.

Goleman, D., Boyatzis, R., & McKee, A. (2002). *Primal leadership: Realizing the power of emotional intelligence.* Boston: Harvard Business School Press.

Heaphy, E. (2007). Bodily Insights: Three lenses on positive organizational relationships. In J. Dutton & B. Ragins (Eds.), *Exploring positive relationships at work* (pp. 47–71). Mahwah, NJ: Lawrence Earlbaum.

Hochschild, A. R. (1983). *The managed heart: The commercialization of human feeling.* Berkeley: University of California Press.

Humphrey, R. H. (2006). Promising research opportunities in emotions and coping with conflict. *Journal of Management and Organization, 12*(2), 179–186.

Isen, A. M., & Daubman, K. A. (1984). The influence of affect on categorization. *Journal of Character and Social Psychology, 47*(6), 1206–1217.

Izard, C. E. (1991). *The psychology of emotions.* NY: Plenum.

Jardim, A. (1970). *The first Henry Ford: A study in personality.* Cambridge, MA: MIT Press.

Johnson, S. M. (1994). *Character styles.* NY: W. W. Norton.

Kets de Vries, M. F. R., Carlock, R. S., & Florent-Treacy, E. (2007). *Family business on the couch: A psychological perspective.* Chichester, UK: John Wiley.

Kets de Vries, M. F. R., & Miller, D. (1984). *The neurotic organization.* San Francisco: Jossey-Bass.

Kisfalvi, V. (1995). Laisser nos émotions à la porte? *Gestion, 20*(3), 110–113.

Kisfalvi, V. (2000). The threat of failure, the perils of success and CEO character: Sources of strategic persistence. *Organization Studies, 21*(3), 611–639.

Kisfalvi, V. (2002). The entrepreneur's character, life issues, and strategy making: A field study. *Journal of Business Venturing, 7*(5), 489–518.

Kisfalvi, V., & Maguire, S. (2011). The nature of institutional entrepreneurs: Lessons from Rachel Carson. *Journal of Management Inquiry, 20*(2), 152–177.

Kisfalvi, V., & Pitcher, P. (2003). Doing what feels right: The influence of CEO character and emotions on top management team dynamics. *Journal of Management Inquiry,* 12, 42–66.

Klein, M. (1948). *Contributions to psychoanalysis, 1921–1945.* London: Hogarth.

Kong-Hee, K. (2012). Emotion and strategic decision-making behavior: Developing a theoretical model. *International Journal of Business and Social Science, 3*(1), 105–113.

Lazarus, R. S. (1982). Thoughts on the relations between emotion and cognition. *American Psychologist, 37*(9), 1019–1024.

Lazarus, R. S. (1984). On the primacy of cognition. *American Psychologist, 39*(2), 124–129.

LeDoux, J. E. (1996). *The emotional brain: The mysterious underpinnings of emotional life.* NY: Simon & Schuster.

Liggan, D. Y., & Kay, J. (1999). Some neurobiological aspects of psychotherapy: A review. *Journal of Psychotherapy Practice and Research, 8*, 103–114.

Locke, E. A. (2005). Why emotional intelligence is an invalid concept. *Journal of Organizational Behavior, 26*, 425–431.

Lord, R. G., & Hall, R. J. (2005). Identity, deep structure and the development of leadership skill. *The Leadership Quarterly, 16*(4), 591–615.

Mano, H. (1994). Risk-taking, framing effects, and affect. *Organizational Behavior & Human Decision Processes, 57*, 38–58.

Matsumo, D., & Williamson, B. (2009). Spontaneous facial expressions of emotion in congenitally and non-congenitally blind individuals. *Journal of Personality and Social Psychology, 96*(1), 1–10.

Mayer, J. D., Salovey, P., & Caruso, D. (2002). *The Mayer-Salovey-Caruso emotional intelligence test (MSCEIT).* Toronto, Canada: The Multi-Health Systems.

Mesquita, B. (2003). Emotions as dynamic cultural phenomena. In R. J. Davidson, K. R. Scherer, & G. H. Hill (Eds.), *Handbook of affective sciences. Series in affective science.* NY: Oxford University Press, 871–890.

Moore, B. E., & Fine, B. D (1990). Psychoanalytic terms and concepts. NY: The American Psychoanalytic Association, 123.

Muyia, H. M. (2009). Approaches to and instruments for measuring emotional intelligence: A review of selected literature. *Advances in Developing Human Resources, 11*(6), 690.

Pavlovich, K., & Krahnke, K. (2012). Empathy, connectedness and organization. *Journal of Business Ethics, 105*(1), 131–137.

Polychroniou, P. V. (2009). Relationship between emotional intelligence and transformational leadership of supervisors. *Team Performance Management, 15*(7), 343–356.

Reich, Wilhelm (1933). *Character analysis.* NY: Orgone Institute Press.

Riggio, R. E., & Reichard, R. J. (2008). The emotional and social intelligences of effective leadership: An emotional and social skill approach. *Journal of Managerial Psychology, 23*(2), 69–185.

Schneider, S. C., & Shrivastava, P. (1988). Basic assumptions themes in organizations. *Human Relations, 41*(7), 493–516.

Schwartz, D., & Malach-Pines, A. (2007). High technology entrepreneurs versus small business owners in Israel. *The Journal of Entrepreneurship, 16*(1), 1–17.

Segal, H. (1981). The *work of Hanna Segal. A Kleinian approach to clinical practice.* NY: Jason Aronson.

Simons, T., Pelled, L. H., & Smith, K. A. (1999). Making use of difference: Diversity, debate, and decision comprehensiveness in top management teams. *Academy of Management Journal, 42*(6), 662–673.

Skinner, C., & Spurgeon, P. (2005). Valuing empathy and emotional intelligence in health leadership: A study of empathy, leadership behavior and outcome effectiveness. *Health Services Management Research, 18*(1), 1–12.

Solms, M. (2000). Preliminaries for an integration of psychoanalysis and neuroscience. In J. A. Winer (Ed.), *The annual of psychoanalysis* (vol. 28, pp. 179–200). Hillsdale, NJ: The Analytic Press.

Stein, S. J., Papadogiannis, P., Yip, J. A., & Sitarenios, G. (2009). Emotional intelligence of leaders: A profile of top executives. *Leadership & Organization Development Journal, 30*(1), 87–101.

Turnbull, O. H., & Solms, M. (2007). Awareness, desire, and false beliefs: Freud in the light of modern neuropsychology. *Cortex, 43*(8), 1083–1090.

Wälder, R. (1936). The principle of multiple function: Observations on over-determination. *Psychoanalytic Quarterly, 5*, 45–62.

Walter, F., Cole, M.S., & Humphrey, R.H. (2011). Emotional intelligence: Sine qua non of leadership or folderol? *The Academy of Management Perspectives, 25*(1), 45.

Westen, Drew (1990). Psychoanalytic approaches to personality. In L.A. Pervin (Ed.), *A handbook of personality: Theory and research* (pp. 21–65). NY: Guilford Press.

Westley, F., & Mintzberg, H. (1989). Visionary leadership and strategic management. *Strategic Management Journal, 10*, 17–32.

Winnicott, D.W. (1953). Transitional objects and transitional phenomena—A study of the first not-me possession. *International Journal of Psycho-Analysis, 3*, 89–97.

Winnicott, W.D. (1965). *The maturational processes and the facilitating environment: Studies in the theory of emotional development.* NY: International Universities Press.

Wright, W.F., & Bower, G.H. (1992). Mood effects on subjective probability assessment. *Organizational Behavior & Human Decision Processes, 52*, 276–291.

Zajonc, R.B. (1980). Feeling and thinking: Preferences need no inferences. *American Psychologist, 35*(2), 151–175.

Zajonc, R.B. (1984). On the primacy if affect. *American Psychologist, 39*(2), 117–123.

Zaleznik, A. (1977). Managers and leaders—Are they different? *Harvard Business Review, 55*(3), 67–78.

Zaleznik, A., & Kets de Vries, M. (1975). *Power and the corporate mind.* Boston: Houghton-Mifflin.

6 Empathy

A Leadership Quintessential

Samuel M. Natale, Anthony F. Libertella, and Caroline J. Doran

INTRODUCTION

Empathy is the ability to understand what others feel and experience (Goleman, 1995; Natale & Sora, 2010). As a critical adjunct to understanding, empathy ties directly to leadership. First and foremost, the application of empathy to the leadership context fosters a new understanding of other persons' wants and needs, and requires a paradigm shift (Patnaik & Mortensen, 2009). This change calls for a relational understanding of people and requires one to protect their well-being and guide them toward a moral imperative (McIntosh, 2011; Van Lange, 2008). In short, it has the compelling quality of "ought" associated with its implementation. Fundamentally, empathy becomes demanded and not optional. Within the empathic paradigm shift, the leader has a visceral understanding of the human dynamic as encapsulated within the organization. Empathy is essentially constrained by the value-based structure that preexists within the organization.

Yet in earlier studies, leadership theorists eschewed the notion of empathy as too "soft" a concept (Pink, 2005). Consequently, the ability to lead from the outside rather than the inside seemed to be an easier task to undertake for stakeholders. In a society where financial measurements singularly predominated (Friedman, 1970), it was easy to dismiss empathy as a valid measurement tool. Leaders emphasized the "cognitive" (McBane, 1995) nature of decision making, forgetting the critical maxim by Jonathan Swift, "Man is not a rational animal [only] but an animal capable of reasoning" (Davis, 1940). A considerable subterranean reservoir of ambiguous drivers remained, albeit ignored. These externally oriented perceptions created an organizational framework that was essentially hierarchical. While this framework assured unity of command, it required the price of distancing the decision-making structure from the affective needs of the stakeholders. It was not until 1972 that studies emerged supporting the teaching of ethics, and the concept of empathy was recognized as being capable of operationalization (Natale, 1972).

Empathy, on the other hand, allows the leader to understand individuals on a more profound emotional and intellectual level. This understanding helps the leader to build positive relationships, which creates a sense of community, morality, and social accountability (Batson et. al., 1995). The application of empathy to the leadership process develops engagement and caring in an environment where stakeholders' needs are addressed, and necessary corrective actions are undertaken. Concomitantly, empathy incorporates aspects such as vision, modeling, and service with "empowerment", "collaboration", and "connectivity" (Goleman, 1998).

This chapter examines empathy as a quintessential leadership quality from multiple viewpoints. By briefly exploring the nature of empathy and its general application to business, we examine case studies from various organizations within which leaders applied empathic concepts and generated a positive impact on the organization's achievements and competitive advantage. We will also identify the lessons learned from these cases and provide concluding commentary.

THE NATURE OF EMPATHY

The psychological and scientific research discoveries continue to demonstrate the multifaceted viewpoints on the nature of empathy. The psychological findings strongly suggest that empathy could serve as the primary driver for "altruistic behavior and cooperation" as well as prosocial behavior (DeVignemont & Singer, 2006; Eisenberg, 2005; Hoffman, 2001; Gano-Overway et al., 2009). In short, empathy is the learned ability to understand the feelings of others and to be able to reconfigure one's own understanding to "listen with the third ear", or to actually walk in the other person's shoes (Natale & Sora, 1972). Beyond these psychological models, there is increasing biochemical evidence for the biological foundations of empathy (Brothers, 1989) More specifically, biological research findings have produced new leadership dynamics regarding the emotional connection to peoples' behavioral tendencies by emphasizing mirror neurons and the limbic system (Goleman, 2006; Patnaik, 2009).

Empathy demands, from the leader, an understanding of the centrality of the person in decision making and professional judgments. It requires that one adhere to the basic moral principle that the rights of others enjoy the same status as one's own. The paradigm shift towards a leader's holistic understanding of empathy fosters a sense of "social responsibility" (Goleman, 2006). Concurrently, empathy enables the leader to develop an organizations.

> Conscience, to care for the human element . . . to care for the society, to create a profitable environment for the corporation that goes beyond revenue but looks at affect . . . and finally becomes a source of goodness in the society in which it finds itself. (Natale & Sora, 2010, p. 315).

The leader's quest is to inculcate the empathic paradigm throughout the organization. The question becomes: How does one expand and intensify or institutionalize the empathic paradigm to influence the organizations constituents? Institutionalized empathy provides leaders and the leadership team with pertinent information to improve organizational outcomes. To achieve their outcomes, the leadership team must institutionalize empathic principles company-wide while fostering proper "balance" and "self-regulation" (Klemp, 2005). This can be accomplished by continuous training and development specifically focused on the components of empathic awareness.

The subsequent section discusses significant leaders from diverse fields who demonstrate various practical applications of empathy to enhance their leadership effectiveness. The empathic approach enabled these leaders to achieve significant organizational successes and advanced a moral commitment to their communities.

LEADERS: EMPATHY PERSONIFIED

A. G. Lafley: Empathic Engagement for Innovation

Founded in 1837, Procter & Gamble (P&G) has been a world-renowned health, beauty, baby, family, and household product manufacturer (Procter & Gamble, 2012). P&G's growth over the years remained impressively consistent until 2000, whereupon its stock declined with a concomitant loss of "$85 billion in market capitalization" (Tichy, 2009). The general consensus was that P&G had expanded too rapidly while its crippling "bureaucratic structure" increasingly distanced the corporation from its consumers (Whitman & Hamilton, 2010).

To address the crisis, A. G. Lafley was elected in 2000 as P&G's CEO with the mandate to revive the struggling company. His preferred strategy was to restore P&G to its roots with a customer-centric focus that incorporated innovation and empathic awareness (Lafley & Charan, 2008). P&G's leadership had come to view the consumer as a simple income stream, while disregarding the genuine needs, concerns, and aspirations the consumer might have. Lafley, however, argued for a paradigm shift that required emphasis on empathic engagement to "translate purpose into action and show up in everyday behaviors, beginning with how we treat the consumer and each other" (Lafley & Charan, 2008, p. 11). The empathic engagement precepts were at the heart of P&G's innovative growth and required the company to step into the shoes of their consumers to gain a better understanding of consumer perspective, the virtual definition of empathy.

Lafley initiated a campaign to reinvent P&G by incorporating empathic insights into his innovation strategy. This new perspective impacted P&G's market research, driving an exclusively "consumer immersion focus". He committed "a billion dollars" to market research that eventually acted as a catalyst toward the aforementioned market perspective (Lafley & Charan, 2008). This ultimately enabled the P&G'ers to adopt a transformative mindset that allowed them to read the pulse of their consumers that empowered P&G to improve the success rate of their core brands.

In line with this thinking, Lafley created a "consumer closeness program" entitled Living It (Lafley & Charan, 2008). This program required P&G'ers to spend time in the customers' environments to learn from their perspectives. Lafley explained, "We live with consumers in their homes, shop with them in stores, and observe their daily behaviors for days, weeks and even months at a time" (Procter & Gamble, 2008, p. 5). The connectivity with consumers required oneself to see the problem from their viewpoint and create the best solution from the consumers' outlook. A follow-up program entitled Working It (Lafley & Charan, 2008) expanded upon the Living It model by having P&G'ers function as sales counter clerks in various retail outlets. Working It enabled P&G's sales personnel to develop insight into the consumers' decision-making process such as price point limitations, behavioral considerations, and alternative competitive product choices. In essence, this new role modification produces an emotional connection creating a synergy, whereby loyalties develop on both sides of the business equation. Empathic engagement results in mutuality and concern.

As a consequence of these activities, the consumer, the employees, and other constituents worked together by providing ideas, constructive criticism, and possible solutions that would strengthen the chances for continuous enhancement of a successful brand. To reinforce these changes, Lafley led by example and went once a month to meet with P&G's customers. He indicated that this initiative "gave clarity and meaning to our business strategy . . . it pulled us together . . . it was crystal clear, compelling and inclusive" (Lafley & Charan, 2008, p. 72). Lafley's empathic leadership created a deeper engagement that led to community.

Lafley's insistence on institutionalizing his customer-centric focus permeated the complete organization. For example, Meg Whitman, as a P&G board director, traveled to China to experience the empathic understanding toward the customer. Whitman visited the homes of families to observe, understand, and question the women that used the P&G brand products. The family visits convinced her that Lafley's emphasis on acquiring insight into the consumer's feelings provided invaluable input that no other "metric" methodology could uncover (Lafley & Charan, 2008). The by-product of Whitman's journey reaffirmed Lafley's determination that the acceptance of his customer-centric focus for the organization needed top-to-bottom support.

Lafley continued experimenting with new methodologies to develop a deeper understanding of consumer's feelings and concerns; two notable examples were the "Clay Street" and the "Baby Discovery Center" programs (Lafley & Charan, 2008, pp. 223, 232). Each of these strategies was a cross-functional team effort to address specific challenges confronting P&G's various product lines. The methodologies utilized required an intrapsychic perspective of each team member as well as a deep, genuine behavioral understanding of the consumer. The Clay Street project, regarding P&G's *Herbal Essences* product, led the team to drill down into the potential market; the team went into the marketplace acting as prospective buyers as well as meeting with real buyers to explore generational differences. Their research indicated that "Gen-Y" was not attracted to the overall packaging of the product, but wanted Herbal Essences to emphasize, in the case of women, "feminine sensuality". The newly created packaging of Herbal Essences enabled the product to become "another one of P&G's billion-dollar brands" (Lafley & Charan, 2008, pp. 228–230). Similar experiments performed in the Baby Discovery Center program resulted in the significant development of the *Pampers* product, culminating in a "$7 billion brand" (Lafley & Charan, 2008). Once again, empathic engagement supported by research had won the day.

Lafley's experimentation culminated in the development of the "Connect and Develop" (C&D) model (Lafley & Charan, 2008). P&G's C&D approach to innovation focuses on an empathic connectivity that utilizes "external" partnerships with P&G's "internal" sources for creative ideas and product enhancements. The underlying concept of C&D is to build relationships (Eisberg, 2007). The leadership mindset for each partnership developed required the utilization of empathic precepts to establish a win-win situation.

The empathic insight utilized by Lafley during his 10-year tenure established one point incontrovertibly. By understanding the needs, feelings, and aspirations of their consumers, P&G identified a product need as well as an affective bond with the product that generated a sustainable competitive advantage with long-term financial success.

Meg Whitman: Engaged Action-Orientation

To understand eBay and its story requires understanding the revolution in technology that was its context. eBay existed in virtual space and exploited the Web as a means for economic exchange. In spite of being Web based, eBay provided a humanistic environment that enabled the company to communicate empathically with its users. The human perspective became the hallmark of the company and enticed Meg Whitman to take the reins as CEO in 1998. As CEO, Whitman not only created significant financial success for eBay, but enhanced its human image by "amplifying our [its] humanity in extraordinary ways" by providing the customer with tools that would "institutionalize listening and enfranchising" (Whitman & Hamilton, 2010, p. 7) and emphasize transparency. Accordingly, this "values-based approach to management" created "a new model for success with lessons that go beyond business" (Whitman & Hamilton, 2010, p. 11).

eBay engaged their customers empathically, assuming that "most were essentially good people" (Whitman & Hamilton, 2010); a principle inculcated in Whitman's thinking by her mentor, and eBay's founder, Pierre Omidyar.

This was not done naïvely, however, as the company also implemented a vigilant Trust and Safety Division with the use of software to examine patterns that might signal less-than-honest interactions (Whitman & Hamilton, 2010). To this more mechanistic model, Pierre Omidyar institutionalized a feedback section where buyers could not only evaluate their transactions, but also be of assistance to each other. eBay understood that its success came from intensely listening to its community of users. McConnell and Huba (2003) argue, a company that encourages a "democratic" structure, allows a community of users to have the freedom to provide feedback and new ideas. This listening with the "third ear" is the hallmark of empathy.

Whitman's insight along with her prior P&G experience, created the Voices of the Customer program: "We invited members of the community, usually ten or so at a time, to sit down with us at headquarters, and we listened to their ideas, their complaints, and their suggestions" (Whitman & Hamilton, 2010, p. 167). This kind of listening is a continuous process that results in immediate feedback regarding the emotional mindset of the consumer.

Listening to, and understanding its customers required empathic engagement that, in turn, enhanced relationships. Whitman indicated, "An emotional connection is central to any great relationship in business and in life" (Whitman & Hamilton, 2010, p. 179). Oftentimes, those relationships were based on mutual trust between eBay and their users for the enhancement of the company's success. The trust and attention eBay gave its customers allowed the company to become "a powerful brand" that established the basis for it's sustainable competitive advantage.

This listening and trusting begins with leaders understanding their own needs as well as recognizing that all growth will require continual modification and change. Whitman realized that culture and values is an executive leadership prerogative. She understood that identifying executives with the kind of reputation eBay wanted to be known for affected the qualities the company's employees would ultimately have. Whitman explained, "The most effective executives model and live the same behaviors they demand of their organizations" (Whitman & Hamilton, 2010, p. 73).

All empathic engagement requires a sense of affective bonding as well as self-awareness. This awareness and customer sensitivity moved eBay in its acquisition of PayPal. The company realized that a bottleneck in the sales transaction process between buyers and sellers was the payment for goods. The acquisition of PayPal instituted a seamless transition (Whitman & Hamilton, 2010).

Nor is this empathic engagement limited only to the interpersonal. When significant problems arose in China, Whitman and some of her staff relocated there to manage the issues (Whitman & Hamilton, 2010). In this case, learning, not predicted success, was the result. The formula appears clear: Empathic engagement stemming from effective leadership engages people, modifies systems, energizes corporate success, and increases learning. This experience taught Whitman and her leadership team that differences in cultural dynamics must be fully explored and understood in order to be successful. Only by becoming culturally empathic with these differences at an affective level could effective change be implemented. Further, these changes can require considerable time, trust, and concern.

Due to her respect-driven empathic engagement, Whitman believed, "the hard-nosed business values and the 'softer,' ethical values—were complementary" (Whitman & Hamilton, 2010, p. 9). Pierre Omidyar, as cited in Whitman & Hamilton (2010), stated, "We don't have to invent values. This community already has values. We need to align ourselves with their values or it's not going to work" (p. 5). eBay fosters a belief that people, although diverse, have basic human morality; encourages mutual respect; and promotes an open environment that develops outstanding employees.

Whitman understood that to create "The Power of Many", you could not rely on "bullying people into doing what you want and trying to make every day an excruciating mind game to figure out what the boss really wants" (Whitman & Hamilton, 2010, p. 200). For Whitman, this was reminiscent of her experience as a partner at Bain & Co., in which new hires were placed in a situation that promoted a survival of the fittest environment (Whitman & Hamilton, 2010). Whitman eventually convinced Bain to make changes, and the company chose to have her design a training program. She concluded, "The results played out just as we had predicted they would: We improved both individual performance and retention, and boosted morale and loyalty" (Whitman & Hamilton, 2010, p. 202).

The training program also changed the culture of the organization and emphasized the concept of "enfranchising". Enfranchising emphasizes teamwork and helps one another to acquire a strong empathic engagement. By enfranchising, Whitman means "convincing every stakeholder . . . that we have a shared mission that we can best achieve by working together rather than attacking and undermining one another" (Whitman & Hamilton, 2010, p. 203). This enfranchising model was later utilized by Whitman as she implemented her empathic approach at eBay.

During the now famous June 10, 1999, eBay outage, Whitman's empathic understanding of the concerns and feelings of her users immediately initiated enfranchising precepts. Whitman and her management team personally called thousands of eBay's top customers to apologize, which resulted in positive feedback from skeptical sellers (Whitman & Hamilton, 2010). The crisis enhanced eBay's connectivity process with all stakeholders. The experience allowed eBay to show its users that the company shared in their anguish and, in turn, developed a mutual understanding of collaboration and trust. Furthermore, the personal nature of eBay's apology displayed a sense of humility that characterizes the true nature of empathy.

Whitman refers to her ability to decide when and how to act as "a bias for action", which enables a leader to swiftly adjust in times of crisis, without having all the information at hand (Whitman & Hamilton, 2010). To accomplish this, you must have an understanding of and confidence in, your own abilities as a leader. Whitman's engaged action-orientation, with intrapsychic perspectives, founded on customer needs and the concerns of others within the company, is the hallmark of what empathic engagement can offer.

Pete Carroll: Empathy a Continuous Learning Process

Celebrated and successful football head coach of the University of Southern California (USC), Pete Carroll from 2001 to 2008 "won seven straight PAC 10 Championships, amassed an impressive 86% win record, won two national championships, and set an all-time record for being ranked the number one team in the nation by the Associated Press 33 straight weeks" ("Pete Carroll USC Head Football Coach", n.d.). Coach Carroll stands apart from an array of other college head coaches in his creative implementation of a varied model of motivation and support for his players.

Carroll was influenced by the theories of Abraham Maslow (1962), Tim Gallwey (1997), and Michael Murphy in crafting his empathic paradigm shift. In a model that traditionally demanded its head coach to be dictatorial, intimidating, and emotionally detached, he assumed an antithetical posture. In his evolving shift, Carroll moved from exemplification to humanization of his role as leader.

Maslow's influence is evident in Carroll's relational approach to player engagement. After reading Maslow's book *Toward a Psychology of Being* (1962), Carroll, as cited in Malcomson (2007), asked himself: "What if my job as a coach isn't so much to force or coerce performance as it is to create situations where players develop the confidence to set their talents free and pursue their potential to its full extent?" Tim Gallwey (1997), author of *The Inner Game of Tennis*, encouraged Carroll to assist players in developing a quieted and highly focused mind, which, in turn, improved player performance. Gallwey's influence can be seen in Carroll's willingness to live in his players' shoes in order to understand their feelings, concerns, and aspirations. This engagement enhanced player confidence, which manifested itself in intense concentration attended by an obvious absence of doubt or fear.

Carroll was looking to transform his players and found a supporting theory in Michael Murphy's teachings. He indicated "Michael was one of the first researchers to explore the transformational potential of sport, not only in terms of performance, but also in terms of how these experiences can drive you to be the best human being you can be" (Carroll & Roth, 2010, p. 23). Clearly, Carroll's leadership engaged players at an affective and empathic level through an understanding that the whole person was involved in the sport. This was a significant change from the more mechanistic model espoused by so many coaches.

Carroll emphasized the human and affective dimension of the players to achieve a deeper understanding of their personal motivation. Carroll noted "This kind of thinking would have been laughed right out of the locker room" (Carroll & Roth, 2010, p. 20). Carroll endured, however, and insisted "It is through the strength of my relationships with my players that I gain insight into how to guide and challenge them to be their best. If you really care about helping people maximize their potential, then you must try to uncover who they are and what they are all about" (Carroll & Roth, 2010, p. 135).

Fundamental to this paradigm shift, Carroll's utilization of mentoring allowed him to create a network of support to implement his developing model. The six years of working under some of the leading coaches in college football enabled Carroll to gain invaluable experience and develop a network of coaches that provided the mentoring needed to enhance his philosophy (Carroll & Roth, 2010). In addition, working under various National Football League coaches taught Carroll the art of leadership and the importance of observing human behavior as well as the utilization of intuitive powers in understanding the way people and teams work. Observing these coaches by whom he was mentored, Carroll understood that a consistent philosophy on leadership was quintessential. Not only did his philosophy engage his players. It required self-understanding and resonance between his feelings and those of others. This is the intrapsychic component of empathy: "the importance of being able to organize your thoughts and feelings about your work" (Carroll & Roth, 2010, p. 28).

These experiences enabled Carroll to become head coach of two NFL teams, the New York Jets and the New England Patriots. The story does not magically end here. Carroll was not able to function at peak performance because, as mentioned earlier, he realized that he needed to engage a 360-degree network that required support from those above, below, and beside him to assure effective empathic deployment. His dismissal from the New England Patriots provided an opportunity to refine his philosophy when he was named head coach at USC, which was attempting to regain national prominence.

Carroll focused his approach to coaching USC on key empathic elements that led to outstanding success. He acknowledged that unity, communication, trust, understanding, and respect must all be present in order for the team to achieve its goals (Carroll & Roth, 2010). Here his earlier experiences proved invaluable. He now had a significant understanding of himself and his ability to articulate the critical importance of empathy to the owners, front office, and support staff. Carroll knew that concurrence was needed throughout the entire organization, arguing, "The strongest [teams], I firmly believe, are those that are the most unified as an organization" (Carroll & Roth, 2010, p. 72). Empathy flows from unity, which results in cohesive team building. This cohesion encourages the team understanding that each member is crucial. In short, self-awareness is synergistic with empathy.

To acculturate his players, Carroll developed the "Win Forever Pyramid" (Carroll & Roth, 2010, p. 79). Mimicking Maslow, he included important empathic elements in his structure such as respect and trust, both in oneself and in one's team. Carroll points out, "It [*the Win Forever philosophy*] is about maximizing the potential of everyone in a program or organization" (Carroll & Roth, 2010, p. 116). When a coach, a manager, or a CEO focuses on maximizing each individual's performance, it further fosters motivation and success. To support this premise, Carroll encouraged players to create their own philosophies. "Every player in our program is a unique individual from a specific background, and before we can effectively reach and connect with him we must develop a relationship. Then we must formulate an approach that will enable the teaching and learning process" (Carroll & Roth, 2010, p. 128). The engagement with the players allows a coach to develop a plan that would enable them to learn and generate mutual respect, understanding, and appreciation. Carroll understood this concept, which in turn convinced him to drill down into the players' psyche, to enhance their performance. He and his coaching staff observed and listened to players in all situations, enabling them to acquire an understanding into a player's inner core values.

A key component to empathic leadership is to engage other followers in the organization to acquire a sense of empathy. Carroll not only focused on his players, but his fellow coaches as well. He insisted that each coach "be themselves", and encouraged all of them to create their own teaching style and visions. One particular experience that he describes is his working relationship with his assistant coaches. In the beginning, Carroll noticed that they began by "coaching hard", yelling and screaming at the players. However, he intuitively knew it was not their true nature. He notes, "After a few weeks, I sat down with each of them individually to discuss their approach. We discussed how they were coaching outside their personalities . . ." (Carroll & Roth, 2010, p. 117). Carroll's attunement to his coaches drove his intervention. By speaking to each of them respectively, he exhibited his understanding and developed open communication, which is crucial to empathic leadership.

Listening and communication are critical in empathic leadership (Goleman, 2006). Carroll kept communication lines open between him, his coaches, and the players. He noted, "By encouraging our players to communicate in such ways, we developed a positive mentality for the entire team" (Carroll & Roth, 2010, p. 111). His listening capabilities and open-door policy allowed for everyone in the organization to express their feelings in a healthy manner. When people can communicate and listen effectively with one another, it is easy to see where the other person is coming from.

An open environment leads to a more nuanced understanding that requires sensitivity to body language or facial expressions (Goman, 2011). Carroll enhanced the learning environment by implementing rules. He realized each player needed to be able to see the team's failures and successes through their teammates' eyes. So he insisted that players change seats each time, to get a new perspective on the situation (Carroll & Roth, 2010). Carroll also created a mantra "learn your learner", which became the guiding precept at USC. Carroll, as cited in Malcomson (2007), explained, "By paying close attention to the actions, mannerisms, and traits of our players . . . we get mountains of information". By learning about the person who is taking instruction from you, empathic engagement is enhanced.

Carroll emphasized his empathic insight into other aspects of his coaching philosophy. As Tim Gallwey indicated, players in all sports are looking for relief from fear and anxiety in order to play at peak performance (Gallwey, 1997). Carroll, influenced by both Gallwey's philosophy and his own past experience as a player, understood the players' anxieties. Therefore, he placed a strong emphasis on strenuous practices so that their mindset would develop self-confidence to minimize those anxieties; this intrapsychic perspective acts as an enabler for empathy.

Another important aspect of utilizing empathy applied to the recruitment process when Carroll and his coaching staff visited the home of a prospect (Carroll & Roth, 2010). They would observe, listen, and ask questions to gain better insight into the whole person and the family. They dug deep into the hearts of the parents and the player to understand their concerns, values, and aspirations. In turn, the empathic process becomes a two-way street. The parents and the player also have the opportunity to step into Carroll's and his coaches' shoes to better understand their core values regarding integrity, care, and sensitivity. Empathy is a mutual relationship-building process.

To develop and foster empathic leadership is a constant learning process that takes time, fortitude, and patience. Although labor intensive and demanding, empathy acts as a key catalyst for leaders to achieve long-standing, sustainable success.

Jack Mitchell: Customer-centric Passion

Founded in 1958, Mitchells/Richards/Marshs (MRM) is an upscale clothing company that boasts sales of "over $65 million dollars" and has customers that includes CEOs, top level senior executives, and managers from many Fortune 500 companies (Mitchell, 2003). The man behind the company's success, Chairman and CEO Jack Mitchell, has implemented a focused and empathic approach with his customers. Recently, *Inc.* magazine named Mitchell as one of the top 10 most fascinating entrepreneurs listed alongside such famous names as Richard Branson and Michael Dell (McCuan, 2005). Mitchell (2003) acknowledged that in business, "Today it's not enough to just make a sale" (p. 16). By viewing the customer as an actual person, rather than as another dollar earned or unit of inventory sold, the company develops a sense of bonding with its buyers. This understanding and attentiveness enhances the customer's sense of importance to the company beyond financial concerns.

Unlike many other companies in the retail business, MRM did not employ a "hi" and "bye" model. Instead, Mitchell instructed his sales associates to step into the shoes of his clients in order to glean information about what the customer needs (Mitchell, 2003). When the sales associate asks questions such as, What type of colors do you like best? or Are you looking for an outfit for a particular occasion?, empathic engagement and bonding is born.

The empathic engagement of asking meaningful questions and trying to understand the customer's needs and concerns makes it easier to determine what products that company should be creating. This is empathic engagement at its best and embraces the customer completely. Mitchell (2003) emphasized, "By customer-centric, I mean the customer is the center of the universe" (p. 19). The customer-centric focus enabled his sales associates to step into the customers' shoes to understand what they want in a product, as opposed to telling them what they want to buy.

Empathy generates customer loyalty beyond the product line. Customers return when they feel that their needs are being met and that the decision process is dialogic in nature. Mitchell (2003) argued, "When you have strong relationships, customers will do more buying from you. They'll refer other customers. They'll communicate with you better and tell you what they like and what they don't like, in turn making your business more efficient and effective" (p. 19). Customer engagement generates trust, a positive word-of-mouth network, and a window into the company's directional choices in terms of product enhancement and inventory control.

When the company supports relationship development with customers, employees are also more engaged. When you know someone personally you want to be more helpful because you understand how you would want to be treated, especially by someone whom you know by name. In this model of empathic engagement, both the customer and the employee develop an enhanced sense of value-based interactions.

It is not sufficient for individual workers to be engaged, as would be common in many companies. Rather, the goal would be to institutionalize this engagement through careful listening and attentiveness to nuance. At MRM employees not only know their top "1,000 customers", but also their database has the capability to understand their clients' spending habits and product preferences ("Retailer of the Year", 2001). Although this process seems initially improbable, Mitchell's methodology confirms that institutionalizing empathy can enhance corporate learning, which impacts the bottom line.

The corporate listening and learning approach generated an IT system that reflected each customer's values, attitudes, needs, and expectations regarding purchases. The outcome was a "comprehensive Customer Relationship and Point of Sale software" (Mitchell, 2003, p. 127). By knowing what people like, understanding their buying patterns and particular tastes, the company had the ability to make their product and service even better.

MRM required all employees to work on the floor at some point, which provided them an opportunity to meet and interact with customers in the buying environment. Mitchell (2003) explained, "The reason I want everyone on the selling floor at some point is that's where it's easiest to see, touch, and feel real live customers" (p. 25). Being able to interact directly with the people who purchase your product gives managers, tailors, sales associates, and executives the ability to know their customers. This interaction is quintessential, as we have seen in previous cases where leaders even relocated to absorb the cultural values that were initially alien. Again, the empathic engagement enhanced corporate profitability and bonding.

To improve interactions and awareness, Mitchell emphasized a "flat organization" (Mitchell, 2003). When employees feel they can talk with their supervisors it promotes a sense of pride in oneself. Employees at MRM were encouraged to discuss concerns at weekly meetings, which bolstered self-awareness, other-directed understanding, and more effective problem solving. These meetings also provided an opportunity for Mitchell to step into the shoes of his employees' to understand their needs and aspirations regarding their careers, which in turn would maximize their full potential.

As a result of the above changes, the company had a more clearly articulated value hierarchy, as well as an expansive moral compass. The order of concern within the company is "People-Service-Product" (Mitchell, 2003). This emphasis on the employee was not naïve. Rather, the employees were the external face of the company and represented its values. Mitchell (2003) argued, "If you don't give them the right support and latitude, they'll stagnate. The most important thing in our organization, everyone is enabled" (p. 97). Making the employee feel special is one method Mitchell employed to retain and motivate his workers.

MRM has taken their customer-centric focus, which is emphasized in every department, and merged it with psychological awareness of consumer behavior to provide valuable feedback. Mitchell (2003) explained, "Studies show that it costs six times more to get a new customer than it does to keep an existing customer. That's why our focus has always been on better servicing our existing customers" (pp. 82–83). Service and empathic engagement remain the elixir of success. Service is its outward manifestation. By the deft use of empathic awareness and engagement, Mitchell has created success and sustained creativity for MRM. As Mitchell (2003) proudly concluded, many pundits have recognized that MRM has become "one of the most successful—if not the most successful—high-end clothing businesses of our size in the country, and maybe in the world" (p. 5).

LESSONS LEARNED

Empathy has recently attracted the interest of business leaders, as shown in the previous cases. Our objective in the subsequent section is to glean from the cases lessons to be learned by current leaders and nascent leaders in their quest to enhance their own leadership capabilities.

Listening: The Third Ear

Demonstrating empathic leadership requires a significant ability to listen. It is this listening with the "third ear" that enables one to sense the conflicts and needs of the stakeholders. The listening skill is a driving force for successful empathic leadership as Whitman, cited in Bethel (2009), admonished, "Listen. Listen. Listen. You will learn what people think the problem is, and maybe you'll learn what the solution is" (p. 301). The failure to intensely listen to your customer base, due to a sense of "arrogance", is financially detrimental to a company's survival, as illustrated by such companies as The Great Atlantic and Pacific Tea Company (A&P), Ames Department Store, and Circuit City (Collins, 2009, p. 37). In addition, as P&G and eBay learned from their early global expansion setbacks, "listening with the third ear" is a necessity for a leaders' global success. Concomitantly, leaders must learn to modify their ethnocentric perspective toward an expansive viewpoint that incorporates "mindfulness, dignity, and moral inclusion" (Johnson, 2012, p. 371).

Financial Myths Debunked

In a difficult global economy the financial drive is intensified. While financial drivers are crucial, the cases explored demonstrate that financial rewards and the use of an empathic approach to leadership are not exclusive. For P&G, Lafley's 10-year tenure demonstrated both empathy and monetary savvy as reflected in P&G's having "increased sales 110%, to $84 billion, and nearly tripled profits, to $12 billion" (Procter & Gamble, 2008, p. 2). Similar to Lafley's empathic and financial success, Whitman, upon retiring, had grown eBay from "$4 million in 1998 to approximately $8 billion in 2008, with an employee base from 50 employees to 15,000 employees globally" (Cohen, 2008). Also, Carroll's empathic leadership reign enhanced the financial position of USC's athletic department, with revenues "increasing from $47 million to $76 million, enhancing football scholarships and supporting almost all of USC's twenty other varsity sports" (Horowitz, 2008). The cases demonstrate that empathy serves as a key driver in creating a profitable environment within an empowered, collaborative, and connected context.

The Moral Compass: Building Community

The empathic interactions in the cases described produce a moral compass that is both culturally contextual and person oriented (Lennick, Kiel, & Jordan, 2011). The moral compass heightens sensitivity to employee and consumer needs, and enhances the flow of conversation throughout the organization.

Lafley's drive toward understanding the consumer's needs and concerns generated a moral imperative within the organization. This stepping into the shoes of his constituents moved Lafley beyond financial concerns and into a moral realm. P&G's sense of morality and social responsibility is manifest in a variety of moral considerations, such as the provision of safe drinking water in over 50 countries, supplying essential vaccinations to women and children, and building schools in China to make education available to poverty-stricken areas (CPXample, 2010). In line with Lafley's moral considerations, Carroll's creation of A Better L.A. Foundation reached out to reduce gang violence, thereby promoting a safe haven as a result of his empathic engagement with the Los Angeles neighborhoods (Malcomson, 2007).

Whitman's stance against pro-Nazi paraphernalia advertised on eBay exemplifies the impact that empathy poses on a company's moral perspective. For Whitman to eliminate such abhorrent material proved contrary to eBay's belief in the principles of "free speech" and a "free open marketplace": the bedrock to eBay's corporate philosophy. Nevertheless, after much debate, Whitman and the board approved that regardless of eBay's protected legal rights, it was more important for the company to support behavior that is morally correct, thereby resulting in the removal of such paraphernalia, as well as any other such abhorrent material in the future (Whitman & Hamilton, 2010). eBay, by stepping into the shoes of the victims' families, empathically understood how the sale of such products would cause them pain and suffering.

These examples underlie that empathy is contagious and action oriented, which, in turn, promotes a moral imperative.

Organizational Restructuring: Institutional Imperative

The command-control structure dominating many organizations appears to be giving way to empowerment models (Tappin & Cave, 2010). Mitchell (2003) argued for a "flat organization", stating, "Bureaucracy kills warmth and openness. It doesn't allow for a culture of always being open to ourselves" (p. 66). The command-control format is often too linear in structure and is not as quickly responsive to the changing socioeconomic environment (Tappin & Cave, 2010).

Institutionalizing empathy, as demonstrated in the aforementioned cases, is a company-wide implementation model that requires concurrence and synchronization. This model produces a team dynamic that, if successful, creates an organization that achieves sustainable success. P&G is a prime example of the value of employing empathy in a team-based model. The Clay Street program previously mentioned in this chapter is just one example of the power of incorporating empathy into a team-based structure.

The team approach is necessarily reflected in the hiring processes. Larry Bossidy, former CEO of Allied Signal, commented that, "the job no leader should delegate [hiring]—having the right people in the right place" (Bossidy & Charan, 2002, p. 109). All the leaders in the cases addressed the hiring process and emphasized the importance of person-environment fit. P&G's

Lafley developed a "Build From Within" program that would track the performance of managers throughout their succession in the company based on business acumen and value-based qualities. This program acts as an inside hiring concept, which developed capable leaders and resulted in "lining up three replacement candidates for each of P&G's top 50 executives within the organization" (Kimes, 2009). Similarly, Carroll emphasized the importance of recruiting the best skilled players with the proper core values to ensure a sustainable winning team environment. For all leaders, the person-environment fit is enhanced by utilizing empathic principles in the hiring process to uncover the values and emotional mindset of the potential employee.

EMPATHY: TEACHABLE DIMENSION

It should be noted that empathy appears to exist in various degrees in different peoples. Since empathy is a complex phenomenon based on primitive instinct as well as psychological self and other awareness, it is tricky to teach. Nevertheless, the cases have demonstrated that empathy can be bolstered by various methodological approaches. First and foremost, the mentoring process offers the most significant benefits. Both Whitman and Carroll demonstrated the significance that proper mentoring can have on one's success. Whitman's constant referencing to Pierre Omidyer provided the culture that contributed to her leadership enhancement. In line with Whitman's mentoring experience, the various coaches under whom Carroll worked enhanced his leadership.

Another methodology to bolster a leader's empathic nature was formal education. Carroll's higher education training provided him with an appreciation for the emotional components of empathy. The study of Maslow, Gallwey, and Murphy laid the foundation for his paradigm shift to empathic instrumentation.

The cases also illustrate the importance of real-world experience in developing an empathic approach toward leadership. The leaders studied valued their varied business experiences, which enabled them to gain a holistic understanding of the nature of stakeholder's needs, concerns, and aspirations.

All of the above methodologies can assist in teaching empathy. Regardless of the methods chosen, the cases establish that empathy can be taught despite personal variance.

CONCLUSION

The cases have demonstrated how tightly empathy is bound to effective leadership. The leader must be present and engaged in the life of the stakeholders, living with them affectively to provide appropriate responses. Further, as we have seen, the empathic engagement is intrapsychic, interpersonal, and encompasses value-based cultural differences. Most significantly, a critical requirement of employing empathic leadership involves moral qualities that include humility, selflessness, and concern. In essence, the motivation of the leader must be congruent with the greater good of all.

Finally, we have chosen not to define in detail the various models that leaders have implemented in these cases. Rather, what is universal in these models is that empathy is the condition sine qua non that drives awareness, trust, and creativity. Perhaps our case explorations are best summarized by Col. Eric Kail in *The Washington Post* (who argues on 10/28/2011):

> Perhaps the most pervasive axiom on the topic of leadership is that leadership is all about people. This simple statement reveals two critical principles of effective leadership. First, leadership is more than accomplishing a goal or mission. Second, seeing as the word "people" is plural, the focus of who benefits from leadership should be on the followers, not the leader. These truths, in turn, rest upon empathy, one's capacity to comprehend or experience the emotions of another. . . .
>
> Interestingly, the followers decide how empathic a leader really is, and this is how the most powerful and effective leaders receive their influence. Leadership, after all, is a relationship. We cannot expect others to go very far with us in a relationship until we reveal who we are and in turn learn who they are in a meaningful manner.
>
> Powerful leaders value their followers as individuals. They are also tolerant, willing to investigate the perceptions and positions of others objectively. Empathic leaders leverage diversity because of individual differences, not in spite of them. Each person brings unique perceptions, experiences, strengths and challenges to a team . . . In this way, empathy is far more critical to good leadership than any technical knowledge, skill or ability. . . .

REFERENCES

Batson, D., Batson, J., Todd, M., Brummett, B., Shaw, L., & Aldeguer, C. (1995). Empathy and the collective good: Caring for one of the others in a social dilemma. *Journal of Personality and Psychology, 68*(4), 619–631.

Bethel, S. M. (2009). *A new breed of leader*. NY: Penguin.

Bossidy, L., & Charan, R. (2002). *Execution*. NY: Crown Business.

Brothers, L. (1989). A biological perspective on empathy. *The American Journal of Psychiatry, 146*, 1.

Carroll, P., & Roth, Y. (2010). *Win forever*. NY: Penguin.

Cohen, A. (2008, January 25). [Web log message]. Retrieved from http://theboard. blogs.nytimes. com/2008/01/25/going-going-gone-meg-whitman-leaves-ebay/

Collins, J. (2009). *How the mighty fall*. NY: Harper Collins.

CPXample. (2010, June 29). *Procter & Gamble: Helping kids live, learn and thrive*. Retrieved from http://www.cpxample.com/2010/06/procter-gamble-helping-kids-live-learn-and-thrive/

Davis, H. (Ed.). (1940). *Gulliver's travels. The prose works of Jonathan Swift, XI,* 267. London: Chatto & Winders.

DeVignemont, F., & Singer, T. (2006). The empathic brain: How, when and why? Trends in *Cognitive Sciences, 10*(10), 435–441.

Eisberg, N. (2007). Collaborate to innovate. *Chemistry & Industry,* (12), 25–26.

Eisenberg, N. (2005). Moral motivation through the lifespan. In *Current Theory and Research in Motivation.* Nebraska: University of Nebraska, 51.

Friedman, M. (1970, September 13). The social responsibility of business is to increase profits. New *York Times Magazine,* 32–33, 122–126.

Gallwey, T. W. (1997). *The inner game of tennis: The classic guide to the mental side of peak performance.* NY: Random House Trade.

Gano-Overway, L. A., Michelle Magyar, T., Kim, M. S., Newton, M., Fry, M. D., & Guivernau, M. R. (2009). Influence of caring youth sport contexts on efficacy— Related beliefs and social behavior. *Developmental Psychology, 45*(2), 239–340.

Goleman, D. (1995). *Emotional intelligence: Why it can matter more than IQ.* NY: Bantam.

Goleman, D. (1998). *Working with emotional intelligence.* NY: Bantam Dell.

Goleman, D. (2006). *Social intelligence.* NY: Bantam.

Goman, C. K. (2011). *The silent language of leaders.* San Francisco: Jossey Bass.

Hoffman, M. L. (2001). Toward a comprehensive empathy-based theory of pro social moral development. In A. C. Bohart and D. J. Stipeck (Eds.), *Constructive and destructive behavior: Implications for family, school, and society.* Washington DC: American Psychological Association; Cambridge: Cambridge University Press, 61–86.

Horowitz, J. (2008, December 26*). The Pete Carroll effect.* Retrieved from www.petecarroll.com /2008/12/26/the-pete-carroll-effect/

Johnson, C. E. (2012*). Meeting the ethical challenges of leadership.* Thousand Oaks, CA: Sage.

Kail, E. (2011, October 28). *Leadership character: The role of empathy. Washington Post.* Retrieved from http://www.washingtonpost.com/blogs/guestinsights/post/leadershipcharacter-the-role-of-empathy/2011/04/04/gIQAQXVGQM_blog.html

Kimes, M. (2009). P&G's leadership machine. *Fortune, 159*(7), 22.

Klemp, G. (2005). *Emotional intelligence and leadership: What really matters.* Boston, MA: Cambria Consulting, 1–4.

Lafley, A. G., & Charan, R. (2008). *The game-changer: How you can drive revenue and profit growth with innovation.* NY: Crowne Business.

Lennick, D., Kiel, F., & Jordan, K. (2011). *Moral intelligence 2.0.* NY: Prentice Hall.

Malcomson, B. (2007, August 13). *Making a better L.A.* Retrieved from www.pete carroll.com /2007/08/13/making-a-better-l-a/

Maslow, A. (1962). *Toward a psychology of being.* Princeton, NJ: Van Nostrand.

McBane, D. (1995). Empathy and the salesperson: A multidimensional perspective. *Psychology and Marketing, 12*(4), 349–370.

McConnell, B., & Huba, J. (2003). *Meg Whitman: How eBay rules.* Retrieved from http://www.creatingcustomerevangelists.com/resources/evangelists/meg_whitman.asp

McCuan, J. (2005, April 1). *26 most fascinating entrepreneurs: Jack Mitchell.* Retrieved from http://www.inc.com/magazine/20050401/26-mitchell.html

McIntosh, F. (2011). *The relational leader.* Boston: Course Technology.

Mitchell, J. (2003*). Hug your customers: The proven way to personalize sales and achieve astounding results.* NY: Hyperion Books.

Natale, S. (1972). *An experiment in empathy.* Slough, England: National Foundation for Educational Research.

Natale, S., & Sora, S. (2010). Ethics in strategic thinking: Business processes and the global market collapse. *Journal of Business Ethics, 94*(3), 309–316.

Patnaik, D. (2009). *Widespread empathy: Rewiring your corporation for intuition.* New York, NY: Fast Company. Retrieved from http://www/fastcompany.com/ blog/dev-patnaik/innovation/ widespread-empathy.

Patnaik, D., & Mortensen, P. (2009). *Wired to care.* New Jersey: FT Press.

Pete Carroll USC Head Football Coach. Retrieved from http://www.usctrojans.com/ sports/m-footbl/mtt/carroll_pete00.html

Pink, D. H. (2005). *A whole new mind.* NY: Penguin.

Procter & Gamble. (2008). *2008 annual report.* Retrieved from http://annualreport. pg.com/ annualreport2008/

Procter & Gamble (2012). *Heritage.* Retrieved from http://www.pg.com/en_US/ company/ heritage.shtml

Retailer of the year Mitchells/Richards. (2001, November*)."What are you doing, Dave?"* The computers at Mitchells and Richards know what you did last summer, 56. Retrieved from http://www.mitchellstores.com/site/wp-content/themes/ cadc/images/pr_mitchells_mr1.pdf

Tappin, S., & Cave, A. (2010*). The new secrets of CEO's.* Boston: Nicholas Brealey.

Tichy, N. (2009). Lafley's legacy: From crisis to consumer-driven. *Businessweek Online,* 14.

Van Lange, P. (2008). Does empathy trigger only altruistic motivation? How about selflessness or justice? *Emotions, 8*(6), 766–774.

Whitman, M., & Hamilton, J. O. (2010). *The power of many.* NY: Three Rivers.

Part II

Applied Approaches to Empathy

B: Decision Making

7 Ethical Decision Making in Organizations

The Role of Empathy

Emmanuelle P. Kleinlogel and Joerg Dietz

INTRODUCTION

For a long time, organizational theory focused on rational decision-making processes, and on "how organizations systemize, rationalize, routinize, and bureaucratize human action in an attempt to strip away or control emotion that might interfere with rationality" (Dutton, Worline, Frost, & Lilius, 2006, p. 61). However, as pointed out by Tenbrunsel and Smith-Crowe (2008), emotions are critical for ethical decision making because they help to "draw our attention to moral issues and highlight the moral imperative in situations" (p. 575) (see also Damasio, 1994; Gaudine & Thorne, 2001). Pavlovich and Krahnke (2012) present the emotion of empathy in particular as crucial for organizational functioning and decision making because it fosters connectedness between organizational members and creates cooperative relationships and ethicality.

In this chapter, we propose to review when empathy facilitates and when it undermines ethical decision making. On the one hand, we propose that empathy plays a positive role in ethical decision making through the empathy-altruism hypothesis (Batson, 2008) and through the lens of positive organizational ethics (Stansbury & Sonenshein, 2012). On the other hand, we also propose that empathy can lead individuals to make poor decisions via biased decision-making processes.

The chapter is organized as follows. First, we define the concept of empathy. Then, we discuss the processes that underlie a positive effect of empathy on ethical decision making, followed by processes that explain a negative effect of empathy on ethicality in decision making. These are summarized in a model on the factors that impact on ethical decision making. Finally, we conclude by discussing the limitations of the current research on empathy and the implications of empathy in decision-making processes.

DEFINITION OF EMPATHY

For the purpose of our chapter, we adopt the definition of empathy by Batson (2008, p. 8) as "an other-oriented emotional response elicited by and congruent with the perceived welfare of someone in need". An empathetic response entails two interrelated processes: a cognitive one and an emotional one (Batson, 2008). The cognitive process is activated by an arousal, that is, when an individual observes or interacts with a person in need. It consists in adopting the perspective of the person by imagining "how the person in need is affected by his or her situation" (Batson & Shaw, 1991, p. 112). Empathy has been considered as both a state (Batson, Duncan, Ackerman, Buckley, & Birch, 1981; Stocks, Lishner, & Decker, 2009) and a trait (Detert, Treviño, & Sweitzer, 2008; Duan & Hill, 1996; Verhaert & Van den Poel, 2010).

Empathy can be distinguished from two related concepts: sympathy and personal distress (e.g., Eisenberg & Strayer, 1987). Sympathy can be defined as "an emotional response stemming from the apprehension of another's emotional state or condition, which is not the same as the other's state or condition but consists of feeling of sorrow or concern for the other" (Eisenberg, Valiente, & Champion, 2004, p. 387). Contrary to empathy, which consists in part of the ability for individuals to image how the person in need feels, sympathy mainly refers to a feeling of sorrow for the person in need. Eisenberg and Strayer (1987, pp. 5–6) distinguished empathy from sympathy by arguing that empathy is a "feeling with another" while sympathy is a "feeling for someone".

Empathy differs also from personal distress. A feeling of distress consists of "personal feelings of anxiety and discomfort that result from observing another's negative experience" (Davis, 1980, p. 2). While empathy occurs when someone observes a person in need and takes his or her perspective, personal distress might occur when someone observes a person in need and experiences a strong negative emotional reaction to that (Eisenberg et al., 2004). Contrary to empathy, which involves a minimum "degree of

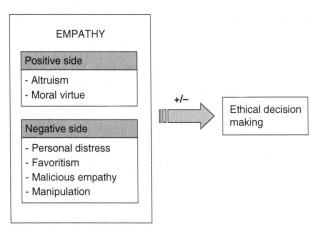

Figure 7.1   Empathy and ethical decision making

self-other differentiation" (Eisenberg & Strayer, 1987, p. 5), personal distress is thus a self-oriented emotion (Hodges & Biswas-Diener, 2007; Tangney, Stuewig, & Mashek, 2007). The factors that impact on positive and negative empathy are presented in Figure 7.1 and discussed in the following sections.

THE POSITIVE SIDE OF EMPATHY IN ETHICAL DECISION MAKING

The Social Psychological View of Empathy

According to the empathy-altruism hypothesis, empathy leads individuals to engage in helping behaviors toward a person in need in order to relieve that need. Research has shown that this behavior is primarily driven by a concern to assist persons in distress and not by egoistic needs (see Batson, 2008, for a review). Batson and his colleagues conducted numerous studies in support of this hypothesis. For instance, they found that the behaviors of empathic individuals were not motivated by (1) a need to reduce one's own distress or negative state (Batson et al., 1981; Batson et al., 1989; Dovidio, Allem, & Schroeder, 1990), (2) rewards (Batson & Shaw, 1991), (3) concerns about negative social evaluations (Fultz, Batson, Fortenbach, McCarthy, & Varey, 1986), or (4) similarity to the person in need (Batson, Lishner, Cook, & Sawyer, 2005).

Furthermore, empirical evidence has shown that empathy as a trait predicts altruistic behaviors (Eisenberg et al., 1999). In a meta-analysis, Eisenberg and Miller (1987) reported that trait empathy generally was associated with prosocial and related behaviors. More recently, Verhaert and Van den Poel (2010) found a relationship between empathic concern and donation decisions.

The Moral Virtue View of Empathy

Drawing on the empathy-altruism hypothesis, empathy is considered as a moral virtue and a human strength for organizations. Through the lens of positive organizational ethics (Stansbury & Sonenshein, 2012), the fundamental position of the "empathy as a virtue" approach is that empathy motivates human behavior that creates positive consequences for other people and stakeholders.

Empathy is considered as "the greatest contributor in strengthening social interaction through its ability to motivate individuals to cooperate, to share resources and to help others" (Pavlovich & Krahnke, 2012, p. 131). For instance, empathy-based behavior is perceived as enhancing compassion and connectedness through altruistic behavior within organizations (Dutton et al., 2006; Pavlovich & Krahnke, 2012). Empathy can therefore be said to motivate a collaborative rather than a competitive mindset. In addition, empathy also leads individuals to consider different points of view before they make decisions. They take the perspective of different stakeholders and consider the possible consequences of different scenarios. In the next section, we review empirical evidence relative to the positive effect of empathy on ethical decision making, starting with our experimental work on the role of empathy in wage-cut decisions.

Empirical Examples

Example 1: The Role of Empathy in Wage-Cut Decisions

We conducted a study to assess the role of empathy in wage-cut decisions (see Dietz & Kleinlogel, in press, for a detailed description of the method and results). In the first stage of the study, participants completed a questionnaire on individual differences including a measure of empathy. Participants' levels of empathy were measured using two subscales developed by Davis (1980, 1983), the perspective taking scale, and the empathic concern scale. The perspective taking scale assesses "the tendency or ability of the respondent to adopt the perspective, or point of view, of other people" (p. 6). A sample item is "Before criticizing somebody, I try to imagine how I would feel if I were in their place". The empathic concern scale indicates "the tendency for the respondent to experience feelings of warmth, compassion, and concern for others undergoing negative experiences" (p. 6). A sample item is "I often have tender, concerned feelings for people less fortunate than me".

In the second stage, four weeks later, participants worked on an in-basket exercise in which they played the role of a manager and had to make decisions regarding several managerial dilemmas. The task of interest concerned a potential wage-cut for overpaid personnel. Participants received a memorandum from the president of the company explaining that economic conditions had driven wage levels down for easily replaceable, unskilled labor and that the company paid their personnel in this category 9% above the market wage rate. Participants were randomly assigned to one of the two experimental conditions: Request to cut wages (Condition 1), and request to hold wages constant (Condition 2). In the cut-wages condition, the president of the company mentioned that the best decision would be to respond to the problem by immediately cutting the wages of those people who were overpaid. In the hold-wages-constant condition, the president mentioned that the best decision would be to hold the wage levels constant. Following the request from the president to cut wages (Condition 1) or to hold wages constant (Condition 2), participants were asked to make a decision either to cut wages (coded as "1") or not (coded as "0").

We were interested in whether and how participant levels of empathy had an effect on the decision to cut wages as a function of a request to cut or hold them constant. Past research has shown that when individuals received an instruction, they consistently demonstrated compliance even if the instruction was unethical (Brief, Dietz, Cohen, Pugh, & Vaslow, 2000; Petersen & Dietz, 2008). This effect is explained by the role obligations of individuals, that is, as subordinates they have to comply with the instructions received from an authority figure (Brief et al., 2000). We therefore expected an effect on the president's instruction on the decision to cut wages. We also expected an interaction between these instructions and participant levels of empathy and proposed that empathic individuals, through their capacity to take the perspective of others and their concern toward persons in need, would refrain from complying with an instruction that would harm others. We therefore hypothesized that in the cut-wages condition, participants with higher levels of empathy would be less likely to make the decision to cut wages. However, in the hold-wages-constant condition, participant levels of empathy should not affect decision making.

As expected, results revealed an effect of the experimental manipulation demonstrating that participants in the cut-wages condition were more likely to cut wages than participants in the hold-wages-constant condition. Results also provided evidence that the effect of the experimental manipulation on the decision to cut wages was dependent on participants' level of empathy. Consistent with our prediction, in the cut-wages condition, participant levels of empathy had a negative effect on the decision to cut wages, while in the hold-wages-constant condition, participant levels of empathy did not affect the decision to cut wages. Hence, empathy led to noncompliance with organizational pressures because empathic individuals violated traditional norms of organizational compliance only when the well-being of other stakeholders was at risk.

Example 2: The Role of Empathy in Moral Disengagement
Detert et al. (2008) conducted a multiwave survey study to assess the role of empathy and moral disengagement (i.e., processes through which individuals justify unethical behaviors) on unethical decision making. Students participated in the three surveys spanning two semesters. Surveys 1 and 2 aimed to measure participants' individual differences, including their levels of empathy and moral disengagement. Empathy was measured in Survey 1 using the sympathy scale from the International Personality Item Pool (IPIP) (e.g., Goldberg et al., 2006). To assess participants' level of moral disengagement, the authors adapted the measure developed by Bandura, Barbaranelli, Caprara, and Pastorelli (1996). Survey 3 aimed to collect data on participants' unethical decision making. Participants were asked to read eight ethically charged scenarios and had to indicate how likely they would engage in the behaviors described in each of the scenarios.

Detert et al. (2008) proposed that empathy was related to unethical decision making through moral disengagement, such that empathy was negatively related to moral disengagement, which in turn would have a negative effect on the ethicality of decisions. Their argument was that empathic individuals are able to imagine how a person is affected by a situation and are concerned about how the person feels, and, hence, are less likely to morally disengage. Furthermore, the link between moral disengagement and unethical behavior could be explained by a lack of self-censure and reduced feelings of guilt under conditions of high moral disengagement. The findings of their study supported these predictions. More precisely, they found an effect of empathy on moral disengagement and an effect of moral disengagement on unethical decision making. Results also provided evidence of the mediating effect of moral disengagement on the relationship between empathy and unethical decision making.

Example 3: The Role of Empathy in Ethical Decision Making

Mencl and May (2009) studied the effect of empathy on individuals' ethical decision making. Human resource professionals participated in a study composed of two parts: a scenario and a survey including a measure of empathy. First, participants read a scenario describing an employee experiencing health problems (participants were randomly assigned to one of the six different variations of the scenario), and filled out the ethical decision-making components scale (see Mencl & May, for more details about the scenarios and the measure). This scale was composed of four subscales on moral recognition, principle-based moral evaluation, utilitarian moral evaluation, and moral intention. To measure participants' level of empathy, the authors created two measures based on two of the four empathy subscales from Davis (1980) (i.e., empathic concern and perspective taking).

Mencl and May (2009) proposed that cognitive empathy would not have the same effect as affective empathy on individual ethical decision-making processes (i.e., on the four components of the ethical decision-making measure). They found that cognitive empathy was related to principle-based evaluations that placed the individual's own responsibilities toward others and the well-being of others first. Consistent with their reasoning, they also found that empathy was not related to utilitarian evaluations that relied on cost-benefit analyses. In addition, the authors reported an effect of cognitive empathy and a marginally significant effect of affective empathy on ethical decision making. Taken together, these findings suggested that empathic decision makers were more concerned with the well-being of others than with the consequences of the decision in terms of social benefits or costs, which then resulted in other-oriented ethical behavior.

Example 4: The Role of Empathy in Negotiation

Cohen (2010) studied the effect of empathy in a negotiation context by conducting two survey studies. Empathy was measured using the two Davis (1980) subscales of empathic concern and perspective taking. As dependent variables, participants filled out the Self-Reported Inappropriate Negotiation Strategies II scale (SINS II; Lewicki, Saunders, & Barry, 2007). This measure was composed of seven subscales describing different unethical bargaining tactics (e.g., traditional competitive bargaining, false promises, and inappropriate information gathering).

The author proposed that the individual difference characteristic of empathic concern was related to the disapproval of ethically questionable tactics of negotiation while the individual difference characteristic of perspective taking was not. She argued that as opposed to individuals who took the perspective of others, individuals high on empathic concern understood how other persons felt and took this into account in their decision making. The results supported these predictions, providing evidence that the affective component of empathy (i.e., empathic concern) led to the disapproval of unethical tactics of negotiation while the cognitive component of empathy (i.e., perspective taking) did not.

Summary

The reviewed studies showed that empathy could play a critical role in ethical decision making. In our experimental study, we demonstrated that empathic participants were less likely to make a decision to cut wages than low empathic participants when they received the request to do so. We also reported empirical evidence showing that empathy can foster ethical decision making through less moral disengagement (Detert et al., 2008), through principle-based evaluations and moral intention (Mencl & May, 2009), and through the disapproval of ethically questionable negotiation tactics (Cohen, 2010). A general pattern across these studies is that by virtue of their ability to take the position of others and to feel like them, empathic individuals frequently make other-oriented decisions, thereby suppressing self-favoring or egoistic tendencies. Although the emotion of empathy has a positive connotation as pointed out above, empathy can also undermine the ethicality of decision-making processes. In the following section, we present the negative side of empathy in ethical decision making (see Figure 7.1).

THE NEGATIVE SIDE OF EMPATHY IN ETHICAL DECISION MAKING

As reviewed above, empathy can improve ethical decision-making processes. However, it can also lead to poor decisions and unfair outcomes. Particularly, empathy can negatively affect individual decision making processes when it leads to (1) personal distress, (2) favoritism, (3), abuse of the ability of perspective taking, or (4) when it results from a manipulated empathic reaction.

Empathy versus Personal Distress

As highlighted earlier, empathy might turn into personal distress when an individual's emotional response to the observation of someone in need is too strong (Eisenberg et al., 2004). The emotional reaction then switches from an other-oriented feeling to a self-oriented feeling (Tangney et al., 2007). Contrary to individuals feeling empathy who focus on the need of the other person and on how to help this person, individuals feeling personal distress focus on their own experience and on how to reduce their discomfort. Individuals may decide either to help the person in need, or to leave the situation depending on what best relieves their personal distress. In short, empathy that turns into distress leads individuals to no longer engage in altruistic behaviors but rather in self-oriented behaviors aimed at reducing their personal distress.

Empathy and Favoritism

Empathy might also bias decision-making processes resulting in favoritism for targets of the empathy. According to the empathy-altruism hypothesis, when someone observes another person in need and experiences empathic concern, he or she engages in helping behavior (Batson, 2008). Accordingly, if empathy is felt for a specific person, the empathic individual would focus on helping this person in particular and potentially at the expense of others. By overfocusing their attention on a given person, empathic individuals might fail to notice the distress of other persons. The ethicality of the decision-making process would therefore be undermined if the empathic person decided to help only the person to whom empathy is felt, while he or she should also help other needy persons at the same time.

Malicious Empathy

As reviewed in the previous section, Cohen (2010) found that the affective component of empathy, namely, empathic concern, was related to the disapproval of ethically questionable tactics of negotiation while the cognitive component of empathy, namely, perspective taking, was not. In this regard, Hodges and Biswas-Diener (2007) proposed that the cognitive component of empathy, the "mindreading" ability (p. 391), can have negative consequences for the persons to whom empathy is felt. Particularly, individuals with high mindreading ability can abuse their capacity to understand others to serve their own interest. Consequently, empathy, or more precisely the ability to take another person's perspective, can result in unethical conduct.

The Manipulation of Empathy by a Target

Empathy is a complex emotion that includes diverse feelings. Particularly, empathic individuals can experience positive empathic feelings such as delight and joy when the observed person "is in a state of benefit, having achieved a goal or won a prize, or is playing gleefully" or negative empathic feelings such as sorrow and pity when the observed person "is in a state of need, having failed at a task or suffered a loss, or is enduring pain" (Batson, 1990, p. 339). In this regard, we propose that individual empathic reactions differ depending on the victims' state.

Our argument is that individuals are generally more sensitive to the distress than to the well-being of others, and focus on helping people who signal distress, while failing to help people who might need help just as much, but do not signal it. Consequently, a person in need might decide to accentuate his or her distress in order to arouse observers' empathic reactions. The ethicality of decision-making processes would thus be undermined if empathic individuals help only persons displaying need and distress, and not persons in need who fail to display their distress.

Research on the negative side of empathy in ethical decision making is sparse. In the next part, we review some empirical studies that, from our point of view, raise some important issues about potential negative effects of empathy in decision-making processes and are partially reflective of our theoretical arguments above. We review two studies demonstrating how empathy can lead to selfish behavior through personal distress, and to favoritism. Then, we present a study showing how individual empathic reactions are a function of the emotional state of the person in need.

Empirical Examples

Example 1: Empathy as Distress and Selfish Behavior

As mentioned earlier, empathy can lead to personal distress when the emotion is too strong. This switch of emotion can have negative consequences for the person in need as demonstrated by Carrera, Ocejo, Caballero, Munoz, Lopez-Pérez, and Ambrona (2012). These authors conducted two studies aiming at assessing the effect of empathy and personal distress on helping behavior. In one of their studies, participants were asked to read a story describing a person in need and to look at the picture of that person. Afterwards, they completed a questionnaire including a measure of empathy composed of five of the adjectives commonly used by Batson and his colleagues (Batson et al., 1991), and three items related to the story (see Carrera et al., 2012, for more details about the measure of empathy). Personal distress was measured using the six following adjectives: worried, distressed, disturbed, upset, troubled, and agitated. For each scale, participants were asked to indicate to what extent they experienced these emotions when they read the story. Participants then had the opportunity to indicate whether they would like to help the needy person by filling out a Helping Form.

Carrera et al. (2012) proposed that participants who felt empathy toward a needy person would be more likely to engage in helping behavior than participants who felt personal distress. Findings were supportive of this prediction. Helping behavior was more likely when participants felt empathy than when they felt personal distress. Results also indicated that the behavior of participants who felt personal distress was driven by egoistic motives. Their unique goal was to reduce their personal distress and, so, they were willing to help the person in need only if they thought it was a way to reduce their own discomfort. These findings provide evidence for the switch from altruistically driven behavior when individuals feel empathy, to egoistically driven behavior when individuals feel personal distress.

Example 2: Empathy and Favoritism

Batson, Klein, Highberger, and Shaw (1995) studied whether empathy-induced altruism can lead to immoral decision making by conducting two experiments. In one of their studies, participants were randomly assigned to one of the three experimental conditions in which participants' empathy was manipulated. In two conditions, participants had to read a text describing something negative that happened recently to a person. Previously, they had either been asked to take an objective perspective when reading the text (i.e., low empathy condition) or to imagine how the person felt about what was described (i.e., high empathy condition). In the third condition, participants did not read any text. Then, participants had to make decisions that would affect the well-being of other persons, including the person described in the text.

The authors proposed that empathy could induce target specific altruistic behaviors. They hypothesized that participants induced to feel empathy toward a specific person (i.e., high empathy condition) would not respect the moral principle of justice by favoring the person described in the text. Thus, empathy would lead to favoritism for the person for whom they felt empathy for at the expense of the other persons affected by the situation, while the moral principle of justice would not be violated in the low empathy condition. Findings supported the predictions. Participants who were induced to feel empathy toward a specific person were inclined to favor this person over other persons, while participants not induced to feel empathy engaged in a fair decision-making process, and thus respected the principle of justice. Oceja (2008) recently replicated these findings in two experiments. These findings provide further evidence for partiality when individuals display empathy for a specific person. In addition, in these experiments, empathy resulted in unfair decision making when participants did not personally know the individual in need for whom they were induced to feel empathy. Empathy may lead to even more partiality when the empathic individual personally knows the person in need. In summary, empathy comes with the risk of favoritism, in particular when the targets are personally known, and this partiality undermines ethical decision making.

Example 3: Empathy and the State of the Targeted Person

Lee and Murnighan (2001) proposed the empathy-prospect model stating that depending on how the situation of the observed person was, and particularly depending on whether the person was in a state of loss or of benefit, individuals were more or less likely to engage in helping behaviors. To test their propositions, Lee and Murnighan conducted two studies. In one of their studies, students participated in a scenario study, in which they had to take the role of a supervisor who overheard a discussion between two employees about an incident that happened with one of their colleagues who was a supervisor as well. Participants were randomly assigned to one of the eight different variations of the next part of the scenario. In each of the versions, the consequences of the incident on the colleague supervisor were manipulated (i.e., positive consequences versus negative consequences for him). After the scenario, participants filled out a questionnaire in which they had to indicate what they would do and why. Empathy was measured using the items developed by Batson and his colleagues (Batson, Bolen, Cross, & Heuringer-Benefiel, 1986).

Results provided evidence on the empathy-prospect model by demonstrating that participants were more likely to feel empathy when they learned their colleague faced a loss than when they learned he faced a gain. In addition, they found that the loss situation had an effect on participants' empathy through a stronger perception of need, which then led to a stronger intention to help. These findings suggest that empathy, when characterized by negative feelings such as sorrow and pity, is more likely to have an impact on individuals' behaviors than when empathy is characterized by positive feelings such as delight and joy.

Summary

The studies reviewed above indicate that empathy can undermine the ethicality of decision-making processes that produce outcomes that are unfair to at least some of the involved parties. Empirical evidence shows that empathy can lead to selfish behavior (Carrera et al., 2012), to favoritism (Batson et al., 1995), and that empathy is more likely to affect individuals' helping behavior when individuals observe a person experiencing negative events than when they observe a person experiencing something positive (Lee & Murnighan, 2001) In addition, as pointed out by Hodges and Biswas-Diener (2007), empathy can also have negative consequences for the actors themselves if empathic individuals engage in behavior that is costly for them. It might happen when, for instance, helping others "result in material and opportunity costs, as the empathic person may sacrifice some of his or her own resources" (Hodges & Biswas-Diener, 2007, p. 392).

CONCLUSION

Limitations in the Research on Empathy

The reported studies point to some limitations in the research on empathy. First, different measures of empathy are used across studies. For instance,

Detert et al. (2008) measured empathy using the sympathy scale from the International Personality Item Pool (Goldberg, 2001, Goldberg, et al., 2006). Dietz and Kleinlogel (in press), Mencl and May (2009), and Cohen (2010) measured empathy using Davis's (1980) scale, and Carrera et al. (2012) used the measure developed and commonly used by Batson and his colleagues (Batson et al., 1991). The use of different measures implies that empathy is conceptualized differently across studies. In some studies, empathy is measured as a one-dimensional concept (Detert et al., 2008), while in others there is a distinction between cognitive and affective components of empathy (Mencl & May, 2009). It is obvious that both the conceptualization and operationalization of empathy need to be further investigated. Second, empirical research on the effects of empathy on decision making is sparse. More evidence is therefore needed to be able to draw more robust conclusions of the effects of empathy on ethical decision making processes.

Discussion

This chapter illustrates that empathy can have positive consequences (e.g., ethical decision making), as well as negative consequences (e.g., favoritism) on ethical decision making (see Figure 1 for an illustration of the positive and negative sides of empathy for ethical decision making). In our opinion, the dual and contradictory effects of empathy might be explained by a distinction between mindful and mindless empathy. Mindful empathy is empathy that is supplemented and evaluated by a consideration of the decision-making context, while mindless empathy refers to an automatic application of empathy. For example, empathy for members of underprivileged groups may be mindful if it is supplemented by a consideration of long-term consequences of different helping behaviors for members of these groups (e.g., whether to sponsor them financially or enable them to generate their own income). Empathy for members of underprivileged groups is mindless if it results in automated helping reactions that may satisfy immediate needs without considering long-term implications.

Indeed, it would be naïve to make decisions solely based on empathy. While empathy is an important element for making ethical decisions, it is just one piece of the puzzle that is needed for organizational decision-making processes that create value for all stakeholders. For instance, in our wage-cut experiment, empathy played a role in participant decisions to cut wages or to keep them constant, but economic considerations were also likely considered by our participants. In the case of wage cuts, which have been shown to also produce negative outcomes for employers (and not just employees) as employees reciprocate by lower efforts (e.g., Kube, Maréchal, & Puppe, 2006), empathy was a productive ingredient in the decision-making process. Narrowly focused economic thinking alone might have also motivated a different and poorer decision. However, in some cases empathy can undermine the ethicality of decision-making processes, particularly when empathic decision makers decide to favor the well-being of those for whom they feel empathy at the expense of the well-being of other stakeholders. In our experiment, if the decision to cut wages would have been vital for the survival of the organization, empathic-based decision making would have led to an inefficient decision for the organization, which eventually would have had a negative impact on the employees (e.g., bankruptcy).

To conclude, we suggest that organizational functioning would benefit from the inclusion of empathy (and possibly other emotions) in decision-making processes. Organizing through empathy can contribute to enhance the ethicality of decision-making processes and enhance prosocial and altruistic behaviors within organizations. Therefore, taking into account managers' moral virtues such as empathy seems like an obvious intervention for improving ethical decision making, but can only be effective if organizations have practices and procedures that allow organizational members to express and act on their moral virtues. For instance, organizations may explicitly protocol that decisions should be emotionally comfortable for the decision makers. Otherwise the lack of comfort should be explored explicitly. Hence, emotional reactions can become a check or a warning signal for morally inappropriate decisions. Yet, moral virtues should only be one ingredient in the decision-making process. It is also important for decisions to be rationally sound to avoid decision making based on pity or favoritism as reviewed in this chapter.

REFERENCES

Bandura, A., Barbaranelli, C., Caprara, G. V., & Pastorelli, C. (1996). Mechanisms of moral disengagement in the exercise of moral agency. *Journal of Personality and Social Psychology, 71*, 364–374. doi: 10.1037/0022-3514.71.2.364

Batson, C. D. (1990). How social an animal. The human capacity for caring. *American Psychologist, 45*, 336–346. doi: 10.1037/0003-066X.45.3.336

Batson, C. D. (2008). *Empathy-induced altruism motivation*. Paper presented at the Inaugural Herzliya Symposium on "Prosocial Motives, Emotions, and Behavior", Herzliya, Israel.

Batson, C. D., Batson, J. G., Griffitt, C. A., Barrientos, S., Brandt, J. R., Sprengelmeyer, P., & Bayly, M. J. (1989). Negative-state relief and the empathy altruism hypothesis. *Journal of Personality and Social Psychology, 56*, 922–933. doi: 10.1037/0022-3514.56.6.922

Batson, C. D., Batson, J. G., Slingsby, J. K., Harrell, K. L., Peekna, H. M., & Todd, R. M. (1991). Empathic joy and the empathy-altruism hypothesis. *Journal of Personality and Social Psychology, 61*, 413–426. doi: 10.1037/0022-3514.61.3.413

Batson, C. D., Bolen, M., Cross, J., & Heuringer-Benefiel, H. (1986). Where is the altruism in the altruistic personality? *Journal of Personality and Social Psychology, 50*, 212–220. doi: 10.1037/0022-3514.50.1.212

Batson, C. D., Duncan, B. D., Ackerman, P., Buckley, T., & Birch, K. (1981). Is empathic emotion a source of altruistic motivation? *Journal of Personality and Social Psychology, 40*, 290–302. doi: 10.1037//0022-3514.40.2.290

Batson, C. D., Klein, T. R., Highberger, L., & Shaw L. L. (1995). Immorality from empathy-induced altruism: When compassion and justice conflict. *Journal of Personality and Social Psychology, 68*, 1042–1054. doi: 10.1037/0022-3514.68.6.1042

Batson, C.D., Lishner, D.A., Cook, J., & Sawyer, S. (2005). Similarity and nurturance: Two possible sources of empathy for strangers. *Basic and Applied Social Psychology, 27*, 15–25. doi: 10.1207/s15324834basp2701_2

Batson, C.D., & Shaw, L.L. (1991). Evidence for altruism: Toward a pluralism of prosocial motives. *Psychological Inquiry, 2*, 107–122. doi: 10.1207/s15327 965pli0202_1

Brief, A.P., Dietz, J., Cohen, R.R., Pugh, S.D., & Vaslow, J.B. (2000). Just doing business: Modern racism and obedience to authority as explanations for employment discrimination. *Organizational Behavior and Human Decision Processes, 81*, 72–97. doi:10.1006/obhd.1999.2867

Carrera, P., Oceja, L., Caballero, A., Munoz, D., Lopez-Pérez, B., & Ambrona, T. (2012). I feel so sorry! Tapping the joint influence of empathy and personal distress on helping behavior. *Motivation and Emotion*. Advance online publication. doi: 10.1007/s11031-012-9302-9

Cohen, T.R. (2010). Moral emotions and unethical bargaining: The differential effects of empathy and perspective taking in deterring deceitful negotiation. *Journal of Business Ethics, 94*, 569–579. doi: 10.1007/s10551-009-0338-z

Damasio, A.R. (1994). *Descartes' error: Emotion, reason, and the human brain.* NY: G.P. Putnam.

Davis, M.H. (1980). A multidimensional approach to individual differences in empathy. *JSAS Catalog of Selected Documents in Psychology, 10*, 85.

Davis, M.H. (1983). Measuring individual-differences in empathy: Evidence for a multidimensional approach. *Journal of Personality and Social Psychology, 44*, 113–126. doi: 10.1037//0022-3514.44.1.113

Detert, J.R., Treviño, L.K., & Sweitzer, V.L. (2008). Moral disengagement in ethical decision making: A study of antecedents and outcomes. *Journal of Applied Psychology, 93*, 374–391. doi: 10.1037/0021-9010.93.2.374

Dietz, J., & Kleinlogel, E.P. (in press). Wage cuts and managers' empathy: How a positive emotion contributes to positive organizational ethics in difficult times. *Journal of Business Ethics.*

Dovidio, J.F., Allen, J.L., & Schroeder, D.A. (1990). Specificity of empathy-induced helping: Evidence for altruistic motivation. *Journal of Personality and Social Psychology, 59*, 249–260. doi: 10.1037//0022-3514.59.2.249

Duan, C.M., & Hill, C.E. (1996). The current state of empathy research. *Journal of Counseling Psychology, 43*, 261–274. doi: 10.1037/0022-0167.43.3.261

Dutton, J.E., Worline, M.C., Frost, P.J., & Lilius, J. (2006). Explaining compassion organizing. *Administrative Science Quarterly, 51*, 59–96. doi: 10.2189/asqu.51.1.59

Eisenberg, N., Guthrie, I.K., Murphy, B.C., Shepard, S.A., Cumberland, A., & Carlo, G. (1999). Consistency and development of prosocial dispositions: A longitudinal study. *Child Development, 70*, 1360–1372. doi: 10.1111/1467-8624.00100

Eisenberg, N., & Miller, P.A. (1987). The relation of empathy to pro-social and related behaviors. *Psychological Bulletin, 101*, 91–119. doi: 10.1037/0033-2909.101.1.91

Eisenberg, N., & Strayer, J. (Eds.). (1987). *Empathy and its development.* Cambridge: Cambridge University Press.

Eisenberg, N., Valiente, C., & Champion, C. (2004). Empathy-related responding: Moral, social, and socialization correlates. In A.G. Miller (Ed.), *The social psychology of good and evil* (pp. 386–415). NY: Guilford.

Fultz, J., Batson, C.D., Fortenbach, V.A., McCarthy, P.M., & Varney, L.L. (1986). Social evaluation and the empathy-altruism hypothesis. *Journal of Personality and Social Psychology, 50*, 761–769. doi: 10.1037//0022-3514.50.4.761

Gaudine, A., & Thorne, L. (2001). Emotion and ethical decision-making in organizations. *Journal of Business Ethics, 31*, 175–187. doi: 10.1023/A:1010711413444

Goldberg, L. R., Johnson, J. A., Eber, H. W., Hogan, R., Ashton, M. C., Cloninger, C. R., & Gough, H. C. (2006). The International Personality Item Pool and the future of public-domain personality measures. *Journal of Research in Personality, 40*, 84–96. doi: 10.1016/j.jrp.2005.08.007

Hodges, S. D., & Biswas-Diener, R. (2007). Balancing the empathy expense account: Strategies for regulating empathic response. In T.F.D. Farrow & P.W.R. Woodruff (Eds.), *Empathy in mental illness* (pp. 389–405). Cambridge: Cambridge University Press.

Kube, S., Maréchal, M. A., & Puppe, C. (2006). Putting reciprocity to work: Positive versus negative responses in the field (Working Paper No.2006–27). Retrieved from the Social Science Research Network website: http://ssrn.com/abstract = 944393

Lee, J. A., & Murnighan, J. K. (2001). The empathy-prospect model and the choice to help. *Journal of Applied Social Psychology, 31*, 816–839. doi: 10.1111/j.1559-1816.2001.tb01415.x

Lewicki, R. J., Saunders, D. M., & Barry, B. (2007). *Negotiation: Readings, exercises, and cases* (5th ed.). Boston: McGraw-Hill/Irwin.

Mencl, J., & May, D. R. (2009). The effects of proximity and empathy on ethical decision-making: An exploratory investigation. *Journal of Business Ethics, 85*, 201–226. doi: 10.1007/s10551-008-9765-5

Oceja, L. V. (2008). Overcoming empathy-induced partiality: Two rules of thumb. *Basic and Applied Social Psychology, 30*, 176–182. doi: 10.1080/01973530802209236

Pavlovich, K., & Krahnke, K. (2012). Empathy, connectedness, and organisation. *Journal of Business Ethics, 105*, 131–137. doi: 10.1007/s10551-011-0961-3

Petersen, L.-E., & Dietz, J. (2008). Employment discrimination: Authority figures' demographic preferences and followers' affective organizational commitment. *Journal of Applied Psychology, 93*, 1287–1300. doi: 10.1037/a0012867

Stansbury, J., & Sonenshein, S. (2012). Positive business ethics: Grounding and elaborating a theory. In K. S. Cameron & G. M. Spreitzer (Eds.), *The Oxford handbook of positive organizational scholarship* (pp. 340–352). New York: Oxford University Press.

Stocks, E. L., Lishner, D. A., & Decker, S. K. (2009). Altruism or psychological escape: Why does empathy promote prosocial behavior? *European Journal of Social Psychology, 39*, 649–665. doi: 10.1002/ejsp.561

Tangney, J. P., Stuewig, J., & Mashek, D. J. (2007). Moral emotions and moral behavior. *Annual Review of Psychology, 58*, 345–372. doi: 10.1146/annurev.psych.56.091103.070145

Tenbrunsel, A. E., & Smith-Crowe, K. (2008). Ethical decision making: Where we've been and where we're going. *The Academy of Management Annals, 2*, 545–607. doi: 10.1080/19416520802211677

Verhaert, G. A., & Van den Poel, D. (2010). Empathy as added value in predicting donation behavior. *Journal of Business Research, 64*, 1288–1295. doi: 10.1016/j.jbusres.2010.12.024

8 The ACES Decision-Making Technique as a Reframing Tool for Increasing Empathy

Larry E. Pate and Traci L. Shoblom

Could a greater miracle take place than for us to look through each other's eyes for an instant?

Henry David Thoreau

INTRODUCTION

Chris Pressman is a software developer who works for the same company you do. It is 6:30 pm and you walk by his office and see him staring at his computer screen with his head in his hands. You stick your head in his office and ask, "Hey, Chris, are you okay?" He replies, "I have no idea how this happened, but I lost every piece of code that I have written for the last week. It's just gone, and we're supposed to deliver the finished product to the client by tomorrow night. What am I going to do?"

What you think, feel, and do in the above situation, as well as the empathy you might feel and express, will largely be determined by your mental model and interpretation of events. Singer and Lamm (2009) suggest that "empathy is a highly flexible phenomenon and that vicarious responses are malleable with respect to a number of factors—such as contextual appraisal, the interpersonal relationship between empathizer and other, or the perspective adopted during observation of the other" (p. 83).

For example, imagine an individual who does not have a particularly close working relationship with Chris, or one who is diligent about backing up his or her own work, or who has only a half hour to get to his or her son's soccer game. In such situations the individual might feel indifferent toward Chris's plight and say, "*That's too bad, man. I hope it works out for you*". However, if the individual has experienced a similar loss of computer data, or is personally invested in meeting the client's deadline, or has a close working relationship or friendship with Chris, the individual might feel empathy for him and say, "*Oh no! What can I do to help?*"

The above example illustrates the often complex nature of human interaction as an individual's cognitions and emotions both influence and determine the individual's behavioral responses, in this case when one observes another person's distress. In some situations an individual might be able to cognitively "relate" to another's plight without feeling empathic. In other situations, an individual might be able to feel similar emotions as the other person without fully understanding why.

This chapter examines both cognitive and emotional components of empathy and suggests that empathy is strongest when an individual *cognitively* understands another person's plight and also *emotionally* feels what the other person is feeling. Further, we suggest that an individual's mental model and psychological perspective of the situation will affect the degree of empathy that individual will feel toward another. Finally, we suggest that the ACES Decision-Making Technique (ACES) can be useful in shifting an individual's mental and emotional framework from one of indifference to one of empathy.

LITERATURE REVIEW

Researchers have been studying the concept of empathy for hundreds of years, in fields as disparate as philosophy, psychology, theology, sociology, and neuroscience, among others (Hatfield, Rapson, & Le, 2009; Singer & Lamm, 2009). Yet, despite an interdisciplinary study of the phenomenon of empathy—or perhaps because of it—there has been little agreement among practitioners and researchers on a clear definition of the term or its origin. Perhaps the most widely accepted definition to date has come from the Perception-Action Model, or PAM for short (Preston, 2007; Preston & de Waal, 2002).

According to PAM, empathy is defined as *a shared emotional experience* occurring when one person (the subject) comes to feel *a similar emotion* to another (the object) as a result of *perceiving* the other's state. This process results from the fact that the subject's *representations* of the emotional state are *automatically* activated when the subject pays attention to the emotional state of the object. The *neural mechanism* assumes that brain areas have processing domains based on their cellular composition and connectivity; as such, there is no "empathy area", and brain areas are recruited when the relevant domain is required by the task (Preston, 2007, p. 428, emphasis added).

Much research shows that shared emotional experiences are precursors to feelings of empathy (Cox et al., 2012; de Vignemont & Singer, 2006). To feel empathy for Chris, in our example, the individual would need to have had one or more—or perhaps even a set of—shared emotional experiences with Chris. This similar emotional experience between the observer and Chris is imbedded in each individual's mental state, thereby giving both Chris and the individual mental representations of that emotional state. Consequently, when the individual attends to Chris and his plight, the individual's mental representation is, according to PAM, automatically activated. The individual first perceives Chris's state and then, because of the common mental representation of a similar experience, the person automatically feels what Chris is feeling.

But what happens if there is no *empathy area* of the brain under that scenario? How do distinct cognitive and emotional components of empathy develop? Is it true that having a cognitive representation of someone's plight will automatically trigger an emotionally similar response? What other factors moderate these relationships?

Researchers have attempted to answer these and related questions about the causes and consequences of empathy from primarily four perspectives: (1) *emotional contagion*, (2) *cognitive perspective taking*, (3) *prosocial behavior*, and (4) *self-awareness*. We will now briefly review the literature from each of these four perspectives.

EMOTIONAL CONTAGION

Most researchers agree that empathy has both cognitive and emotional components (Cox et al., 2012; Singer & Lamb, 2009). Some research (e.g., Shamay-Tsoory, Aharon-Peretz, & Perry, 2009) suggests that there are two distinct neurological systems for empathy—a basic *emotional contagion* system and a more advanced *cognitive perspective-taking* system.

Research conducted using patients with brain lesions (e.g., Shamay-Tsoory, 2011; Shamay-Tsoory et al., 2009) suggests cognitive empathy and emotional empathy originate in different places in the brain, providing support for the assertion that they are separate and distinct processes entirely. In other words, the cognitive roots of empathy and the emotional roots of empathy are discrete neurological processes. If so, this may explain why a person can intellectually empathize with someone else's plight but not feel emotionally connected to it. This may also explain why an individual can emotionally empathize with someone even if the person lacks an intellectual understanding of what he is going through.

The term *emotional contagion* refers to the phenomenon of "catching" someone's mood (Hatfield et al., 2009). A classic example of emotional contagion is when babies who hear other babies crying begin to cry themselves. Most people have had the experience of developing a good or bad mood based upon the moods of the people around them. Walk into a room with angry, hostile people, and the individual is likely to pick up on those emotions. Similarly, walk into a party or celebration of some kind, and the individual's mood is likely to be lifted.

Finally, emotional contagion is not equivalent to or synonymous with empathy. It has, however, been called *primitive empathy* (Hatfield et al., 2009), meaning that it is more likely a precursor to empathy. Put another way, emotional contagion occurs when "*I see that you are feeling anxious and I begin to feel anxious, too"*. These feelings may have nothing to do with a cognitive awareness of the other person's plight.

COGNITIVE PERSPECTIVE TAKING

The concept of *cognitive perspective taking* is an intellectual "relating" to another person's situation. It is looking at the other person's plight and observing that the other person is having difficulty, without necessarily "feeling the pain" of the other person. DeVignemont and Singer (2006) describe it this way. "Based on my knowledge of you, I infer from your behavior that you are anxious, but I do not feel anxious" (p. 435).

In the example of Chris, an individual might cognitively understand what Chris is going through, yet not have emotional feelings of empathy about Chris's plight to actually feel what Chris is feeling or, further, to feel compelled to offer help.

The cognitive perspective-taking position is that an individual cannot be empathic to the plight of another if the individual does not first cognitively recognize that plight. For example, if a coworker walks past Chris's office but fails to notice that Chris has a problem, that coworker cannot feel empathy for Chris. Similar to PAM, perceiving the other's state is the necessary first step in the development of an empathic response. Additionally, cognitive recognition, while necessary, is insufficient. Even if an individual identifies that Chris is in distress, that individual might not care enough to do anything.

Emotionally feeling what the other person is feeling is also a necessary, but insufficient, condition. A coworker can walk past Chris's office and feel upset for Chris even though the individual may not have an adequate understanding of what Chris is going through. But, as noted, emotional contagion is not empathy; it is primitive empathy.

In short, one must both recognize the plight of another and also emotionally connect with the experience of the other for empathy to occur. These two distinct systems—one cognitive, one emotional—interact and mutually cause feelings of empathy for another.

PROSOCIAL BEHAVIOR

The compelling reason many researchers have studied empathy is to better understand the dynamics that both increase and decrease the likelihood of *prosocial behavior* (Rameson, Morelli, & Lieberman, 2012). In a practical sense, it may matter less that an observer actually feels empathy for another and more that the observer is motivated to offer help.

Pavlovich and Krahnke (2012) identify two ways in which empathy can lead to prosocial behavior through connectedness. First, empathy creates an unconscious sharing of neuro-pathways that remove perceived barriers between the self and another. This, in turn, allows a sense of connectedness to develop between the individuals, thus enabling them to find common ground for solution building. Second, the development of empathy enhances connectedness through altruistic behavior.

Singer and Lamm (2009) also describe the process by which prosocial behavior may evolve. They say, "In most cases, mimicry or emotional contagion precedes empathy, which precedes sympathy and compassion, which in turn may precede prosocial behavior" (p. 82).

How, then, does a person develop the ability to cognitively identify when another person is in distress? The answer lies, partly, in research and theory on self-awareness.

SELF-AWARENESS

Gallup and Platek (2002) suggest that cognitive empathy is a by-product of *self-awareness*. In order to be able to recognize the plight of another, one must have an awareness of one's self. In other words, the use of one's own experience as a model to make inferences about the experiences of others is a necessary precondition for the development of cognitive empathy.

Oddly enough, research on contagious yawning supports this thinking. It is a commonly observed phenomenon that when one person yawns, often other people around him or her will also yawn. Research indicates people can only "catch" another person's yawn when they have a sense of self and the ability to empathically identify another's mental state (Platek, Critton, Myers, & Gallup, 2003).

Similarly, research on individuals with disorders along the autism spectrum showed a strong relationship between a lack of self-referential cognition and low scores on empathy assessments (Lombardo, Barnes, Wheelwright, & Baron-Cohen, 2007). Those with autism often do not have as clear a sense of self as non-autistic individuals, and also are not as empathic toward others. Non-autistic individuals with a clear sense of self have been found to be more empathic to others. Figure 8.1 illustrates this progression from self-awareness to prosocial behavior.

While a complete examination of the relationship between self-awareness and empathy is beyond the scope of this chapter, it is nonetheless necessary to distinguish two separate forms of self-awareness—*objective self-awareness* and *subjective self-awareness*. Silvia and Duval (2001) offer the following definition and description of these two forms of self-awareness.

> Just as people can apprehend the existence of environmental stimuli, they can be aware of their own existence. When attention is directed inward and the individual's consciousness is focused on himself, he is the object of his own consciousness—hence 'objective' self-awareness. This is contrasted with 'subjective self-awareness' that results when attention

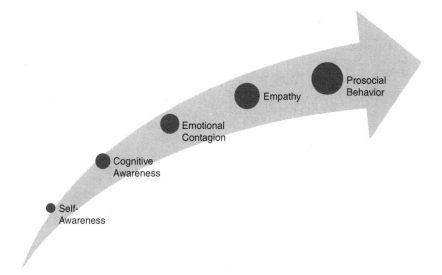

Figure 8.1   The progression from self-awareness to prosocial behavior

is directed away from the self and the person "experiences himself as the source of perception and action". (p. 235)

In this way, looking inward to develop awareness of one's self and one's mental processes is an important step toward developing empathy. Essentially, an individual must be able to perceive himself/herself as distinct from another, as reflected in a mental model of one's own experiences, in order to be cognitively aware of another and, thereby, feel the emotions another person is feeling. If the observer is not distinctly different from another individual, the observer cannot have empathy for another.

The next section of this chapter integrates these four perspectives— *emotional contagion, cognitive perspective taking, prosocial behavior,* and *self-awareness.*

INTEGRATING THE FOUR PERSPECTIVES

Collectively, these four perspectives tell us that mental maps represent objects, actions, and people differently, depending on how psychologically distant the individual perceives the various items to be (Trope & Lieberman, 2010). The more psychologically distant the item is perceived to be, the more abstract the individual's thinking about it. Conversely, the more psychologically close an item is perceived to be, the more concretely the individual will think about it.

Because we have examined empathy, in part, as the shared emotional experience of another, though, in order to develop empathy one must be able to come back out of one's own experience and share the emotional experience with the other. The ability to shift back and forth between abstract and concrete thinking is an important skill in the development of empathy. Woltin, Corneille, Yzerbyt, and Förster (2011) suggest that a detailed and concrete processing style, as opposed to an abstract processing style, facilitates an individual's propensity to care about others' feelings. They write:

> Empathic concern requires self-other differentiation and consists of 'zooming in' on concrete other-oriented feelings of warmth and compassion (i.e., feelings different from those of the other). Building upon this reasoning, it stands to reason that empathic concern should be facilitated when people engage in a more detailed and concrete form of processing. (p. 419)

This ability to "toggle" back and forth between psychological distance and proximity will become an important consideration in our discussion of how to increase empathy.

Thus far, we have reviewed theoretical foundations of empathy. Throughout we have emphasized the importance of (1) an *objective awareness of self*, (2) a *cognitive awareness of another*, and (3) an *emotional connection to the other's feelings* as necessary conditions for the development of empathy. Additionally, we have talked about the importance of (4) *shifting back and forth between abstract and concrete thinking* to alter one's perception of the psychological distance between self and other.

Where, then, does the disconnect occur? Why does a person feel empathy in some circumstances and not others? Why does one person feel empathy and another feels indifferent toward another person in distress? The answer to these questions can be found by examining the core assumptions the individual makes about the given situation.

A WORKING MODEL OF EMPATHY

We began this chapter with a brief story of a software developer, Chris Pressman, who lost a week's worth of data. What are the factors that will determine whether or not an individual will feel empathy or indifference toward him?

An individual's mental model about Chris's situation is based on the individual's experience. If an individual experienced something similar in the past and has personal knowledge of the anxiety Chris is facing, the individual is more likely to have a mental model that engenders empathy. Such an individual will make certain assumptions about Chris (e.g., "*It happened to me; it could happen to anyone*"), Chris's level of responsibility for his plight (e.g.,

"*I backed up my data all the time and it still happened to me*"), and the possible outcomes of Chris's problem (e.g., "*When this happened to me, we all had to pitch in together to get the project done to meet the client deliverable*"). Such assumptions are likely to lead to empathy and prosocial behavior.

But, what if the individual's mental model is one that does not support empathy toward Chris? If the individual does not particularly like Chris, for example, he or she may assume Chris's plight could have been easily avoided (e.g., "*Chris is so arrogant he probably didn't back up his data properly*"). Similarly, if the individual is in a hurry to get to a son's soccer game, the individual might not attend to Chris's distress at all (e.g., "*This isn't my problem. Someone else on the team can help him*"). These or other similar assumptions are likely to lead to a lack of empathy for Chris.

Lamm, Meltzoff, and Decety (2010) conducted research using functional Magnetic Resonance Imaging (fMRI) to look at the neural underpinnings of empathy. They noted that "when strong emotional response tendencies exist, these tendencies have to be overcome by executive functions" (p. 362). They further noted that "regulation of one's egocentric perspective is crucial for understanding others" (p. 362).

Over the past 25 years, Pate (1987, 1988) and his associates (Driver & Pate, 2002; Pate & Chesteen, 2000; Pate & Filley, 2002; Pate & Greiner, 1989; Pate & Heiman, 1987; Pate & Nielson, 1996; Pate & Ryder, 1987; Pate, Young, & Swinth, 1988) have identified three key activities—challenging core assumptions, clarifying decision criteria, and expanding the decision maker's evoked set of alternatives—that have helped individuals in a wide variety of settings, from the classroom to the board room, to see problem situations differently and to reframe their mental models.

ACES DECISION-MAKING TECHNIQUE

ACES is a simple four-phase decision-making technique, as shown in Figure 8.2. The acronym "ACES" stands for *A*ssumptions, *C*riteria, *E*voked Set, and *S*trategy. All decisions involve assumptions, the decision maker's beliefs about the problem situation. Similarly, all decisions involve the use of decision criteria, the basis on which decisions can be made, essentially asking the question, "*What do I want?*" Finally, all decisions involve an evoked set of alternatives, the options being considered by the decision maker for solving the problem. By examining these A, C, and E components, the decision maker is able to identify additional information needed for seeing the situation differently and, ultimately, solving the problem. The S worksheet represents a "To Do" list for developing a preliminary plan of action.

Detail on the use of ACES can be found in Pate's (1987, 1988) early articles on the process. Briefly, Phase 1 is merely having the decision maker prepare the four worksheets. Phase 2 has the decision maker working on the lefthand side of the A, C, and E worksheets, to get down on paper the decision maker's initial view of the problem situation. Phase 3 has the decision maker working on the righthand side of the A, C, and E worksheets, to generate an alternative view of the problem situation. Finally, Phase 4 has the decision maker working on the S worksheet, to identify a list of action items necessary for making an informed decision.

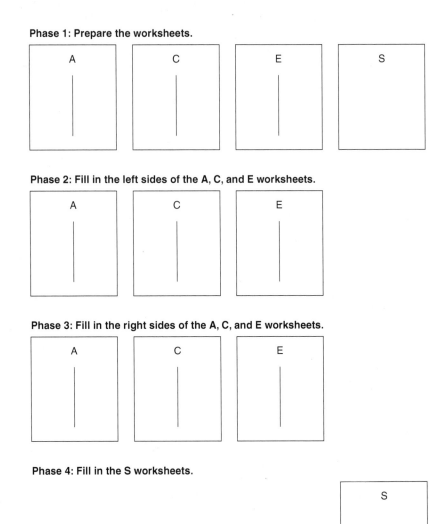

Phase 1: Prepare the worksheets.

| A | C | E | S |

Phase 2: Fill in the left sides of the A, C, and E worksheets.

| A | C | E |

Phase 3: Fill in the right sides of the A, C, and E worksheets.

| A | C | E |

Phase 4: Fill in the S worksheets.

| S |

Figure 8.2   The ACES decision-making technique

EXPECTED OUTCOMES

There are several expected outcomes from the use of ACES as a means of increasing empathy. This section of the chapter reviews a few of the more important outcomes.

Integrating Key Components

ACES offers a concrete method for users to integrate the key components that lead to empathy. ACES allows a person to intentionally shift from a perspective that inhibits the formation of empathy to one that engenders empathy. This shift is done on the basis of the person's values. In this way, one can choose empathy based on his or her authentic values. If you value spending time with your family more than the client deadline, in our Chris Pressman example, you can consciously choose to behave in a way that is consistent with that value. If, on the other hand, you value your friendship with Chris, and it's really not that important for you to get to that soccer game, you can choose to behave in a way that is consistent with that value. ACES allows for the situational development of empathy.

Increasing Self-Awareness

ACES is a tool that can blend the cognitive perspective and emotional connection that is necessary for the development of empathy. Figure 8.3 illustrates how ACES can be used to develop empathy.

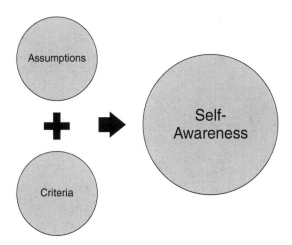

Figure 8.3   The role of the ACES decision-making technique in developing self-awareness

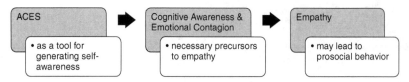

Figure 8.4   ACES and the development of empathy

When a person actively identifies his or her assumptions about a given situation, he or she is examining his or her cognitive perspective. We have shown this to be a necessary condition for the development of empathy. Similarly, when a person examines his or her criteria—what is important to him or her—this evokes the emotional component, "*What do I want?*" It is in this way—blending the cognitive and emotional components—that a person can develop the self-awareness that can lead to empathy.

Once someone has an awareness of their own mental map, then the person can shift their thinking and focus specifically on the "other". As we have said, the ability to toggle between abstract and concrete thinking is an important part of the development of empathy. ACES allows a person to develop a clear self-awareness about the situation and to then focus back out onto the distressed other, to cognitively identify their distress (based on their own awareness of their mental map), and emotionally identify with the other person. This may in turn lead to empathy. Figure 8.4 illustrates the process.

As Peter Senge (1990) wrote in his seminal work *The Fifth Discipline*, "In my experience, as people see more clearly the systems within which they operate, and as they understand more clearly the pressures influencing one another, they naturally develop more compassion and empathy" (p. 34).

TEACHING EMPATHY

ACES enables people to able to shift their perspective to one that could promote empathy. It is in this way that empathy can be "taught". Shapiro (2002) states that, "most formal teaching approaches have focused on teaching empathy as a behavioral skill. In these models, empathy is defined as a set of discrete behaviors that can be analyzed and learned. Typically, such approaches are presented in a concentrated workshop format and as supplemental curriculum with short-term successful outcomes" (p. 323). She also suggests that "limiting the teaching of empathy to a skill-based approach does not reflect the richness of what actually occurs . . . and that it is important to teach empathy comprehensively, acknowledging both behavioral and attitudinal tools" (p. 323).

ACES addresses both the behavioral and attitudinal components of empathy, thereby capturing how empathy is demonstrated in real-life settings.

By learning the ACES process, individuals are able to consider their cognitive map, mental assumptions, emotional feelings, and values about a given situation and then behave with intent.

ACES IN REAL TIME

ACES has been described as a pen-and-paper tool that walks people through a process that enables them to shift their perspective on a problem. ACES has been taught for more than 25 years in companies, universities, and to the public in this way.

However, it is not feasible for a person to stop what they are doing, take out four pieces of paper, and walk through the A, C, E, and S components when they are deciding whether or not to be empathic to the plight of another. Instead ACES must become a mental technique that is employed in the moment to shift a person's mental map. ACES has consistently been found to be an effective tool for reframing one's mental maps and allowing for a shift in one's assumptions. The more one uses it in the traditional pen-and-paper way, the more instinctive the process becomes. Here is how it might look in real time, using the example with Chris Pressman.

It is 6:30 pm and you walk by Chris' office and see him staring at his computer screen with his head in his hands. In order to attend to his situation, you have to be self-aware enough to notice him and what he is doing. If you are thinking about your son's soccer game, you might not even notice that Chris has a problem. But you do notice that Chris seems upset and you have had the experience of being upset and staring at your computer, too. You have cognitive awareness that Chris is in distress.

You stick your head in his office and ask, "Hey, Chris, are you okay?" He replies, "I have no idea how this happened, but I lost every piece of code that I have written for the last week. It's just gone, and we're supposed to deliver the finished product to the client by tomorrow night. What am I going to do?"

If you find yourself having an initially non-empathic reaction to Chris, mentally walk through the ACES technique to reframe your assumptions. If, for example, you find yourself thinking, "I knew this would happen. Chris never backs up his data", consider the opposite assumption. *"Maybe Chris actually did back up his data".*

Think about what is important in the situation. Is it important to get out the door and to your son's game? Is it important to help Chris? Is it important to meet the client deadline? How important is each of these things? Once you initially consider the importance of each item, then question the weight you gave to each item. Maybe it is not as important to go to your son's game as you thought because your spouse will be there too. Maybe the deadline is less important than you originally thought. Maybe it is really important to help Chris because he helped you out of a similar bind once. Maybe it is not as important that you, personally, help Chris as you initially thought.

Also consider your alternatives. You could stay and help Chris. You could leave and go to the game. You could call someone else to come help Chris. Think about the various things you could do in the situation. See if the new assumptions (A) and any revised weights for your criteria (C) cause you to think of any new alternatives (E).

Then, take an action based on your new framework. You may check to see if you can quickly help Chris find his data, make a phone call, or just leave for the game. In this scenario, you had a sense of self-awareness (you were aware of yourself in the situation, as opposed to thinking of something else) that allowed you to have a cognitive awareness of Chris's plight. Although you initially may have not felt an emotional connection to Chris's situation, you were able to develop one by questioning the assumptions you were making about Chris and the situation at hand. You looked at what was most important to you in the situation and based your actions on that. As we have noted, it is the combination of self-awareness, cognitive recognition, and emotional connection that can lead to empathy. In this example, feelings of empathy might have led you toward prosocial behavior (e.g., helping Chris).

This example illustrates how ACES can be used to increase feelings of empathy by allowing an individual to reframe his or her assumptions about the plight of another. An initially non-empathic individual could use the ACES technique, in real time, to reframe his or her mental map, gain insight and greater self-awareness, and with it develop empathy.

Finally, as noted, although ACES is initially taught as a pen-and-paper exercise, the more often a person uses it the more it becomes a natural way of thinking. Identifying assumptions and then automatically questioning them becomes a part of the person's innate decision-making process. Looking at what is important in a situation and weighting (and reverse weighting) the items allows a person to react in a way that is consistent with his or her values. Once this becomes an instinctive technique, the person is better able to use it in real time to shift from indifference to empathy and to behave in a way that is consistent with his or her authentic values.

REFERENCES

Cox, C.L., Uddin, L.Q., Di Martino, A., Castellanos, F.X., Milham, M.P., & Kelly, C. (2012). The balance between feeling and knowing: Affective and cognitive empathy are reflected in the brain's intrinsic functional dynamics. *Social Cognitive and Affective Neuroscience, 7*(6), 727–737.

de Vignemont, F., & Singer, T. (2006). The empathic brain: how, when and why? *Trends in Cognitive Sciences, 10*(10), 435–441.

Driver, M. J., & Pate, L. E. (2002). Decision making. In F. Luthans (Ed.), *Virtual Organizational Behavior.* (pp. 1–26). NY: McGraw-Hill.

Gallup, G. G., & Platek, S. M. (2002). Cognitive empathy presupposes self-awareness: Evidence from phylogeny, ontogeny, neuropsychology, and mental illness. *Behavioral and Brain Sciences, 25,* 36–37.

Hatfield, E., Rapson, R. L., & Le, Y. L. (2009). Emotional contagion and empathy. In J. Decety & W. Ickes (Eds.), *The Social Neuroscience of Empathy.* Cambridge, MA: MIT Press.

Lamm, C., Meltzoff, A. N., & Decety, J. (2010). How do we empathize with someone who is not like us? A functional magnetic resonance imaging study. *Journal of Cognitive Neuroscience, 22*(2), 362–376.

Lombardo, M. V., Barnes, J. L., Wheelwright, S. J., & Baron-Cohen S. (2007). Self-referential cognition and empathy in autism. *PLoS ONE 2*(9): e883. doi:10.1371/journal.pone.0000883.

Pate, L. E. (1987). Improving managerial decision making. *Journal of Managerial Psychology, 2*(2), 9–15.

Pate, L. E. (1988). Using the Four ACES decision-making techniques in the classroom. *Organizational Behavior Teaching Review* (now *Journal of Management Education*), *12*(4), 155–158.

Pate, L. E., & Chesteen, S. A. (2000). Decision-making and work motivation: Reframing the role of the pharmacist from intervention to direct patient care. In C. Nimmo (Ed.), *Staff Development for Pharmacy Practice.* Bethesda, MD: American Society of Health-System Pharmacists.

Pate, L. E., & Filley, A. C. (2002). Leadership and decision-making in medicine. In D. Albert (Ed.), *A Physician's Guide to Healthcare Management.* Malden, MA: Blackwell Science.

Pate, L. E., & Greiner, L. E. (1989). Resolving dilemmas in power and OD with the Four ACES technique. *Consultation: An International Journal, 8*(1), 58–67.

Pate, L. E., & Heiman, D. C. (1987). Organizational schematas: Beyond behavioristic and phenomenological approaches to learning and decision making. *Journal of Human Behavior and Learning, 4*(3), 26–32.

Pate, L. E., & Nielson, T. R. (1996). Empirical findings on the ACES Decision-Making Technique. *Psychological Reports, 78,* 1049–1050.

Pate, L. E., & Ryder, P. A. (1987). Effective decision making and the HRM professional. *Human Resource Management Australia (now Asia Pacific Journal of Human Resources), 25*(2), 72–76.

Pate, L. E., Young, J. E., & Swinth, R. L. (1988). Group processes in solving complex novel problems: Implications for executives' decision making. *Psychological Reports, 62,* 23–29.

Pavlovich, K., & Krahnke, K. (2012). Empathy, connectedness and organisation. *Journal of Business Ethics, 105*(1), 131–137.

Platek, S. M., Critton, S. R., Myers, T. E., & Gallup, G. G. (2003). Contagious yawning: The role of self-awareness and mental state attribution. *Cognitive Brain Research, 17*(2), 223–227.

Preston, S. D. (2007). A perception-action model for empathy. In T. Farrow & P. Woodruff (Eds.), *Empathy in Mental Illness* (pp. 428–447). Cambridge: Cambridge University Press.

Preston, S. D., & de Waal, F.B.M. (2002). Empathy: Its ultimate and proximate bases. *Behavioral and Brain Sciences, 25*(1), 1–71.

Rameson, L. T., Morelli, S. A., & Lieberman, M. D. (2012). The neural correlates of empathy: Experience, automacity and prosocial behavior. *Journal of Cognitive Neuroscience, 24*(1), 235–245.

Senge, P. M. (1990). *The fifth discipline.* NY: Doubleday/Currency.

Shamay-Tsoory, S. (2011). The neural bases for empathy. *Neuroscientist, 17*(1), 18–24.

Shamay-Tsoory, S. G., Aharon-Peretz, J., & Perry, D. (2009). Two systems for empathy: A double dissociation between emotional and cognitive empathy in inferior frontal gyrus versus ventromedial prefrontal lesions. *Brain, 132*(3), 617–627.

Shapiro, J. (2002). How do physicians teach empathy in the primary care setting? *Academic Medicine, 77*(4), 323–328.

Silvia, P. J., & Duval, T. S. (2001). Objective self-awareness theory: Recent progress and enduring problems. *Personality and Social Psychology Review, 5*, 230–241.

Singer, T., & Lamm, C. (2009). The social neuroscience of empathy. J. Decety & W. Ickes (Eds.), *Annals of the New York Academy of Sciences, 1156*(1), 81–96. MIT.

Trope, Y., & Liberman, N. (2010). Construal-level theory of psychological distance. *Psychological Review, 117*(2), 440–463.

Woltin, K. A., Corneille, O., Yzerbyt, V. Y., & Förster, J. (2011). Narrowing down to open up for other people's concerns: Empathic concern can be enhanced by inducing detailed processing. *Journal of Experimental Social Psychology, 47*, 418–425.

Part II

Applied Approaches to Empathy

C: Contextual

9 Predicting Empathy in Medical Students and Doctors

Don Munro, David Powis, and Miles Bore

INTRODUCTION

It is universally acknowledged that empathy is an essential quality in members of the medical and other helping professions, although it is often referred to by other names such as "caring attitude" (e.g., Lown et al., 2007). Selection of students to professional courses therefore requires the identification of those who have the capacity to respond empathically to patients, families, and others. This chapter reviews some of the important issues concerning empathy in medicine, including the conditions that foster it and how to predict it in medical students and medical professionals. We review research carried out by ourselves and others in recent years on methods to measure those aspects of personality that have been found to be related to caring attitudes and behaviors. A particular issue that is addressed is whether it is better to try to identify and select those likely to show a high degree of empathy, or to identify and reject applicants to medicine who have characteristics that are antagonistic to empathy. A tentative model is proposed that takes account such factors as emotional stability, conscientiousness, and self-control, which tend to support the capacity for empathic behaviors in professional people, and some factors such as narcissism that may inhibit them.

EMPATHY IN MEDICINE

Empathy is widely regarded as the sine qua non among desirable characteristics of members of the medical professions, featuring prominently in lists of desirable qualities of "the good doctor" and taken for granted in expectations of nurses. Until relatively recently, however, the use of the term even by medical educators was casual, the expectation being that everybody knew what it meant and how important it was. However, in the second half of the 20th century, arguably in response to increasing bureaucratic pressures to evaluate medical practice more formally and accurately, there was greater interest in measuring empathy in medical settings. In the 21st century, there is widespread recognition of its importance for the healing process, and even of a basis in neurobiology (Riess, 2010). This has resulted in efforts to predict clinical empathic behavior and to select from among applicants to medical professions those with the greatest capacity for empathy, and the motivation to apply it in the interests of patients (e.g., Haque & Waytz, 2012; Haslam, 2007).

One of the first influential discussions about the qualities required of a good doctor was by Price et al. in 1971. They sampled over 1,600 people in the United States, including doctors and other medical professionals, asking them to list the qualities of a "good practicing physician". Eighty-seven qualities were listed as positive, the majority of them referring to technical skills and procedural appropriateness, but including some personal qualities that seem to involve empathy, for example, "Has sustained general concern for patients during their illness and convalescence" (ranked 18th), "Is willing to take needed time to listen to patients' problems sympathetically and helpfully' (24th), "Is an understanding sort of person" (35th), and "Has warm, outgoing, friendly personality" (72nd). Twenty-nine negative characteristics were also listed, including No 15: "Is not interested in, and does not want to be bothered with, patients' subjective difficulties and problems". Much more recently, Cullen, Bury, and Leahy (2003) did a similar survey of 599 members of the public in Ireland, finding that "Both interpersonal and cognitive characteristics . . . are important qualities for doctors to possess" (Abstract, p 38), with cognitive aspects such as general mental ability and medical knowledge leading in importance, but the fifth most important group of characteristics being "Understanding/compassionate/considerate/sensitive/acceptable/discerning".

Further confirmation comes from a study of health professionals ranging from medical students to faculty members (Mann, Reudy, Millar, & Andreou, 2005), using ratings of 25 descriptions of doctors' behavior, including "Displays compassion and empathy in patient care". The results were presented in terms of five factors calculated from the similarity of groups of ratings: "Teamwork and interpersonal skills", "Duty and responsibility", "Professionalism and values", "Communication and interpersonal skills" (including the example item), and "Trustworthiness and ethical behavior", in descending order of explanatory power.

Two things might be noted about these factors. First, it is clear that all five contain reference to personal characteristics, and while empathy is only explicitly mentioned as part of the third factor, there are aspects of caring for the patient implicit in all of them. Secondly, while they are in descending order of their statistical power to account for the original ratings, this does not necessarily mean a reducing in importance from first to last: The statistical methodology of factor analysis points rather to five qualitatively different groups of characteristics in the collective mind of the respondents, differently supported by groups of respondents. It is arguable therefore that caring or empathy and other humanistic impulses are seen as bound up in different aspects of the most important responsibilities of the doctor. It has also been suggested that empathy varies in its importance for medical specialisms. Hojat et al. (2005) showed that not only did empathy vary according to students' family background, but that higher scores on the Jefferson Scale of Physician Empathy (Hojat, Mangione, & Nasca, 2001) predict greater interest in the "people-oriented" specialisms.

While the empathic personality is regarded as a valuable characteristic in medicine generally, some have questioned whether very strong empathy is altogether advantageous. Hojat, Vengare, and Maxwell (2009), in their longitudinal study of erosion of empathy in medical school, remarked that "Cognitively defined empathy always leads to personal growth, career satisfaction, and optimal clinical outcomes, whereas affectively defined sympathy can lead to career burnout, compassion fatigue, exhaustion, and vicarious traumatization" (p. 1183). This points to a distinction between empathy as a behavior that is consciously directed, and an emotionally based form that they regard as more suitably called sympathy. On the same page, Hojat et al. (2009) explain, "a pro-social behavior that is induced by empathic understanding is more likely to be elicited by a sense of altruism. A prosocial behavior that is prompted by sympathetic feelings, however, is more likely to be triggered by egoistic motivation to reduce personal distress". This distinction, and the possibly negative consequences of very high empathy scores, will be raised again in the context of the present authors' work, to be discussed later.

Another writer (Macnaughton, 2009) goes even further in questioning the place empathy has in medicine, in an article entitled "The dangerous practice of empathy". Largely on philosophical grounds, she criticizes the way in which empathy has come to be regarded as a skill, as a part of medical practice, and as something that can be measured: "I have suggested that true empathy derives from an experience of intersubjectivity and this cannot be achieved in the doctor–patient relationship" (p. 1941). Perhaps the conclusions drawn by Haque and Waytz (2012) provide a reasonable viewpoint: "The aim for a physician will be to cultivate the practical wisdom to find the golden mean in different situations that optimizes overall care" (p. 181).

Hojat (2007) has provided one of the most comprehensive accounts of empathy in the medical context, ranging from the origin of the term to recent research on its application in patient care, including neurobiological and developmental aspects not covered here. A theme that runs through the book is the distinction between the cognitive aspects of empathy, which the author sees as of primary importance; and the affective aspects, which he would prefer to be labeled as sympathy. Another emphasis is on the complex interactions of a number of influences on empathy, such as previous learning, family, and the clinical setting, in a dynamic system in which each component acts on the others, with feedback that constantly influences the outcome behaviors. Furthermore, it is pointed out that much remains to be learned about how these influences work, either singly or in a system together. In this chapter, we do not take issue with Hojat's general approach, and there are several references to particular findings by his research group, though we focus rather more narrowly on the issue of selecting medical students on entry than on a wider consideration of how empathy develops. On that point, Hojat (2007) summarizes his own and others' findings to the effect that measures of personal qualities including "sociability, satisfactory interpersonal relationships, and self-esteem" are more useful in predicting clinical performance, and "essential humanistic qualities, such as empathy" than the typical cognitively oriented selection test used in medical schools (p. 210).

THE MEASUREMENT OF EMPATHY

Empathy is typically defined as an ability or inclination to adopt the point of view of another person and to respond to the perceived emotional state of the other. Although discussions of empathy often treat it as unitary, even this simple definition suggests that it is comprised of both a deliberate action (based on cognition) and a more autonomic response (based on affect). Whether these should be treated as different aspects of a singular empathy, or as different types of empathy, is one of the issues that have arisen from attempts to measure the degree to which individuals are empathic.

In the last half century or so, numerous instruments have been devised to assess empathy. Some of these have used empathy as a kind of personality trait, such as the scales by Hogan (1969), Mehrabian, and Epstein (1972) and Davis (1983) that have been used extensively in academic research on the concomitants of empathy and as a basis for the development of further scales (including those by the authors, to be described later). Others have seen empathy, or concomitants of it such as sympathy, as part of more inclusive traits, or of even broader dispositions such as altruism. For example, the Goldberg version of the widely accepted "Big Five" personality theory and measures (Goldberg et al., 2006) takes sympathy to be a facet of the primary trait, Agreeableness. However, it quickly became clear that such scales do not correlate well with each other, or correlate differently with other personality measures, or factor into different components, and it was concluded that they measured different aspects or types of empathy. For example, Chlopan, McCain, Carbonell, and Haagen (1985) showed that the Mehrabian approach related more to vicarious emotional arousal while the Hogan scale related to role-taking ability—reflecting the affective versus cognitive distinction mentioned above.

In the medical field, much research, especially in North America, has used the Jefferson Scale of Physician Empathy (Hojat et al., 2001; Chapter 7 in Hojat, 2007). This scale asks respondents to indicate their agreement or disagreement with 20 statements about the importance of different aspects of empathy in medicine, such as whether they contribute to better care or patient response. Both cognitive aspects (e.g., observing, seeing things from the patient's perspective, understanding, sense of humor, knowing the details of patients' lives) and affective (patients' and doctors' feelings, emotional ties, facial expression and body language, family relationships) are taken into account. Obviously, being able to respond appropriately to the scale requires some experience in the medical field, and so its usefulness with junior level students is limited. Another possible limitation is that none of the items refers to actual empathic or caring behavior, being devoted to opinions about the importance of different expressions of empathy.

Research on empathy in the medical field, especially that focusing on students, frequently makes use of observations by more experienced staff members of behavior in clinical settings or simulated interactions with patients (or standardized patients; see Schnabl, Hassard, & Kopelow, 1991). Although these observations are systematic within studies, they are typically not standardized across studies, so comparisons can be difficult. However, it is clear that different kinds of measure produce different results. For example, Jarski, Gjerde, Bratton, Brown, and Maatthes (1985) compared four measures of empathy, one of which was the Hogan (1969) self-report scale mentioned above, and three other scales based on observations of simulated student-patient interactions, showing that the latter correlated significantly with each other but not with the self-report scale. Similarly, Layton and Wykle (1990) found only partial support for their hypothesis that four empathy instruments would be positively related. Evans, Stanley, and Burrows (1993) suggested that the reason for this is that "pencil-and-paper tests of empathy cannot incorporate the range of complex cognitive, emotional, and behavioral components of the empathy construct" (Abstract, p. 121).

EMPATHY IN MEDICAL STUDENTS

Several studies have examined the development of empathy in medical students (e.g., Chen, Lew, Hershman, & Orlander, 2007; Hornblow, Kidson, & Jones, 1977). Some investigations have focused on the reasons for the individual differences that are observed, while others have attempted to show that these differences are consequential for the development of professional competence in medical school and beyond. It has generally been found (e.g., Hojat et al., 2002) that empathy variations are related to gender (females scoring significantly higher on most measures), and that these variations are more predictive of clinical skills than performance in examinations that assess knowledge and reasoning. However, it should be pointed out at this stage that results for examinations of the latter kind are much more easily obtainable in conventional medical schools, and statistically reliable, than evaluations of clinical skill, which are often based on the subjective impressions of many faculty members in situations that are variable and complex.

Lown et al. (2007) are of the view that caring attitudes are generally officially valued in medical schools but are inconsistently fostered. They suggest that what is often missing is support for faculty development, and an emphasis on caring attitudes by assessing them in students and in applicants for faculty posts. They also mention earlier work that pointed to the amount of work stress in staff and its effect on communication with patients as being important inhibitors of caring behavior (and, presumably, the modeling of caring behavior by students).

Several efforts have been made to deliberately foster empathy in medical students. Sanson-Fisher and Poole (1978) set up an experiment that involved ratings of empathy based on videotaped interviews with patients before and after eight two-hour video training sessions; they found the experimental group changed significantly. More recently, Fernandez-Olano, Montoya-Fernandez, and Salinas-Sanches (2008) found a "slight improvement" following a communication skills workshop. Specific experiences that expose the student to doctor-patient interactions that are sensitive to feelings and thoughts, such as psychiatric interviews (Elizur & Rosenheim, 1982), accompanying a patient around a hospital (Stepien & Baernstein, 2006), or even "guided reflective writing" (Misra-Hebert et al., 2012) may also be good training in empathy. It may be that a continuous emphasis on the importance of relating well to patients may be more effective than "one-off" courses; the University of Amsterdam, for example, found it useful to monitor its students during clinical rotations for several qualities including handling emotions and showing empathy (ten Cate & De Haes, 2000).

ROLE MODELS

There has been considerable interest in the impact of role models on the fostering of empathy and a range of related behaviors, including the maintenance of ethical and professional standards (Lynoe, Lofmark, & Thulesius, 2008), doctor-patient relationships and the importance of interpersonal skills (Siegler, Reaven, Lipinski, & Stocking, 1987) and the handling of specific encounters with patients such as terminal illness (Wear, 2002). Finding an exceptional role model has been found to be one of the most impactful events in medical school (Murinson et al., 2010). Joubert et al. (2006) argued for the importance of teaching "soft skills" as well as clinical skills "at the bedside", and pointed out that poor role models affect students negatively, due to the fact that their unacceptable behaviors are often imitated and passed on to others (though in some cases students realize that such behaviors are precisely what should be avoided). The authors exhorted medical schools to take more care with the allocation of teachers to students for this reason, echoing the views of Kenny, Mann, & MacLeod, 2003), who pointed out that doctors are not merely playing a role (as actors) but embodying the cognitive, behavioral, and emotional processes necessary for being a good doctor. Shapiro (2002) showed that experienced primary care physicians might differ about whether empathy is a skill or an attitude, but most used both clinical settings and "debriefing" sessions to teach both the behavioral and attitudinal aspects comprehensively. Matthews (2000) found with students and faculty in Saudi Arabia that the best-remembered thing about former role models' behavior was their positive attitude towards patients. Elzubeir and Rizk (2001) found "personality" to be among the highest ranked desired characteristics of role models (together with teaching and clinical skills), meaning "positive, respectful attitudes toward patients and their families, and staff and colleagues; honesty; politeness; (and) enthusiasm" (Abstract, p. 272).

A curious aspect of empathy in medical students that has been noted several times is that it varies across years of study, typically falling to a low by the third year of the course (Chen et al., 2007; Hojat et al., 2009; Spencer, 2004). This has been attributed to the pressures of the medical course leading to defensive changes in emotion, lack of sympathetic role models, and to acculturation by the ways in which the wider profession depersonalizes medical conditions and handles emotional situations: "Over-reliance on computer-based diagnostic and therapeutic technology . . . market-driven health care . . . can also lead to a false idea that empathy is outside the realm of evidence-based medicine" (Hojat et al., 2009, p. 1188). Haslam (2007) has characterized these processes as *dehumanization*. However, Colliver, Conlee, Verhulst, and Dorsey (2010) have recently questioned whether the phenomenon is significant, especially as the evidence is largely based on self-reports by students. Austin, Evans, Magnus, and O'Hanlon (2007) found that male empathy scores increased between Years 1 and 2, while female scores decreased.

EMOTIONAL INTELLIGENCE

The notion of emotional intelligence (EI) emerged in the 1980s and was popularized by Mayer and Salovey (1997) and Goleman (1998). It is usually defined in terms of either an ability or a disposition to be aware of emotions (including feelings, fears, motives and related thoughts) in oneself and others and to use this awareness to better control one's own behavior and social interactions. It is therefore more comprehensive than empathy as an account of sensitivity to others, and its broad definition has been seen by some psychologists as undermining its value as a predictive variable compared to more specific personality or ability constructs (e.g., Matthews, Zeidner, & Roberts, 2007). However, this does not necessarily mean that is less useful in applied fields such as medical education. Arora et al. (2010) in a review of studies in medicine reported that EI had been found predictive of empathy, doctor-patient relationships, teamwork and communications skills, and also qualities of interest to institutional management, including stress management, organizational commitment, and leadership. On the other hand, Weng et al., (2011) found in a study of 50 surgeons and over 500 of their patients in follow-up visits, that long-term patient satisfaction was affected more by their empathy ratings than by their emotional intelligence, although before surgery the reverse was true.

Turning to medical students, Austin, Evans, Goldwater, and Potter (2005) found that a self-report measure of EI was only modestly predictive of first-year examination performance on general aspects of medicine and communication skills, with gender effects (females scoring higher on EI) overshadowing others. Empathy was not assessed separately. An Australian study of the correlations between an ability-based measure of EI and ability test, school performance, and entrance interview results (Carr, 2009) showed no significant results. Minor changes in EI have been noted between the first and third years of a medical course (Stratton, Saunders, & Elam 2008), a result similar to that mentioned earlier for empathy. Finally, Borges, Stratton, Wagner, and Elam (2009) used a variety of ability-based and self-report personality measures of EI, but failed to find significant relationships with career choice differences between primary care and other branches of medicine.

Our conclusion must be that, despite the intuitive appeal of emotional intelligence as an alternative to empathy as a measure of ability or disposition to be sensitive to patient needs, there is insufficient evidence to displace empathy from its role as the generic construct in the medical field. Ickes (Flury & Ickes, 2006; Mast & Ickes, 2007) have suggested that a middle ground is "empathic accuracy", which goes beyond simple empathic responding to making use of one's empathic understanding to correctly infer the thoughts and feelings of the other person, and which can be regarded as the essence of EI. However, despite the half century of interest in the topic outlined in Mast and Ickes (2007), application to the medical field, for example in terms of improved diagnostic ability, seems to be lacking.

NARCISSISM

Discussions of empathy in the medical literature generally seem to assume that the construct is a unipolar one, with high empathy regarded as positive and low empathy as neutral or negative. The possibility must be considered, however, that empathy is bipolar, with a negative pole that is the opposite of, or antagonistic to, empathy. Paulhus and Williams are credited with the idea that the "Dark Triad" of narcissism, Machiavellianism and psychopathy provide this negative pole, in that representative measures of them share negative correlations with empathy measures (Paulhus & Williams, 2002). Wai and Tiliopoulos (2012) argue for a lead role for "primary psychopathy" but this is dependent on the way the variables are measured. In this chapter, we concentrate on narcissism as the prototypical antagonist of empathy, partly on the basis of its nature and partly on the basis of our findings, to be discussed later.

Numerous descriptions of narcissism and narcissists are available in published material and on the Internet, often written by colleagues, marital partners, and others who have suffered damaging relationships with those who are described as narcissists. Some more formal definitions of narcissism refer to the nine criteria for diagnosis with Narcissistic Personality Disorder according to the DSM guidelines (e.g., American Psychiatric Association, 1994), which are currently under revision. Different forms or expressions of narcissism have been identified, notably the Arrogant or Grandiose form, characterized by grandiosity, self-centeredness, competitiveness, demands for admiration from others and the belittlement of others; and the Shy or Vulnerable form, characterized by hypersensitivity, inhibition, and social withdrawal. To these has recently been added a third expression, the Psychopathic form, characterized by superior self-regard, exploitativeness, and aggression (thus incorporating to a degree the other components of the Dark Triad; Houlcroft, Bore, & Munro, 2012). The common factor in these descriptions could be regarded as a focus on the self and its needs and desires, together with the disadvantaging of others and their needs and wishes, and hence the inhibition of any inclination to empathy and caring.

One of the earliest and most used measures of narcissism was the self-report Narcissistic Personality Inventory of Raskin and Hall (1979, 1981), which includes several types of item, including belief in one's authority, self absorption/admiration, an attitude of superiority and arrogance, and feelings of entitlement and exploitation of others; these cover substantially the same behaviors as the DSM criteria. Several other inventories and checklists have been produced for clinical use, including the Pathological Narcissism Inventory of Pincus et al. (2009).

MORALITY AND EMPATHY

The work carried out over the last decade or so by the present authors originated with a request from a medical school for improved tests for the selection of medical students. Despite the use of earlier tests of moral development and a selection interview, it had been found that a small proportion of students showed behavior during the medical course that was unacceptable to members of staff and indicated the likelihood of unprofessional conduct after graduation. As the problem was identified as one of ethics (Lowe, Kerridge, Bore, Munro, & Powis, 2001), an instrument was constructed to assess moral dispositions in beginning students. An initial decision was made to avoid the weaknesses shown in previous measures of morality, which were largely based on the hierarchical developmental theory of moral reasoning proposed by Kohlberg (1981, 1984), which categorized responses to moral dilemmas into six stages.

This theory had been criticized on a number of grounds, and the measures of morality arising from it had not proved to be able to predict moral behavior independently from educational level. Bore, Munro, Kerridge, and Powis (2005a) suggested that one of the reasons for the latter is that the measures rely on postdecisional rationalizations of decisions rather than predecisional moral reasoning. In view of these issues, a new approach to the assessment of morality was adopted, based not on measuring the degree of moral maturity or sophistication, but on "moral orientation", or the respondent's moral position along a dimension from libertarianism to communitarianism (valuing the rights of the individual more than the group, versus valuing the rights of the group more than the individual). The central portion of this dimension was labeled a "dual" moral orientation, representing those people who equally value the rights of individuals and the rights of the group (Bore, Munro, Kerridge, & Powis, 2005b).

Given the importance of empathy for the medical professions, a measure was also included in the validation research we undertook for the measure of moral orientation. Due to the unsuitability of the Jefferson Scale of Physician Empathy for use with applicants who had no experience of medicine, other measures were sought. In view of the known weaknesses of existing empathy measures, discussed above, items were selected and/ or adapted from a wide variety of sources for a novel scale. In addition, interviews with medical faculty members revealed that the problems presented by a small proportion of students revolved around descriptions of behavior that were very similar to those for Narcissistic Personality Disorder (American Psychiatric Association, 1994). Furthermore, it could be observed that many of these descriptions were the polar opposites of those for empathy. Accordingly, a similar number of items for narcissism were produced, adapted from a variety of sources such as Raskin and Hall's (1979) Narcissistic Personality Inventory. These items were assembled together in scales and subjected to the normal processes of scale development and validation (Munro et al., 2005). Factor analysis revealed that some items intended as indicators of empathy loaded negatively on narcissism factors, and vice versa, while some items formed unpredicted factors. The outcome was the production of a reliable set of scales measuring four traits: Narcissism, Aloofness, Confidence and Empathy (hence NACE as the name of the instrument). Although statistically independent, these can also be used together in a bipolar measure of Detachment versus Involvement (comprising the Narcissism and Aloofness, and Empathy and Confidence, respectively), yielding a single score.

In extensive further use of the scales in research and selection in several countries, both the individual scales and the composite scale have shown a high degree of internal consistency (Cronbach alpha coefficients of around 0.90) and reliable correlations with each other, with Bore's moral orientation measure (see above), and with standard measures of personality (see http://www.pqa.net.au/files/pqa_pub.html).

Research presented in the original companion papers (Bore et al., 2005a; and Munro, Bore, & Powis, 2005) and later by the present authors and others (e.g., Bore, Munro & Powis 2009; Gibbons, Bore, Munro, & Powis, 2007; Powis, Bore, Munro, & Lumsden 2005) have confirmed the expected relationships with other constructs and measures related to altruistic and caring versus selfish and antisocial attitudes and behaviors in medical students and other professional trainees. Typical gender differences recur, with females scoring higher on Involvement and its components, and lower on Detachment. In general, those high in Involvement are socially outgoing and agreeable, and also (perhaps surprisingly) conscientious, while Detached people share the opposite characteristics. An expected positive relationship between Involvement and Emotional Intelligence has also been noted. Ongoing work (e.g., Adam, Bore, McKendree, Munro, & Powis, 2012) also point to positive relationships with ratings of constructive student behavior in medical school tutor groups and with the development of clinical skills.

Scores from the two measures, of Libertarianism—Communitarianism and Involvement—Detachment, have also been combined in a model indicating probable attitudes and behaviors that would be problematic in a clinical setting (see Figure 9.1). For example, the model suggests that people who are highly Involved (being highly empathic and confident in dealing with others) and highly Libertarian in their moral orientation would tend to be permissive in their dealings with others, while people highly Involved but Communitarian in moral orientation would tend to be paternalistic toward others; the Detached Libertarian would be manipulative and narcissistic while the Detached Communitarian would be intolerant of people who hold perceived unconventional views and attitudes. The center portion of the model represents the mid-range of each dimension and, given the normal distribution of each dimension, the location of the majority of people. Most people are empathic and concerned for others, but not excessively, and most people balance the needs and rights of individuals with the needs and rights of society; our model proposes that this is the category of applicants to medicine that should be favored, and that those who are more extreme should be either rejected or subjected to further assessment.

In more recent applications of the model to the actual selection of medical students, other dimensions of personality that have been shown to be important for good performance in medical schools have also been taken into account, particularly conscientiousness and emotional stability (Munro et al., 2008). What is implicit in the overall approach is that the capacity for empathy in medical students, or the disposition to behave empathically, is not something that can be narrowly defined and measured, nor can it be predicted by a single narrow personality trait. Rather, it is part of a "well rounded" character with a set of abilities and dispositions that are brought into play in response to circumstances. These include emotional balance, so that performance as a doctor is not impaired by chronic stress or emergencies; conscientiousness, so that impediments to normal

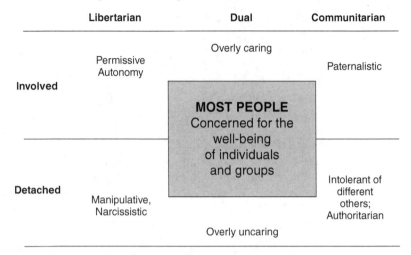

Figure 9.1   Behaviors associated with Libertarianism—Communitarianism and Involvement-Detachment

functioning are overcome by perseverance and determination; and warm involvement with other people, so that they are seen as unique individuals with specific needs. These characteristics are seen as mutually compensatory to a degree, in that a temporary deterioration in one or the other does not lead to a failure of the caring response. There is some similarity here to the notion that the "alpha" superfactor of the Five Factor Model (comprised of agreeableness, conscientiousness and emotional stability) might form a useful general-purpose predictor of occupational proficiency (e.g., Allessandri & Vecchione, 2012).

Another feature of the model is that it does not aim to select only those who are excellently empathic but rather to deselect those who are unlikely to be able to function as empathic doctors even with the benefit of encouragement and specific training and the presence of good role models. It assumes that the majority of people who are in the normal or average category in terms of the relevant personality traits will be able to do so, and seeks to exclude those for whom the "dark side" of personality (Hogan & Hogan, 2001; Knights & Kennedy, 2006) is likely to be crippling. And in relation to the last point it is recognized, if only because people change, that perfect prediction is beyond the scope of any test of personality—we can only specify that the degree of risk increases the more extreme the score.

EMPATHIC BEHAVIORS

Throughout this article we have used the rather informal definitions of empathy that are in everyday use, taking account only of the cognitive versus affective distinction that has been widely accepted by researchers. Possibly the reason that empathy has not usually been more carefully defined is that it is not recognized as a major syndrome or symptom of disorder, as is narcissism (American Psychiatric Association, 1994). While this can be accepted on the basis that everybody knows what empathy is, it may create a practical problem for medical educators who want to teach empathy to medical students, or for bodies desiring to improve professional practices. The question might be, "What exactly does a doctor have to do to be empathic?" This requires something beyond simple exhortations such as "Try to put yourself in the shoes of the patient".

One source of answers to that question might be found in the scales that have been used operationally to measure empathy. Hojat et al.'s (2001) Jefferson Scale of Physician Empathy, for example, contains items such as "paying attention to their nonverbal cues and body language" and "hav(ing) a good sense of humor", though most of the items refer to attitudes and motives rather than to explicit behaviors. The only behavioral items in the Mehrabian Measure of Emotional Empathy (1972) concern "being upset", while Hogan's Empathy Scale (1969) similarly mentions only being upset or angry, versus behaving "normally" or "cool and collected". To a large extent, such items provide guidance on what behaviors to avoid rather on how to appear empathic, insofar as they go beyond appropriate feelings (e.g., of concern), thoughts (e.g., being aware of another person's behavior), and motives (e.g., wanting to help). Actual helping or "caring for" has been mentioned in some instruments, as have behaving ethically and professionally, but these are not specific actions. Self-disclosure in order to encourage patient disclosure has been suggested, though this can be seen as a counseling method rather than empathic behavior as such. Finally, the empathy items in the authors' NACE instrument (see above) contain a few specific behaviors: discussing thoughts and feelings and problems, showing sympathy, speaking to someone who is bereaved, providing "a shoulder to cry on", and expressing affection for another person.

Recent research on apparently empathic (or altruistic) behavior in animals may be worth noting, as the experimental observations are necessarily of behavior rather than inner states. The ethologist and primatologist Frans de Waal (2009) identifies empathy as a "very ancient, very general capacity" based on virtually universal infant nurturing behaviors of the most highly evolved mammals, and as the basis for morality in groups. Among the behaviors that have been identified as indicators of empathy and that might be used by humans to demonstrate empathy are eye contact, various (species specific) facial expressions, consolation behavior (comforting gestures such as touching and embracing), "mirroring" or imitation of body postures and semiautomatic actions such as yawning, and producing reassuring words and noises.

Of course, in professional encounters the use of these would need to be carefully regulated, for example, to avoid empathy becoming intimacy.

Also, there is a risk that the deliberate use of such expressions of empathy might be seen as false by patients and others, and thus counterproductive; while humans as well as animals often react to emotive signals with astonishing speed and accuracy, it is also true that attempts to manipulate situations by simulating empathy or sympathy are readily detected. Research on individual differences among doctors and patients on their sensitivity to such situations remains to be done, though useful clues may be buried in writings on related topics, and indeed in the unrecorded experiences of health professionals.

OVERVIEW AND CONCLUSIONS

In this chapter we have not attempted a comprehensive account of empathy, as such is beyond the scope of a single chapter, and other authors will more adequately complete the picture we have drawn. We have focused on those aspects and issues that are relevant to the practice of medicine, more particularly to the development of empathic caring in medical students, and specifically to the question whether it is possible to predict empathy in medical school and to select students who will be most likely to demonstrate it naturally or to learn it from experienced professionals. We have taken it for granted that empathy is "a good thing" in medical professionals, and have also assumed that there are individual differences in the capacity for caring that are relatively enduring, that these can be measured reasonably accurately, and that they might (therefore) be predictable from suitable indicators even as early as before entry into medical school in the late teenage years. Based on the available evidence from research in the last half century, albeit still rather thin, we believe these assumptions are reasonable.

A major theme that emerges from the review is that empathy, at least as practiced in medicine, is not a pure clear substance that might be absorbed by students, but rather an amalgam of positive and negative components that may take different forms in different contexts. On the one hand, we have the findings of those such as Hojat (2007) and Mann et al. (2005), who have found empathy to be embedded in a complex of attitudes and behaviors that relate to the provision of humanitarian medical treatment. It may be that patients with different psychological needs will respond differentially to the different ways in which doctors present the various components of their approach to treatment, ranging from basic examination techniques, through diagnoses and prognoses, then treatment techniques, to communications and attention to the patient as an individual. Surprisingly little attention has been paid to the issue of what specific kinds of behavior by medical professionals is regarded as empathic or caring by patients (and much of that by nursing professionals; see Larsson, Sahlsten, Segesten, & Plos, 2011).

Similarly, when we attempted to devise a measure of empathy that might be applied to medical students, it became clear that a number of related variables had to be taken into account, including negative tendencies such as narcissism, and a composite index seemed most useful. Other even broader approaches might have been usefully included, such as emotional intelligence, and in later work we have taken account of conscientiousness, emotional stability and self-control to make up a more complete profile of the responsive medical student. For each dimension, we take the view that extreme scores increase the risk of problematic behaviors.

However, although our conceptual model is becoming clearer, it has to be admitted that much remains to be done to validate it. A major impediment to such an endeavor is the difficulty of carrying out research within medical schools. Apart from better measures of empathy and other personality variables that may be able to predict caring behaviors in doctors, we need indices of such caring behavior that are practical and acceptable to the medical community. Carrying out the research requires substantial reorganization of teaching and assessment procedures, involving the cooperation of medical staff at all levels, not to mention the agreement of students, who are often suspicious of additional assessments. However, with the participation of some medical schools and their staff and students (Adam et al., 2012), it may be possible to lay the groundwork for an improvement in the selection of medical students for their empathic potential, and eventually produce a more empathic and caring medical profession.

REFERENCES

Adam, J., Bore, M., McKendree, J., Munro, D., & Powis, D. (2012). Can personal qualities of medical students predict in-course examination success and professional behavior? An exploratory prospective cohort study. *BMC Medical Education, 12*, 69–76.

Allessandri, G., & Vecchione, M. (2012). The higher-order factors of the Big Five as predictors of job performance. *Personality and Individual Differences, 53*, 779–784.

American Psychiatric Association (1994). *Diagnostic and statistical manual of mental disorders* (4th ed.). Washington, DC: American Psychiatric Association.

Arora, S., Ashrafian, H., Davis, R., Athanasiou, T., Darzi, A., & Sevdalis, N. (2010). Emotional intelligence in medicine: A systematic review through the context of the ACGME competencies. *Medical Education, 44*, 749–764.

Austin, E.J., Evans, P., Magnus, B., & O'Hanlon, K. (2007). A preliminary study of empathy, emotional intelligence and examination performance in MBChB students. *Medical Education, 41*, 684–689.

Austin, E.J., Evans, P., Goldwater, R., & Potter, V. (2005). A preliminary study of emotional intelligence, empathy and exam performance in first year medical students. *Personality and Individual Differences, 39*, 1395–1405.

Bore, M.R., Munro, D., Kerridge, I., & Powis, D.A. (2005a). Not moral "reasoning": A Libertarian-Communitarian dimension of moral orientation and Schwartz's value types. *Australian Journal of Psychology, 57*, 38–48.

Bore, M.R., Munro, D., Kerridge, I., & Powis, D.A. (2005b). Selection of medical students according to their moral orientation. *Medical Education, 39*, 266–275.

Bore, M., Munro, D., & Powis, D. (2009). A comprehensive model for the selection of medical students. *Medical Teacher, 31*, 1066–1072.

Borges, N. J., Stratton, T. D., Wagner, P. J., & Elam, C. L. (2009). Emotional intelligence and medical specialty choice: Findings from three empirical studies. *Medical Education, 43*, 565–572.

Carr, S. E. (2009). Emotional intelligence in medical students: Does it correlate with selection measures? *Medical Education, 43*, 1069–1077.

Chen, D., Lew, R., Hershman, W., & Orlander, J. (2007). A cross-sectional measurement of medical student empathy. *Journal of General Internal Medicine, 22*, 1434–1438.

Chlopan, B. E., McCain, M. L., Carbonell, J. L., & Hagen, R. L. (1985). Empathy: Review of available measures. *Journal of Personality and Social Psychology, 48*, 635–653.

Colliver, J. A., Conlee, M. J., Verhulst, S. J., & Dorsey, J. K. (2010). Reports of the decline of empathy during medical education are greatly exaggerated: A reexamination of the research. *Academic Medicine, 85*, 588–593.

Cullen, W., Bury, G., & Leahy, M. (2003). What makes a good doctor? A cross sectional survey of public opinion. *Irish Medical Journal, 96*(2), 38–41.

Davis, M. H. (1983). Measuring individual differences in empathy: Evidence for a multidimensional approach. *Journal of Personality and Social Psychology, 44*, 113–126.

de Waal, F. (2009). *The age of empathy: Nature's lessons for a kinder society*. NY: Harmony Books/Random House.

Elizur, A., & Rosenheim, E. (1982). Empathy and attitudes among medical students: The effects of group experience. *Journal of Medical Education, 57*, 675–683.

Elzubeir, M. A., & Rizk, D. E. (2001). Identifying characteristics that students, interns and residents look for in their role models. *Medical Education, 35*, 272–277.

Evans, B. J., Stanley, R. O., & Burrows, G. D. (1993). Measuring medical students' empathy skills. *British Journal of Medical Psychology, 66*, 121–133.

Fernandez-Olano, C., Montoya-Fernandez, J., & Salinas-Sanchez, A. S. (2008). Impact of clinical interview training on the empathy level of medical students and medical residents. *Medical Teacher, 30*, 322–324.

Flury, J., & Ickes, W. (2006). Emotional intelligence and empathic accuracy in friendships and dating relationships. In J. Ciarrochi, J. R. Forgas, & J. D. Mayer (Eds.), *Emotional intelligence in everyday life* (2nd ed., pp. 140–165). Hove, England: Taylor & Francis.

Gibbons, J., Bore, M., Munro, D., & Powis, D. (2007). Using personal quality assessment for selection of social work students. *Australian Social Work, 60*, 210–221.

Goldberg, L. R., Johnson, J. A., Eber, H. W., Hogan, R., Ashton, M. C., Cloninger, C. R., & Gough, H. G. (2006). The international personality item pool and the future of public-domain personality measures. *Journal of Research in Personality, 40*, 84–96.

Goleman, D. (1998). *Working with emotional intelligence*. NY: Bantam.

Haque, O. S., & Waytz, A. (2012). Dehumanization in medicine: Causes, solutions, and functions. *Perspectives on Psychological Science, 7*, 176–186.

Haslam, N. (2007). Humanising medical practice: The role of empathy. *Medical Journal of Australia, 187*, 381–382.

Hogan, R. (1969). Development of an empathy scale. *Journal of Consulting and Clinical Psychology, 33*, 307–316.

Hogan, R., & Hogan, J. (2001). Assessing leadership: A view of the dark side. *International Journal of Selection and Assessment, 9*, 40–51.

Hojat, M. (2007). *Empathy in patient care: Antecedents, development, measurement, and outcomes*. NY: Springer.

Hojat, M., Gonnella, J. S., Mangione, S., Nasca, T., Nasca, T. J., Veloski, . . . Magee, M. (2002). Empathy in medical students as related to academic performance, clinical competence and gender. *Medical Education, 36*, 1–6.

Hojat, M, Mangione S., & Nasca T. J. (2001). The Jefferson Scale of Empathy: Development and preliminary psychometric data. *Educational and Psychological Measurement, 61*, 349–365.

Hojat, M., Vengare M. J., & Maxwell K. (2009). The devil is in the third year: A longitudinal study of erosion of empathy in medical school. *Academic Medicine, 84*, 1182–1191.

Hojat, M., Zuckerman, M., Magee, M., Mangione, S., Nasca, T., Vergare, M., & Gonnella, J. S. (2005). Empathy in medical students as related to specialty interest, personality, and perceptions of father and mother. *Personality and Individual Differences, 39*, 1205–1215.

Hornblow, A. R., Kidson, M. A., & Jones, K V. (1977). Measuring medical students' empathy: A validation study. *Medical Education, 11*, 7–12.

Houlcroft, L., Bore, M., & Munro, D. (2012). Three faces of narcissism. *Personality and Individual Differences, 53*, 274–278.

Jarski, R. W., Gjerde, C. L., Bratton, B. D., Brown, D. D., & Matthes, S. S. (1985). A comparison of four empathy instruments in simulated patient-medical student interactions. *Journal of Medical Education, 60*, 545–551.

Joubert, P. M., Kruger, C., Bergh, A.-M., Pickworth, G. E., Van Staden, C. W., Roos, J. L., . . . Lindeque, B. G. (2006). Medical students on the value of role models for developing 'soft skills'—"That's the way you do it". *South African Psychiatry Review, 9*, 28–32.

Kenny, N. P., Mann, K. V., & MacLeod, H. (2003). Role modeling in physicians' professional formation: Reconsidering an essential but untapped educational strategy. *Academic Medicine, 78*, 1203–1210.

Knights, J. A., & Kennedy, B. J. (2006). Medical school selection: Screening for dysfunctional tendencies. *Medical Education, 40*, 1058–1064.

Kohlberg, L. (1981). *The philosophy of moral development: Moral stages and the idea of justice: Vol. I: Essays on moral development.* San Francisco: Harper & Row.

Kohlberg, L. (1984). *Essays on moral development, Vol. II: The psychology of moral development.* NY: Harper & Row.

Larsson, I. E., Sahlsten, M.J.M., Segesten, K., & Plos, K. A. (2011). Patients' perceptions of barriers for participation in nursing care. *Scandinavian Journal of Caring Sciences, 25*, 575–582.

Layton, J. M., & Wykle, M. H. (1990). A validity study of four empathy instruments. *Research in Nursing and Health, 13*, 319–325.

Lowe, M., Kerridge, I., Bore, M., Munro, D., & Powis, D. A. (2001). Is it possible to assess the "ethics" of medical school applicants? *Journal of Medical Ethics, 27*, 404–408.

Lown, B. A., Chou, C. L., Clark, W. D., Haidet, P., White, M. K., Krupat, . . . Anderson, M. B. (2007). Caring attitudes in medical education: Perceptions of deans and curriculum leaders. *Journal of General Internal Medicine, 22*, 1514–1522.

Lynoe, N., Lofmark, R., & Thulesius, H. O. (2008). Teaching medical ethics: What is the impact of role models? Some experiences from Swedish medical schools. *Journal of Medical Ethics, 34*, 315–316.

Macnaughton, J. (2009). The dangerous practice of empathy. *The Lancet, 373*(9679), 1940–1941.

Mann, K. V., Ruedy, J., Millar, N., & Andreou, P. (2005). Achievement of non-cognitive goals of undergraduate medical education: Perceptions of medical students, residents, faculty and other health professionals. *Medical Education, 39*, 40–48.

Mast, M. S., & Ickes, W. (2007). Empathic accuracy: Measurement and potential clinical applications. In T. Farrow & P. Woodruff (Eds.), *Empathy in mental illness* (pp. 408–427). NY: Cambridge University Press.

Matthews, C. (2000). Role modelling: How does it influence teaching in family medicine? *Medical Education, 34*, 443–448.

Matthews, G., Zeidner, M., & Roberts, R.D. (Eds.). (2007). *The science of emotional intelligence: Knowns and unknowns.* NY: Oxford University Press.

Mayer, J.D., & Salovey, P. (1997). What is emotional intelligence? In P. Salovey & D. Sluyter (Eds.), *Emotional development and emotional intelligence: Implications for educators* (pp. 3–31). NY: Basic Books.

Mehrabian, A., & Epstein, N.A. (1972). A measure of emotional empathy. *Journal of Personality, 40,* 525–543.

Misra-Hebert, A.D., Isaacson, J.H., Kohn, M., Hull, A.L., Hojat, M., Papp, K.K., & Calabrese, L. (2012). Improving empathy of physicians through guided reflective writing. *International Journal of Medical Education, 3,* 71–77.

Munro, D., Bore, M., & Powis, D. (2005). Personality factors in professional ethical behavior: Studies of empathy and narcissism. *Australian Journal of Psychology, 57,* pp. 49–60.

Munro, D., Bore, M., & Powis, D. (2008). Personality determinants of success in medical school and beyond: "Steady, Sane and Nice". In S. Boag (Ed.), *Personality down under: Perspectives from Australia* (ch. 9, pp. 103–111). NY: Nova Science Publishers.

Murinson, B.B., Klick, B., Haythornthwaite, J.A., Shochet, R., Levine, R.B., & Wright, S.M. (2010). Formative experiences of emerging physicians: Gauging the impact of events that occur during medical school. *Academic Medicine, 85,* 1331–1337.

Paulhus, D.L., & Williams, K.M. (2002). The dark triad of personality: Narcissism, Machiavellianism, and psychopathy. *Journal of Research in Personality, 36,* 556–563.

Pincus, A.L., Ansell, E.B., Pimentel, C.A., Cain, N.M., Wright, A.G.C., & Levy, K.N. (2009). Initial construction and validation of the Pathological Narcissism Inventory. *Psychological Assessment, 21,* 365–379.

Powis, D., Bore, M., Munro, D., & Lumsden, M.A. (2005). Development of the Personal Qualities Assessment as a tool for selecting medical students. *Journal of Adult and Continuing Education, 11,* 3–14

Price, P.B., Lewis, E.G., Loughmiller, G.C., Nelson, D.E., Murray, S.L., & Taylor, C.W. (1971). Attributes of a good practicing physician. *Journal of Medical Education, 46,* 229–237.

Raskin, R.N., & Hall, C.S. (1979). A narcissistic personality inventory. *Psychological Reports, 45,* 590.

Raskin, R., & Hall, C.S. (1981). The Narcissistic Personality Inventory: Alternative form reliability and further evidence of construct validity. *Journal of Personality Assessment, 45,* 159–162.

Riess, H. (2010). Empathy in medicine—A neurobiological perspective. *Journal of the American Medical Association, 304,* 1604–1605.

Sanson-Fisher, R.W., & Poole, A.D. (1978). Training medical students to empathize: An experimental study. *Medical Journal of Australia, 1,* 473–476.

Schnabl, G.K., Hassard, T.H., & Kopelow, M.L. (1991). The assessment of interpersonal skills using standardized patients. *Academic Medicine, 66*(9), Supplement, 34–36.

Shapiro, J. (2002). How do physicians teach empathy in the primary care setting? *Academic Medicine, 77,* 323–328.

Siegler, M., Reaven, N., Lipinski, R., & Stocking, C. (1987). Effect of role-model clinicians on students' attitudes in a second-year course on introduction to the patient. *Journal of Medical Education, 62,* 935–937.

Spencer, J. (2004). Decline in empathy in medical education: How can we stop the rot? *Medical Education, 38,* 916–918.

Stepien, K.A., & Baernstein, A. (2006). Educating for empathy. A review. *Journal of General Internal Medicine, 21,* 524–530.

Stratton, T.D., Saunders, J.A., & Elam, C.L. (2008). Changes in medical students' emotional intelligence: An exploratory study. *Teaching and Learning in Medicine, 20*, 279–284.

ten Cate, T.J., & De Haes, J.C.J.M. (2000). Summative assessment of medical students in the affective domain. *Medical Teacher, 22*, 40–43.

Wear, D. (2002). "Face-to-face with it": Medical students' narratives about their end-of-life education. *Academic Medicine, 77*, 271–277.

Wai, M., & Tiliopoulos, N. (2012). The affective and cognitive empathic nature of the dark triad of personality. *Personality and Individual Differences, 52*, 794–799.

Weng, H.-C., Steed, J.F., Yu, S.-W., Liu, Y-T., Hsu, C-C., Yu, T.-J., & Chen, W. (2011). The effect of surgeon empathy and emotional intelligence on patient satisfaction. *Advances in Health Sciences Education, 16*, 591–600.

10 The Caring Climate
How Sport Environments Can Develop Empathy in Young People

Lori A. Gano-Overway

INTRODUCTION

When Joe Ehrmann, a high school football coach, contemplated his purpose for coaching he stated, "I coach to help boys become men of empathy and integrity who will lead, be responsible, and change the world for good" (Ehrmann, Ehrmann, & Jordan, 2011, p. 110). What Coach Ehrmann noted is a perspective shared by many researchers and practitioners. That is, a belief that coaches play a key role in helping young athletes not only develop their athletic prowess but, more importantly, develop life skills for personal growth and empowerment as well as help young people learn how to live compassionately and constructively within our communities (Fraser-Thomas, Côté, & Deakin, 2005; Gould, Flett, & Lauer, 2012). One aspect of this personal growth for youth is the development of empathy (Benson, 2006; Eccles & Gootman, 2002; Lerner, Fisher, & Weinberg, 2000). By developing empathy, youth learn to attend to emotional cues, listen, become sensitive to others, understand another's perspective, and read the needs of others, which allows them to work and live with others in the community and act with compassion toward others' needs.

There are many ways that coaches can influence empathy, as well as other facets of positive youth development; however, a foundational aspect is to develop a caring environment. Many researchers have identified caring adults as a critical component of positive youth development physical activity programs (Hellison et al., 2000; Petitpas, Cornelius, Van Raalte, & Jones, 2005). Additionally, researchers have shown the influence of caring environments on empathy within physical activity settings. Newton and colleagues (2007) found that creating a caring environment in a summer youth sport camp resulted in higher levels of empathetic concern among campers compared to campers participating in a traditionally run program. Gano-Overway et al. (2009) extended this work by noting that when youth sport campers perceived a caring climate it was positively associated with empathic efficacy, which, in turn, positively predicted prosocial behaviors. Exploring these connections in the physical education setting, Gano-Overway (in press) found that cognitive empathy mediated the relationship between a perceived caring classroom and prosocial behavior. In exploring caring behaviors, Fry & Gano-Overway (2010) revealed that when young soccer players perceived a caring climate they were more likely to engage in caring behaviors toward their teammates. Therefore, an empirical connection between a caring climate and empathy and helping behaviors exists. Although we need further research to solidify this connection, it does appear valuable now to reflect on and envision what a caring sport climate might entail or how caring coaches engage in the practice of care that could facilitate the development of empathy.

To begin this journey, this chapter explores what we can learn about creating a caring climate from philosophical writings on caring. It is a useful place to begin because it provides insight into why caring is an important endeavor and provides a framework for understanding how we enact caring. Although there are several philosophical viewpoints on caring, two main viewpoints will undergird the explanation of the caring sport climate. These philosophical perspectives include the caring relation and the African ethic of *ubuntu*. While a brief review of each view is provided, it should be noted that each has its own strengths and weaknesses that will not be explicated. Rather, the intent is to glean insight into how effectively to practice care and develop a caring sport climate.

CARING RELATION

Building on the ethic of care (Gilligan, 1993), Noddings (2002, 2003), an educational philosopher, introduced the concept of the caring relation. According to Noddings (2003), the caring relation involves a person caring, referred to as the *one-caring*, and a person receiving care, identified as the *cared-for*. The ethical ideal of the one-caring is derived from two sentiments: a natural sympathy toward others and a "longing to maintain, recapture, or enhance our most caring and tender moments" (Noddings, 2003, p. 104) from natural caring relationships. The one-caring, therefore, has a feeling or sentiment toward caring: a feeling that nudges the person toward an "I must" action not in an obligatory way but in a more natural and desirous way. One wants to care, and this caring is characterized by an attentiveness to the other, that is, engrossment, which leads the one-caring to turn motivational energy, denoted as motivational displacement, toward helping and supporting the cared-for based upon their own caring experiences (Noddings, 2003). However, a caring encounter also depends upon the cared-for acknowledging and responding to the one-caring (Noddings, 2003). Consistent with the ethic of care (Gilligan, 1993), the ethical ideal of the caring relation depends on one's ability to approach the other as one-caring. Therefore, complete self-sacrificial caring is not indicative of a caring relation because the depletion of self, that is, a lack of self-care, diminishes one's ability to care for others (Noddings, 1992).

At the heart of the caring relation is the belief that the primary aim of life involves a sense of relatedness. Specifically, Noddings (2003) contends that the primary aim of life is ". . . caring and being cared for in the human domain and full receptivity and engagement in the nonhuman world" (p. 174). Therefore, by engaging in a caring relation, we not only nurture our ability to care but we also encourage others to join us in the journey by practicing care. In considering this latter point, Noddings (1992, 2002, 2003) contends that through the caring relation, the one-caring can cultivate caring in the cared-for by modeling caring, engaging in dialogue that validates and supports caring, encouraging the cared-for to practice caring, and accepting the cared-for as well as confirming the best possible motives in any given action. Thus, at the core of the caring relation is that we can teach each other to care (Noddings, 2002). As Noddings (2002) states:

> we remain at least partly responsible for the moral development of each person we encounter. How I treat you may bring out the best or worst in you. How you behave may provide a model for me to grow and become better than I am. Whether I can become and remain a caring person—one who enters regularly into caring relations—depends in large part on how you respond to me. (p. 15)

Therefore, a caring relation offers a moral template for life based on relationships. It also provides a framework for moral education that emphasizes the practice of care through engaging in caring relations, thereby, fostering caring in others.

AFRICAN ETHIC OF *UBUNTU*

The African ethic of *ubuntu* is exemplified in the Nguni saying "*Umuntu ngumuntu ngabantu*", that is, "I am because we are" or "a person is a person through other persons" (Metz & Gaie, 2010; Shutte, 1993; Venter, 2004). *Ubuntu* is also often termed *humanness*. According to Tutu (1999), it means, "my humanity is caught up, is inextricably bound up, in yours. We belong in a bundle of life. . . . I am human because I belong, I participate, and I share" (p. 31). It represents not only a sense of communalism in which people share a way of life but also a notion that one achieves humanness and sense of self through the positive interactions with others in the community: in other words, being relational (Metz & Gaie, 2010). So *ubuntu* is "a philosophy that promotes the common good of society and includes humanness as an essential element of human growth" (Venter, 2004, p. 150). Thus, the meaning of one's life, even one's moral obligation, is to achieve humanness, that is, to be relational and communal with others (Metz & Gaie, 2010; Shutte, 2001). However, it is not strictly duty or obligation but rather it exemplifies a way of life in which the person is "wanting to be a real human being or to obtain complete personhood" (Metz & Gaie, 2010, p. 285).

From a relational perspective, the person who possesses *ubuntu* demonstrates respect, empathy, generosity, patience, hospitality, honor, cooperation, and tolerance toward others in the community as well as cares for and helps others (LenkaBula, 2008; Metz & Gaie, 2010; Shutte, 2001; Venter, 2004). Tutu (1999) further elaborates the relational aspect of *ubuntu* by noting:

> A person with *ubuntu* is open and available to others, affirming of others, does not feel threatened that others are able and good; for he or she has a proper self-assurance that comes with knowing that he or she belongs in a greater whole and is diminished when others are humiliated or diminished, when other are tortured or oppressed, or treated as if they were less than who they are. (p. 31)

Thus, those with *ubuntu* engage in practices that promote human flourishing (Shutte, 1993). It should also be emphasized that *ubuntu* is not a doctrine but rather "how to live humanely with others in a given space and time. It is not a device for instrumental formulation of judgment, but a social practice in terms of which to think, to choose, to act and to speak" (Nkondo, 2007, p. 93). This practice or lifestyle would permeate all aspects of one's life.

The communal nature of *ubuntu* occurs when people live in harmony with others (Metz & Gaie, 2010; Venter, 2004). Metz and Gaie (2010) assert that this communal nature includes a duty to identify with others and a duty toward solidarity. The duty to identify with others means that one recognizes that we are all connected. One realizes that the community is self, and the self is community (i.e., one identifies with others). With this realization, a sense of ownership in the good of the community emerges, which nudges the individual to invest in community. The person participates in the practices of the community. Additionally, this notion of community requires a duty toward solidarity. The duty toward solidarity involves the person empathizing and helping others and through this process beginning to recognize the need to be concerned for the common welfare of all in the community. The focus, thus, turns toward solidarity, working together for the common good of those in the community and the community (which are the same). A key practice within community is dialogue (Shutte, 1993). Dialogue is used to develop mutual understanding and empathy, to reach consensus about shared values and purposes, to determine how to achieve common goals, and to handle problems.

The achievement of *ubuntu* is a developmental process in which morals are derived from other fully formed humans (Shutte, 1993).No one is born with *ubuntu*; rather, one's personhood develops over time through interactions with other people, who have sought to achieve *ubuntu*. Shutte

(1993, 2001) provides a three-stage model for how this progression may proceed. In the first stage, an individual needs to become conscious of self. This occurs by being in relation with another caring individual (i.e., a person who recognizes and treats the other as a person). Shutte (1993, 2001) suggests that this can occur in the mother-child relationship where a mother is responsive and caring so that the child is accepted, affirmed, and cared for. The child is valued for her/his own sake. The second stage involves the personal development of self-knowledge and self-affirmation. Although people can grow in self-knowledge and be self-determined on their own, it is unclear whether this knowledge is true. It is through interactions with more knowledgeable others that we come to know whether it is true—others affirm us. Most often, this means that individuals turn to elder members of the community who have a stronger sense of wisdom and *ubuntu*. Further, others teach us how to be because we watch them in action, and they help us shape our affirmations of self and our desires. Accordingly, it is in this stage that the person seeks the help of others to achieve *ubuntu* and personal fulfillment. Thus, education plays a critical role in imparting the philosophical foundations of *ubuntu* to young people (Venter, 2004). The final stage entails self-transcendence and self-donation. The person wants to give self to others and desires to be in relationship. That is, ". . . we want to know and affirm them not primarily so that we will continue to develop as persons, but simply as an end in itself, because they are knowable and affirmable, because it is worthwhile" (Shutte, 1993, p. 87). In the end, a person with *ubuntu* achieves two human desires: to be in community with others and to achieve personal growth (Shutte, 2001). However, it is important to note one caveat. That is, while not all individuals achieve *ubuntu*, it is the ideal for which individuals strive.

Overall, the ethic of *ubuntu* offers a social practice that is both communal and relational. An *ubuntu* community is marked by care, reciprocity, inclusion, forgiveness, and a shared way of life that encourages active participation. Thus, *ubuntu* provides insight into how to live in community by developing solidarity, promoting mutual understanding, and building consensus regarding shared values and practices. Additionally, a person with *ubuntu* engages in a myriad of relational practices in order to nourish and support other human beings, not for personal benefit or gain, but for the other person. Therefore, a structure to nurture *ubuntu* includes developing caring personal relations, teaching *ubuntu* to others, and practicing *ubuntu* in one's community.

The philosophical underpinnings of both the caring relation and the ethic of *ubuntu* provide motivation for and insight into developing a caring climate. Although disparate in some philosophical thinking (e.g., the emphasis on duty and obligation, potential scope of care), they both provide insight into the notion of caring and how it can be fostered and often complement one another. However, how should these notions of caring be put into practice within the youth sport arena? Within this chapter, a three-tiered framework for developing a caring sport climate is proposed. This framework begins with understanding how coaches can develop caring interpersonal relationships that provide a point of connection. The second step of creating a caring climate focuses on how coaches can nurture caring in their athletes. The final step of building a caring climate is to develop a caring team.

CREATING A CARING CLIMATE

Establishing Caring Interpersonal Relationships

To begin, it is important to look at how coaches could pursue caring interpersonal relationships. Noddings (1992, 2003, 2010) provides the most insight through her conceptualization of the caring relation. There are three elements that comprise the caring relation: namely, engrossment, motivational displacement, and recognition. A caring relation begins with receptivity and engrossment by the one-caring. The carer receives the other person by warmly accepting and recognizing the potential in the person (Noddings, 2003). The one-caring is present as an encounter unfolds and is attentive to the expressed needs of the cared-for by listening, empathizing, questioning, rejoicing, and challenging (Noddings, 2003). This engrossment can prompt the one-caring, through sympathetic reactions, to engage in motivational displacement, that is, to help the cared-for (Noddings, 2010). This motivational displacement moves the one-caring's motivational energy away from personal needs and toward supporting the expressed needs of the other. The key to completing the caring relation is that the cared-for needs to recognize the actions of the one-caring and respond (Noddings, 2003). Therefore, the cared-for acknowledges the feelings and sentiments of the one-caring. The cared-for could share accomplishments, hopes, aspirations, dreams, etc., in a sense revealing more about oneself, which is a meaningful gift to the one-caring in and of itself and also provides further insight into how the one-caring can support the cared-for (Noddings, 2003).

The caring relation can take many forms in the athletic environment. For example, upon completing a race, a swimmer is disappointed in her race. The coach approaches her and she shares her disappointment. The coach listens to her and empathizes with her disappointment and frustration. The coach also asks her what she would have done differently. She describes her need to work on her flip turn and her pacing during the race. They agree that they should address these issues in practice next week. Alternatively, caring encounters may not revolve around sport. For instance, a soccer coach sees an athlete enter the locker room visibly upset. When he exits and makes his way to the field the coach decides to walk with him and acknowledges to the player that he sees that he is upset. The athlete begins to describe how he is a failure (i.e., refusing to help his little brother get ready for school, standing by when someone bullies another kid, and failing his first test in chemistry). Throughout this process, the coach listens and empathizes; however, the coach also confirms the potential for a different set of actions for the athlete. The coach sees him, as he wants to be seen, as a caring and intellectually capable young man. The coach provides counterexamples to note how he has been a successful person and notes that it is not too late to rectify these situations. They agree to talk more after practice.

As can be seen in these examples, engaging in a caring relation depends upon dialogue that occurs between the one-caring and the cared-for. It is through dialogue that the one-caring learns of the interests and needs of the cared-for as well as communicates aspects of engrossment. The one-caring takes an invested interest in the cared-for. It is also through dialogue that the one-caring discusses the expressed needs of the cared-for and, if needed, help the cared-for come to understand why some expressed needs may not be supported or should not be pursued. For example, a coach asks a young soccer player, who intentionally pushes an opponent to get the ball, about her action. The child simply states that she wanted the ball so she just pushed the other player out of the way. It would not be enough for the one-caring to state the action was wrong. Rather the caring coach would ask the child what it might have felt like to be pushed away from the ball. The coach may also encourage the child to think about what could have happened if the other girl had fallen and been hurt. The coach may even refer to an incidence a few weeks back when a girl was pushed, fell, and limped off the field crying. The coach may ask the player if she thinks she should apologize for her action. The caring coach would even prompt her to do so. Additionally, the coach would encourage the athlete to think about tactical skills learned in practice to possess the ball. Reminding the player that reaching one's true potential as a soccer player would mean perfecting these tactics rather than pushing, which requires no technical skill. The point of the interaction would be for the young player to learn to become more empathic, see the importance of reducing harm, and inevitably to see the opponent as one-caring. In so doing, the young player comes to realize that intentionally pushing another player is not an appropriate way to achieve the intending goal of possessing the ball. Additionally, it is learned that a better way to achieve what may be the underlying desire of the child, to be a better soccer player, is even jeopardized by such an action. Therefore, it is not to be assumed that the one-caring gives in to the whims of the cared-for. To do so could potentially compromise the ethical ideal of caring or not appropriately prepare the cared-for to live in a civil society. However, what is important is that the one-caring listens to the cared-for and acknowledges the need while providing a rationale for an alternate path through respectful dialogue.

Researchers in the physical activity domain have also acknowledged aspects of the caring relation. For example, Hellison (2011) includes aspects of a caring relation in his framework for Teaching Personal and Social

Responsibility (TPSR), a program that emphasizes building respect, effort and cooperation, self-direction, and caring through physical activity. In the proposed daily curricular components of TPSR, Hellison includes relational time in which the leader is encouraged to interact and get to know each person in the program. The four goals of these "brief relational encounters" are to recognize the strengths and individuality of each person, listen to each person and hear her/his voice, acknowledge the decision-making ability of each person as well as provide an opportunity to practice this ability (Hellison, 2011). In the end, each person is accepted for his/her strengths and individuality and invited to take part in the community. Although these "brief relational encounters" fall short of direct motivational displacement, there is certainly an opportunity for a coach to be motivated to take action to support the athlete if the coach truly becomes attentive to the needs of the athlete. As Hellison (2011) notes, these encounters "help to guide the relational process" (p. 52). Further, in delineating the leader qualities important to being relational, Hellison clearly notes the importance of listening and acting in the best interest of the other that does capture the caring relation.

Overall, creating caring interpersonal relationships requires an intentional approach by the coach that emanates from a genuine commitment to a caring philosophy. This commitment begins with a willingness to truly listen to the athlete and be moved to action on behalf of the other. A caring interpersonal relationship also sets the stage for a caring climate by providing a foundation for trust and mutual respect between the coach and each athlete. This relationship not only fosters a commitment to the community and understanding of the importance of being in relation with others but also helps athletes learn to empathize with and care for others. That is, realizing that others care reawakens our own ability to care for others (Mercado, 1993). We now turn our attention to this endeavor.

Nurturing Care in Athletes

Preparing someone to care is a key element of the caring relation, and this ability to care begins with our experiences in caring (Noddings, 2003, 2010). It is in these experiences that individuals learn the importance of listening to and supporting another individual as well as respecting and accepting others. Additionally, the development of *ubuntu* in young people occurs in relation with others in the family and community (Shutte, 1993, 2001). Thus, it makes sense to begin exploring how coaches can nurture care in their athletes through caring relations. Noddings (2002, 2003) notes that the one-caring can encourage caring in the cared-for through the following four components: modeling, practice, confirmation, and dialogue.

Noddings (2002) notes that there is a rich tradition of modeling within moral education that dates back to Aristotle. In engaging in care, the one-caring is naturally demonstrating to the cared-for what caring is and how it occurs. In a team environment, a coach who is engaging in a caring relation with one athlete provides a model not only for that athlete but also for all athletes on the team. Shutte (1993) in describing the development of *ubuntu* also notes that one learns by observing someone who has *ubuntu*. However, Noddings (2002) notes that the one-caring must be careful not to focus on modeling caring for the benefit of the cared-for but rather focus on the cared-for. Attending to the lesson of caring turns the one-caring's attentional energy away from the cared-for providing a diminished sense of what it means to care. Thus, it should be a model of natural caring. After the fact, the one-caring may engage in self-reflection to determine whether the response was appropriate and effective as well as how things might be done differently in the future (Noddings, 2002). Therefore, as coaches interact with their athletes and engage in caring relations, they should be cognizant of the fact that they are providing a model for how to care and reflect on whether their actions are in line with their philosophy of caring.

Another component of helping individuals learn empathy and caring is to provide opportunities for the practice of care. Noddings (2002) suggests that this is achieved by having individuals engage in caregiving activities or work together. For example, she suggests service learning projects in which the one-caring can have meaningful dialogue and reflections about the experience that connect back to caring. The importance of practicing care and engaging in prosocial behaviors is exemplified in the Child Development Project (CDP), now known as Caring School Community. Battistich and his colleagues created the CDP as an elementary school intervention program focused on nurturing prosocial behaviors in young children (Battistich, Watson, Solomon, Lewis, & Schaps, 1999; Battistich, Watson, Solomon, Schaps & Solomon, 1991; Schaps, 2009). Although it contains many components, relative to our discussion here is their focus on helping activities. Within CDP, children are encouraged to take on responsibilities within the school community like classroom chores, school service projects, or community service projects. Through these activities the children are counseled to reflect on the importance of the activity to the community (e.g., recognizing how their classroom chores help the class function better), encouraged to take on the perspective of another, and learn ways to help others in their community. In the youth sport domain, coaches could assign team members team responsibilities and discuss their importance to the team as well as organize community service events with the assistance of parents to help athletes understand the importance of caring for others in their community.

As the Child Development Project has evolved, an additional emphasis has been placed on children helping other children through cross-age buddy programs (Schaps, 2009). Within these programs, a younger child is paired with an older child, and they work together on service projects, play together during recess and field trips, or the older student helps the younger student with homework. Through this process, kids are practicing caring relations and with self-reflective activities and dialogue with the teacher, the kids learn how to care. Similar ideas have been implemented in physical activity programs. For example, Martinek, Schilling, and Hellison (2006) describe two physical activity programs, the Youth Leader Corp and the Apprentice Teacher Program, that focus on helping youth teach and care for others. The emphasis for these programs is to empower young people by providing opportunities for them to lead others not only in developing sport skills but also in learning social and personal responsibility based on the TPSR framework. Youth leaders, who have participated in the program, create, implement, and evaluate their own lessons for their younger program participants. They also meet with program leaders to hone their physical and social skills and discuss their lessons. Although the lessons vary in their incorporation of TPSR values, youth are given autonomy in the lesson and encouraged, over time, to reflect upon how they can grow as compassionate leaders. Therefore, it is clear that youth sport coaches have a variety of mechanisms for helping young people to practice care, whether that be through buddy systems during practices or creating leadership opportunities that focus not only on demonstrating prowess on the athletic field or promoting a strong work ethic but also by helping to promote shared values surrounding caring.

Flowing directly from the engagement in practice is the act of confirmation. That is, as a child engages in practice, the one-caring looks toward the ethical ideal that the child is capable of achieving and honors the act accordingly. However, when an action is not caring:

> the one-caring considers always the possibility that the one-appearing-to-do-evil is actually in a deteriorated state, that he is acting under intolerable pressure or in error. She retains a responsibility, then, to relieve the pressure and to inform the error; indeed, she remains responsible for the actualization of the other's ethical ideal. (Noddings, 2010, p. 116)

Therefore, confirmation involves affirming the best possible motive for a given action. In the case of an unsuitable act, the other person is given the benefit of the doubt about her/his action while discussing how to more appropriately move toward the desired motive. For example, when a young field hockey player, clearly frustrated by the level of play of one of her teammates, yells at the player and calls her a name. The coach can pull the player aside and affirm her commitment to her team and wanting everyone to play their positions well but discuss alternative methods to communicate this information to her teammates. As Noddings (2002) notes, "it is wonderfully reassuring to realize that another sees the better self that often struggles for recognition beneath our lesser acts and poorer selves" (p. 21).

Underlying the use of modeling, practice, and confirmation in helping young people to understand caring is the need for open dialogue. Dialogue accompanies modeling in that we look at the model, our self or someone else, and discuss what the model did, how the model made others feel, and seek to praise or identify a better action (Noddings, 2010). Dialogue is apparent in sharing our reflections on engaging in caring practices and how these caring practices inform our thoughts and feelings about caring (Noddings, 2002). Dialogue also occurs as the one-caring intentionally recognizes spontaneous engagement in the practice of care by the cared-for and honors this action and/or seeks to help the cared-for refine his/her caring practice. The use of dialogue to confirm the cared-for may also take the form of helping one talk through how to reach her/his true potential and achieve expressed needs in a way that avoids harm and encourages reflection on the consequences of one's actions. As Noddings (2010) states, "There is a commitment to explore with the child the consequences of certain behaviors in light of the conventions of the culture to which the family belongs and to consider alternatives that avoid harm to self and others" (pp. 196–197). The use of dialogue is also key to fostering *ubuntu* as Shutte (1993, 2001) noted in his developmental stages. Therefore, dialogue is a foundational aspect of teaching youth to care and to achieve *ubuntu*.

Overall, the caring relation provides insight into nurturing care within young people by using modeling, practice, confirmation, and dialogue. Incorporating these concepts in their practices, caring coaches can encourage empathy and caring among their athletes.

Developing a Caring Team

In addition to developing caring relations and nurturing caring concepts with athletes, coaches also develop a caring climate by considering how caring permeates all aspects of team culture and community. This harkens back to the *ubuntu* philosophy of sharing a way of life:

> According to Afro-communitarianism, the relevant relationship to prize is not merely one of caring for others' quality of life but, in addition, sharing a way of life. A fundamental moral value for *ubuntu*/botho is identification with others, that is, enjoying a sense of togetherness and coordinating behavior to realize common goals. (Metz & Gaie, 2010, p. 284)

Further, Noddings (2010) does discuss the idea that communities need to be altered so that harmful situations, for example, bullying or antisocial behavior, do not arise because they are counter to the ethic of the community. Thus, care extends beyond a relationship with an individual and just nurturing care to fostering a caring sport community. Caring sport teams can begin by incorporating a set of norms, values, rituals, and language surrounding ideas of caring and *ubuntu*. That is, there is an emphasis on developing a caring sport community. However, building upon practices within *ubuntu* and the caring relation, a caring coach could also incorporate specific caring practices that could further foster a caring sport team. These practices include building solidarity and harmony, promoting inclusion and acceptance, and emphasizing consensus building and community decision making.

Developing the Caring Community

Within a caring team atmosphere, a coach clarifies the norms and values surrounding caring and helps athletes adopt the norms and values of the team. However, individuals are not forced into community; rather, they are helped to see the value of community and sharing a way of life so that they can voluntarily choose to participate (Metz & Gaie, 2010). Therefore, as athletes become familiar with the team norms and values it is hoped that they come to recognize the importance of caring and respectful interactions in a caring sport community and seek to adopt the norms of that community. That is, they know what it feels like to be cared for and want to preserve that community and extend it to others. They come to value the importance of respect, trust, patience, generosity, safety, acceptance, and concern for others by having these values practiced on them. By teaching these norms, practicing them, and encouraging their practice in others, the norms become valued and adopted within the team. Over time, these norms become part of the shared history of the team that each new member learns as they enter the team. That is, storytelling of caring, tough love, respect, learning to appreciate others, joy, overcoming obstacles, etc., are shared with new members and revisited by current and retired members. Those stories of who we are and what we stand for related to caring become part of team lore. Additionally, rituals and symbols that emphasize caring norms are developed. For example, a team that does a high ropes course at the beginning of each season, which focuses on trust, support, and shared commitment, can become a team ritual. This ritual creates a shared emotional experience that reinforces the team norms that are dialogued, modeled, and practiced throughout the athletic season. Through these strategies, coaches help athletes understand the importance of community and invite athletes to take part as noted by Metz and Gaie (2010). Additionally, coaches build the foundation of community by developing a shared history, emotional connections, and shared rituals and symbols (McMillan & Chavis, 1986).

Building Solidarity and Harmony

A distinguishing element of *ubuntu* is the idea that individuals enter into community with others and seek to live in harmony with others while working toward achievement of the common good (Metz & Gaie, 2010). Thus, an individual within community is working toward living in solidarity and harmony. Inherently built into sport is the notion of solidarity. That is, a team working together to achieve a common goal that encourages all athletes to strive for improvement (i.e., personal growth). Shutte (2001) stated that sport provides a good learning ground for teaching the social practice of *ubuntu* because athletes have an opportunity to work toward solidarity and develop team harmony. Young athletes could come to recognize the importance of collective efforts toward achieving goals as well as learn their responsibility to the community in achieving the group's goals. Team members also learn the importance of supporting one another's goals and encouraging others in their pursuit as the individual's goals represent the accomplishment of the team's goals. As athletes engage in these actions, they work toward solidarity; some would say, foster teamwork. However, it goes a bit deeper. What is desired and supported is not only the achievement of the collective goals and how athletes work together to achieve them but also how people support one another's individual accomplishment and the community. Individuals recognize that they are the community, and they become more fully human when they engage in and support the community and its goals. Thus, out of necessity to help the team succeed, athletes learn to consider the needs and perspectives of others and recognize the need to work together and place the team ahead of self. It is also not only about winning and physical improvement but also about fully developing one's humanity. Athletes come to understand how their interactions with others on the team can influence team harmony and learn strategies for maintaining harmony or dealing with conflict that could disrupt harmony. They learn to empathize and care for the betterment of all individuals on the team. They work toward helping one another achieve *ubuntu*. However, just by participating in sport youth will not necessarily learn these lessons. Coaches must teach and reinforce the concepts of harmony and solidarity and then have athletes practice the lessons learned within the context of sport.

Promoting Inclusion and Acceptance

Another element of the caring atmosphere is acceptance and inclusion. In many ways, this reflects the caring relation at a team level. In the athletic realm, this may take the form of the coach helping athletes maintain their own voice or reclaim it by accepting them for who they are while also encouraging them to be in relation with others on a team that promotes the same acceptance. All members of the team feel included, valued, and accepted. This inevitably means that the environment is physically and emotionally safe so that all individuals feel safe to speak their voice and be themselves. This does not necessarily mean that all actions each athlete takes are acceptable, and some actions are unacceptable, but that the athlete is accepted. Additionally, while all team members are accepted for where they are right now, their potential is also confirmed, and they are encouraged to achieve this potential, not only athletic potential but potential as a person. So all team members are welcomed into the community, and each member is encouraged to engage in caring relations (i.e., engrossment and motivational displacement) as well as practice *ubuntu* (i.e., respect others, empathize with and care for others, be generous and patient, hospitable, and tolerant). Athletes get to know one another and support one another as well as accept and affirm one another. As Battistich (2008) contends, a teacher, in our case "coach", creates an environment where relationships among all students are exemplified by caring not just the relationship between teacher and each individual student. All communal relationships are of great value and need to be nurtured (Metz & Gaie, 2010).

Emphasizing Consensus Building and Community Decision Making

Although a team is marked by its traditions, rituals, and rules that guide the community toward its common objective of developing caring young people, this does not mean that the individual team member is not heard or that a coach exercises autocratic power in dictating what occurs on the team. A caring team embodies the *ubuntu* notion of consensus building. Consensus building allows each person to voice concerns as others listen. Once mutual understanding is achieved, group members work toward consensus on the issue at hand. Thus, demanding blind conformity is not desirable and could not be if the one "in power" is practicing *ubuntu*. Rather, team members are exposed to traditions, norms, and rules; critically think about them before adopting them as their own; and are called to think about self within the group rather than the self alone (Metz & Gaie, 2010). In a way youth come to understand the workings of the team because there is a level of transparency, and athletes are encouraged to participate in the community. Further, these norms and traditions can be questioned and through mutual understanding consensus is achieved about whether and how these rules should continue. However, in consensus building all individuals must be open minded (i.e., each person looks toward the other as the cared-for and practices engrossment and motivational displacement). However, where expressed needs of individuals conflict, further discourse occurs until it becomes clear why some expressed needs may not be in the best interest of the individual and/or the community. For example, a coach may have a rule that his middle school basketball players do not engage in trash talk toward their opponents. The practice following a very intense game where trash talking occurred on both sides, the coach discusses the use of trash talking. The coach reminds players of the rule; and one player, who is a frequent offender, notes her opposition to the rule. Under consensus building, what would follow is an opportunity for the player to voice her opposition to the rule and provide a rationale for her position followed by the coach providing a rationale for his position. Other members of the team would also note their thoughts on the rule. Throughout the process, all voices would be heard, and at some point consensus would be achieved. However, this may not be accomplished before this one practice session. It may be a series of conversations and practiced actions where players evaluate the influence of trash talking on them and other individuals before consensus is achieved. As an aside, it is important to note that consensus building will not work effectively if the person does not feel s/he is cared for in the community. Thus, a caring relation and a sense of empathy are clearly intertwined with this notion of mutual understanding and consensus. Further, from a pragmatic standpoint it is important to note that solidarity is sometimes not achieved through consensus building and rather tolerance is pursued.

Another important aspect of consensus building relates to the conception of power. Traditionally, power has been defined as one having power over another; however, power can also be negotiated (Dominelli & Gollins, 1997). Thus, power fluctuates based on situational factors and one's own agency (e.g., one can freely give up power or negotiate for power with another). On a caring team, this can even be more common as there is a mutual dependency for the good of the team. So each person's power can be challenged, and people need to negotiate with one another to reach objectives. This inherently implies that individuals must navigate the use of their own agency in the process while empathetically considering those within the community.

Embedded in consensus building is the notion that each individual is empowered by the community to take an active role, and individuals engage in community decision making because they have a sense of ownership in the community. However, this involvement may be lessened by the knowledge, expertise, and development of the individual. Battistich and his colleagues (1997) believed that community decision making, in which children were involved in setting classroom rules and norms and having choice in learning activities, was a key component of a caring school community. Schaps (2009) also noted the importance of providing students "voice and choice" in the classroom so that students can have a voice in the decision-making process and choice over activities. Noddings (2003) also speaks to this idea by suggesting that a teacher seeks students' perspectives and identifies their needs and interests, which can then be incorporate into curriculum planning. Clearly, a sense of autonomy is encouraged relative to group engagement. By empowering kids to make decisions within the community and holding them accountable for their actions, they learn to take personal and social responsibility (Hellison, 2011) as well as see the influence of their decisions on the community, further developing their empathy. Reviewing the elements of community, Battistich and his colleagues (1997) stated that

> communities are defined as places where members care about and support each other, actively participate in and have influence on the group's activities and decisions, feel a sense of belonging and identification with the group, and have common norms, goals, and values. (p. 137)

Many of those elements are captured in the components discussed here for creating caring teams. By developing norms, values, and rituals based on caring and *ubuntu*, coaches begin the process of developing a caring sport community. The caring sport community is further instilled by building solidarity and harmony, promoting inclusion and acceptance, and emphasizing consensus building and community decision making.

CONCLUSION

The popularity of sport among youth and the communal nature of sport make it a perfect vehicle to help young people develop into more caring and socially and emotionally competent individuals who come to understand the importance of participating in one's community. However, sport participation alone will not guarantee such a transformation; rather, coaches need to create a climate, a caring climate, for this to occur. As noted throughout this chapter, a caring climate is denoted by being in relation with others, nurturing caring in athletes, and developing a caring team. Thus, caring, as informed by, although not completely adopting all aspects of, the caring relation and the African ethic of *ubuntu*, permeates all aspects of the sport team.

Overall, the caring sport climate has the potential to provide an environment where young people can feel safe; cared for; and accepted; and in so doing, help them come to find their own voice and realize their own potential. A caring sport climate also sets the stage for young people to learn how to develop empathy—a key building block—to being in relation and living in community with others, which are important skills for living in a civil society. However, for this to take place coaches need to be intentional in establishing a caring sport climate and authentically practice it. The framework discussed here provides a place to begin that endeavor.

REFERENCES

Battistich, V. (2008). Voices: A practitioner's perspective: Character education, prevention, and positive youth development. *Journal of Research in Character Education, 6*, 81–90.

Battistich, V., Solomon, D., Watson, M., & Schaps, E. (1997). Caring school communities. *Educational Psychologist, 32*, 137–151.

Battistich, V., Watson, M., Solomon, D., Lewis, C., & Schaps, E. (1999). Beyond the three R's: A broader agenda for school reform. *Elementary School Journal, 99*, 415–431.

Battistich, V., Watson, M., Solomon, D., Schaps, E., & Solomon, J. (1991). The Child Development Project: A comprehensive program for the development of prosocial character. In W. M. Kurtines & J. L. Gewirtz (Eds.), *Handbook of moral behavior and development: Vol 3. Application* (pp. 1–34). Hillsdale, NJ: Lawrence Erlbaum Associates.

Benson, P. L. (2006). *All kids are our kids: What communities must do to raise caring and responsible children and adolescents* (2nd ed.). San Francisco, CA: Jossey-Bass.

Dominelli, L., & Gollins, T. (1997). Men, power, and caring relationships. *Sociological Review, 45*, 396–415.

Eccles, J. S., & Gootman, J. A. (Eds.). (2002). *Community programs to promote youth development*. Washington, DC: National Academy Press.

Ehrmann, J., Ehrmann, P., & Jordan, G. (2011). *InSideOut coaching: How sports can transform lives*. NY: Simon & Schuster.

Fraser-Thomas, J. L., Côté, J., & Deakin, J. (2005). Youth sport programs: An avenue to foster positive youth development. *Physical Education and Sport Pedagogy, 10*, 19–40. doi: 10.1080=1740898042000334890

Fry, M. D., & Gano-Overway, L. A. (2010). Exploring the contribution of the caring climate to the youth sport experience. *Journal of Applied Sport Psychology, 22,* 294–304.

Gano-Overway, L. A. (2013). Exploring the connections between caring and social behaviors in physical education. *Research Quarterly for Exercise and Sport, 84(1),* 104–114.

Gano-Overway, L. A., Newton, M., Magyar, T. M., Fry, M., Kim, M., & Guivernau, M. (2009). Influence of caring youth sport contexts on efficacy-related beliefs and social behaviors. *Developmental Psychology, 45(2),* 329–340.

Gilligan, C. (1993). *In a different voice. Psychological theory and women's development.* Cambridge, MA: Harvard University Press. (Original work published in 1982.)

Gould, D., Flett, R., & Lauer, L. (2012). The relationship between psychosocial developmental and the sports climate experienced by underserved youth. *Psychology of Sport and Exercise, 13,* 80–87. doi: 10.1016/j.psychsport.2011.07.005

Hellison, D. (2011). *Teaching personal and social responsibility through physical activity* (3rd ed.). Champaign, IL: Human Kinetics.

Hellison, D., Cutforth, N., Kallusky, J., Martinek, T., Parker, M., & Stiehl, J. (2000). *Youth development and physical activity: Linking universities and communities.* Champaign, IL: Human Kinetics.

LenkaBula, P. (2008). Beyond anthropocentricity—Botho/*Ubuntu* and the quest for economic and ecological justice in Africa. *Religion & Theology, 15,* 375–394. doi: 10.1163/157430108X376591

Lerner, R. M., Fisher, C. M., & Weinberg, R. A. (2000). Toward a science for and of the people: Promoting civil society through the application of developmental science. *Child Development, 71,* 11–20.

Martinek, T., Schilling, T., & Hellison, D. (2006). The development of compassionate and caring leadership among adolescents. *Physical Education and Sport Pedagogy, 11,* 141–157.

McMillan, D. W., & Chavis, D. M. (1986). Sense of community: A definition and theory. *Journal of Community Psychology, 14,* 6–23.

Mercado, C. I. (1993). Caring as empowerment. School collaboration and community agency. *The Urban Review, 25,* 79–104.

Metz, T., & Gaie, J.B.R. (2010). The African ethic of *Ubuntu*/Botho: Implications for research on morality. *Journal of Moral Education, 39,* 273–290.

Newton, M., Watson, D. L., Gano-Overway, L., Fry, M., Kim, M., & Magyar, M. (2007). The role of a caring-based intervention in a physical domain. *The Urban Review, 39,* 281–299.

Nkondo, G. M. (2007). *Ubuntu* as public policy in South Africa: A conceptual framework. *International Journal of African Renaissance Studies, 2,* 88–100. doi: 10.1080/18186870701384202

Noddings, N. (1992). *The challenge to care in schools: An alternative approach to education.* NY: Teacher College Press.

Noddings, N. (2002). *Educating moral people: A caring alternative to character education.* NY: Teacher College Press.

Noddings, N. (2003). *Caring: A feminine approach to ethics and moral education.* Berkeley: University of California Press. (Original work published in 1984.)

Noddings, N. (2010). *The maternal factor: Two paths to morality.* Berkeley: University of California Press.

Petitpas, A. J., Cornelius, A. E., Van Raalte, J. L., & Jones, T .(2005). A framework for planning youth sport programs that foster psychosocial development. *The Sport Psychologist, 19,* 63–80.

Schaps, E. (March/April 2009). Creating caring school communities. *Leadership,* 8–11.

Shutte, A. (1993). *Philosophy for Africa.* Milwaukee, WI: Marquette University Press.

Shutte, A. (2001). *Ubuntu: An ethic for a new South Africa*. Republic of South Africa: Cluster.

Tutu, D. M. (1999). *No future without forgiveness*. NY: Doubleday.

Venter, E. (2004). The notion of *Ubuntu* and communalism in African educational discourse. *Studies in Philosophy and Education, 23*, 149–160.

11 ... Ad Floridam

Joanna Beth Tweedy

Amid the swell of celestial symphony, a measure
of sentience summons the might of a soul:
ours is the distillate hush of
discernment, coalescing
  time, culture, distance;
ours is the welkin mystery of union,
unraveling, cradling, full
of grace and shadow, where the bone
center of everything is liquescent, and we are
in every part the whole.

12 Transcendent Empathy

The Ability to See the Larger System

Peter Senge and Keiko Krahnke

A human being is a part of a whole, called by us the Universe, a part limited in time and space. He experiences himself, his thoughts and feelings, as something separated from the rest—a kind of optical delusion of his consciousness. This delusion is a kind of prison for us, restricting us to our personal desires and to affection for a few persons nearest us. Our task must be to free ourselves from this prison by widening our circles of compassion to embrace all living creatures and the whole of nature in its beauty.

Albert Einstein

INTRODUCTION

We are in a transformative era characterized by complex and systemic changes, and we face unprecedented uncertainty (Kelly, 2006). We have made tremendous advancements in science and technology with which we have attempted to control our world. In spite of the fact that mysteries abound, we still prefer certainty and clarity to make sense of the world, and default to an "either/or" mindset (Kelly, 2006). In fact, we have learned how to influence our environment to the extent that our very survival as a species is now at risk as a consequence of our own power. Many of the social, economic, political, and environmental challenges that we face today are complex, and may be consequences of our own actions and modes of thinking. The issues we face are not only complex, but also confusing and difficult to interpret because of their contradictory nature (Kelly, 2006). For example, the world is becoming increasingly transparent due to our ability to access and distribute so much information, but at the same time we may be experiencing more confusion because of information overload that is leading to "competing interpretations of major world events driven by ideology and informed by selective 'evidence'" (Kelly, 2006, p. 21). Many of the issues are now serious problems that cannot be solved easily or quickly, and could become irreversible if we ignore them.

One such complex issue is climate change, which most people have finally come to believe is really happening. The IPCC (Intergovernmental Panel on

Climate Change) reports that "it is virtually certain that increases in the frequency and magnitude of warm daily temperature extremes and decreases in cold extremes will occur in the 21st century at the global scale" (2012, p. 13). Over the past few decades, as the incidence of extreme storms caused by warming ocean temperatures has grown, the price of property and liability insurance industry has increased to the point that the industry is priced out of many markets. There is growing evidence of interactions among otherwise distinct environmental stresses—like recently discovered links between climate change (caused largely by burning fossil fuels and other greenhouse gases) and ozone loss (caused by commercial and residential use of CFCs) caused by extreme storms sending water vapor into the stratosphere, which further destroys the ozone layer and increases ultraviolet dosage (Anderson, Wilmouth, Smith, & Sayers, 2012). These storms will cause more disasters, and increased UV dosage will pose health risks. Even though scientists have reached consensus on basic conclusions, the process of taking action has been slowed by groups opposing changes in energy policies, many with strong stakes in the energy status quo. It is also a complex process to engage all the necessary parties globally in working toward a solution. If we do not make a concerted effort, increased cases of disaster and illness are predicted.

Planetary resources are also a concern. Humans occupy less than 1% of biomass on the planet but use 24% of all photosynthesis (Rifkin, 2009). It takes the earth one year and six months to regenerate the resources humanity uses in a year, a serious threat to the health of humans and the planet (World Footprint). Extreme poverty and inequality on a global scale are evidence of this threat. "The poorest 40 percent of the world's population accounts for 5 percent of global income. The richest 20 percent account for three-quarters of world income" (Shah, 2010). Wealth disparities are even greater. Poverty kills 22,000 children each year, and in developing countries, 27–28% of all children are underweight (Shah, 2010). Our children's physical and emotional well-being is a good measure of our societal well-being and generativity (Olfman, 2006), and the conditions in which many children live today indicate future risks on a global scale.

Tackling these issues will require different ways of thinking since many of these problems arise from our own habitual ways of thinking or acting. Ironically, we are probably better prepared for sudden, external, dramatic events than ever before. But, we are still slow to recognize threats that come gradually. Our media focuses almost exclusively on short-term "news". The increasing speed of communication has if anything inured us further to slow gradual changes. With ever-shorter attention spans, we find ourselves, ironically, both more well informed and more incapable of addressing the threats that pose the greatest danger to us.

Our addiction to quick fixes combined with deep-rooted ways of thinking based on fragmentation and competition may be to blame for many of the issues we face today, but the good news is that there is also evidence that shifts in thinking are beginning to happen. Increased discussion about connectedness, partnerships (Seitanidi & Crane, 2009), and relationships (Quinn,

2007) is occurring. More and more businesses are recognizing that, as the CEO of Unilever put it recently, "You cannot build a healthy company in an unhealthy society" (Senge, Smith, Kruschwitz, Laur, & Schley, 2008). And, there is growing appreciation for cooperation, and working across institutional boundaries will be vital to achieve needed changes, as illustrated by the 10-year board-to-board partnership between Unilever and Oxfam focused on reducing rural poverty through pro-poor business innovations. Collaborative initiatives are starting to focus on increasingly bold aims. For example, in 2012, the World Bank announced the "50 in 10" project, to bring 50% of the world's fisheries under sustainable management within 10 years—a historic undertaking that can only be achieved by unprecedented levels of collaboration among business, government, and civil society organizations.

As systemic change efforts elicit different kinds of thinking and scales of collaboration, we will learn how to learn differently. We are most accustomed to learning from the past. Although the past provides important lessons, it alone is not a sufficient guide when the future is likely to differ fundamentally from the past. In such times, Scharmer (2007, 2013) suggests that we learn from the future as it emerges. In some ways, both teachers and leaders have to be prophets since we are preparing people for tomorrow. As Kahlil Gibran said in his poem, *Children*, "For their souls dwell in the house of tomorrow, which you cannot visit, not even in your dreams. You may strive to be like them, but strive not to make them like you. For life goes not backwards nor tarries with yesterday" (Gibran, 1923, p. 17).

In this chapter, we explore a new framework for understanding these changes, which builds on something well understood and which has garnered increasing attention in recent years: empathy. We suggest that empathy is something broader than knowing or feeling another person's psychological or emotional state. The fundamental concept of empathy is to care about another as if you were in the shoes of the other. Our purpose here is to expand this caring to the larger living systems of which we are a part. We propose the notion of "transcendent empathy" as the ability to see these larger systems in time and space, to move beyond mere intellectual understanding to embrace "system sensing" as a doorway to both awareness of what exists now and to future possibilities. In the first part of this chapter, we discuss the need to understand a system. We then illustrate different types of transcendent empathy. We also explore the shifting notion of human nature and the concept of self, and finally, ways to cultivate transcendent empathy.

NEED FOR UNDERSTANDING A SYSTEM

Toward Seeing Processes, Patterns, and Wholes

Many of us have been trained in the machine model of thinking and been taught to see "things" instead of "processes" and '"individuals and cause and effect" instead of "webs of interconnectedness". We, especially in the

West, analyze virtually everything by breaking things down to parts and assuming that we can put the parts back together to understand the whole. This fragmentation extends to the learning process itself. Although some educators strive to make learning more connected and meaningful, education for the most part is still fragmented and disconnected from the real world and the learner. The silo model, in which disciplines are isolated from each other and in which disconnected facts are taught, is still the norm, and education is often not directly connected to personal growth in any meaningful way. Kind, Irwin, Grauer, and De Cosson (2005) noted, "Education is longing for a deeper more connected, more inclusive, and more aware way of knowing. One that connects heart and hand and head and does not split knowledge into dualities of thought and being, mind and body, emotion and intellect, but resonates with a wholeness and fullness that engages every part of one's being" (p. 33).

Our habit of analyzing each part is deep seated. Throughout our formal education, we have been conditioned to look at parts in isolation rather than how the parts are interact with each other, whether the subject is biology, physics, or human organization. An organization, just like a natural system, is not a collection of individuals thrown together but a self-creating web of intentions and actions.

Maturana and Varela's work (1980) on autopoiesis and cognition inspires us to better understand a human organization in light of the complexities of natural systems. They define a living system as an "autopoietic" (self-producing) system (Maturana & Varela, 1980) where parts exist in relation to other parts and to the whole. An autopoietic system is a "a network of process of production (transformation and destruction) . . . that produces the components which: (i) through their interactions and transformations continuously regenerate and realize the network of processes (relations) that produced them; and (ii) constitute it (the system) . . . as a concrete unity in the space in which they (the components) exist by specifying the topological domain of its realization as such a network" (p. 79).

Such a view of organization lays a foundation for discussing corporate citizenship or responsibility. As Waddock says, "Corporate citizenship is an integral part of the whole corporation as it exists in whole communities and whole societies, with whole people operating within" (2009, p. 4). The concept of wholes within wholes reminds us of the physicist Bohm's (1980) notion of "enfoldment", where seemingly separate entities are closely connected and that each part contains information about the whole, like the DNA embedded in each cell. This concept also reflects Talbot's argument (1991) that the universe is holographic, meaning that every part of the hologram contains the image of the whole, which is enfolded in every part of the universe.

Reflection and Seeing the Real Issue Beyond the Symptoms

"It is only through reflection that we escape our history", says Maturana. As we go about tackling complex issues within an organization or in society, we tend to forget to ask ourselves what thinking caused the problem and whether or not we are still thinking in the way that created the problem in the first place. When we fail to reflect, we fail to realize the depth of understanding needed to truly find new ways to confront complex issues.

One consequence of our nonreflective approach is the habit of adopting quick fixes to treat problem symptoms and failing to see deeper causes. Treating symptoms may be necessary at times, but we must be careful not to mistake treating symptoms for solving the problem and especially to continue doing so, typically because it is easier and efficient in making the pain or discomfort go away temporarily. Continually opting for short-term relief, we may not realize that symptoms are gradually worsening while the deeper causes of the problem continue to be neglected. Resorting to symptomatic solutions is part of a system archetype called "shifting the burden" (Senge, 1990; Senge, Kleiner, Roberts, Ross, & Smith, 1994; www. pegasuscom.com).

There are many problems in that we attempt to solve by only fixing symptoms, not the core problems, from common treatments in Western medicine to chronic societal problems like inner city crime. We also know that careless treatment of symptoms sometimes brings unintended consequences. For example, overuse of antibiotics has caused an increase in some illnesses such as diabetes, allergies, and asthma, as well as the creation of a drug-resistant microbe populations (Parry, 2011, 2012)—just as building prisons to address crime has created a booming private sector business around incarceration in the United States, and with it a powerful political lobby that reminds Americans that they are safer with criminals securely behind bars.

Similarly, if we just react to the symptom of food shortage, one might assume that mass production or factory farming is a necessary and effective way to treat the symptom of feeding the hungry by generating food as cheaply and quickly as possible. However, hunger is a very complex social, political, and economic problem, and treating this symptom by supposedly efficient mass production may actually be worsening the real problem. Factory farming takes an enormous amount of resources, leaves a large ecological footprint, and contributes significantly to climate change both through shipping food great distances (about 2,000 miles for the average pound of food sold in the United States) and through clearing land for livestock and feed production ("emissions from deforestation, overgrazing, compaction, and erosion"; Lappe, 2010, p. 244). Factory farms use large amounts of fossil-fuel based inputs, pollute water, drive small farms out of business, and destroy natural habitat in the United States and in other countries, negatively affecting biodiversity and contributing to health problems—indirectly perpetuating hunger. Most of these deleterious effects arise as "externalities", compounding side effects of a complex array of symptomatic quick fixes largely invisible to the proponents of the factory farm solution.

In order to see real issues, we need to see connections and patterns. But to see these connections, we must often first recognize our own blindspots. None of us see reality in total or without bias. "All things said are said by somebody", says Maturana (Maturana & Varela 1987, p. 26)—a gentle reminder that we can easily forget our prejudices and think "we have a privileged view of reality", one that actually "sees things as they are", what philosophers often call "naïve realism". Appreciating the challenge of seeing deeply into the nature of real problems leads to a new appreciation of collaboration: Together we can see what none of us can see alone. Only by building capacity to reflect, individually and collectively, can we cultivate an eye with which to see beyond symptoms and comprehend what we are really looking at.

TRANSCENDENT EMPATHY: EMPATHY AS THE ABILITY TO SEE THE LARGER SYSTEM

A variety of disciplines today are focusing on the processes and nature of empathy. Neuroscience research has made a significant impact with the discovery of "mirror neurons", showing that humans are hardwired to feel what another is feeling, and that the ability to empathize extends beyond our species (de Waal, 2006). Empathy is often referred to as an emotional or cognitive state where we experience another's experience or plight. Empathy is "an affective response more appropriate to someone else's situation than to one's own" (Hoffman, 1987, p. 48). Greason and Cashwell state that empathy "requires an ability to suspend judgment and bias to walk in another's shoes" (2009, p. 4).

But, the process of extending our awareness emotionally and cognitively is not limited to interpersonal situations. We believe it is possible to feel the suffering of a family, or a community, or a society—not just as an intellectual extension of feeling the suffering of individual members but as a larger whole. So, too, can you feel the energy and creativity when the larger whole is healthy and vibrant, as in generative teams or artistic communities giving birth collectively to new forms of expression. If we see empathy as that which allows us to sense beyond our immediate environment, we can see how important it is to dealing with interconnectedness. As we have written elsewhere, "Empathy is the force that makes a community whole through recognizing the interconnectedness and interdependencies among us rather than it merely being a collection of individuals" (Pavlovich & Krahnke, 2012, p. 136).

In the broadest sense, empathy is the ability to transcend our ego and see and sense larger systems. We experience empathy when we care about people who have experienced a disaster regardless of where they might be or whether or not we know them. During disasters and tragedies such as hurricane Katrina, the tsunami in Japan, or a mass shooting of school children, many people all over the world reach out to help. The nuclear plant explosion during the Great Tohoku earthquake in Japan made us realize that the event was not just contained in one country, but rather had global ramifications, and we started a more serious discussion about energy sources and consequences of natural disasters.

This "transcendent empathy" also operates when we make a connection and imagine the consequences of our own actions. In a global marketplace, it is not always easy to know where or how the products we use everyday have been produced. Our cell phones may have been assembled by a 13-year-old who had given up school to work in a factory to support a family. It is ironic that a garment that carries a tag that says "A portion of the proceeds goes to help children in need" may have actually been made by a child in need. Do we ever wonder how we may indirectly contribute to deforestation in South East Asia by purchasing products that contain unsustainably produced palm oil? Large-scale deforestation not only impacts our climate through direct release of carbon into the atmosphere and loss of carbon sequestration but it also destroys habitat critical for species, including endangered species such as orangutans.

Our desire to be more cognizant about ways we contribute to problems and make wiser choices that benefit the whole is getting tested in the marketplace around the world today. Fifteen years ago when the "fair-trade" movement was starting, many doubted the extent of market demand for higher-priced products aimed at assuring livable wages for their producers. In fact, fair-trade coffee became the fastest growing segment of the industry, and the bigger problem became lack of credible supply—not lack of demand. While obviously just a single example confined mostly to U.S. and European consumers, there is little doubt among leaders in the corporate sustainability movement that the latent demand of consumers to express their concern about the larger system through their purchases (versus their charitable contributions) is the key to how far this movement will progress.

This concern for others at a distance is but one characteristic of transcendent empathy, which we attempt to illustrate below.

How Wide Can Our "Circle of Compassion" Spread—Empathy as Biosphere Consciousness

Many of us consider ourselves to be caring and empathic individuals. It is easy to empathize with family members or close friends, but less so with neighbors and even less with strangers who live in the same town. We may empathize more with people who have the same culture or religion we do than with people who have other cultures and religions. As we go further and further to outer circles of lesser commonality and contact, the depth of our empathy may diminish.

How far our empathy extends reflects the degree to which we anchor in a localized notion of self. We feel the feelings of others but only to the extent we know them or can identify with them personally. While this may seem understandable, it is so because our culture reinforces identification with a localized self, such as when we think we are our physical body. In other cultures and traditions, people learn to extend their sense of self to sense other beings at a distance and even all of nature. For example, in Buddhist theory, one definition of a Bodhisattva is one who can radiate compassion into an infinite space. While such notions are foreign to our Western culture, they may hold keys to what will be needed in our future.

A recent NPR special on encroaching seawaters along the coast of New England included a poignant interview with a third-generation resident of Plum Island. When her grandfather built her home, it was 300 yards from the ocean, meaning that "We would always be safe even in severe storms". Today the sea has reclaimed this treasured safety buffer and water now comes below the foundation, meaning very possibly that the next major storm could lead the house to collapse and be pulled into the sea. Today ocean levels are rising due to warming and melting glaciers and ice sheets. The oceans have been here before. The last time the earth had no ice was about 30–40 million years ago, only about 1% of the planet's history. Inland seas covered much of the land, radically altering the familiar outlines of the continents. Aradhna Tripati, a UCLA scientist, and her colleagues report that average global mean temperatures were 5–10 degrees Fahrenheit (3–6 degree C) higher than they are today (Wolpert, 2009). One can almost sense the rise and fall of oceans as a grand cycle that influences all life in its ebb and flow.

Will we learn to sense the fluxes of the larger earth system—especially in time to nurture an expanded empathy for the well-being of our species and the biosphere? Perhaps the same communication technology that has dissolved physical distance and makes us feel others in times of need will help. A mere century ago, it would have been unthinkable for people to empathetically respond when disasters befell people they do not know on the other side of the planet. In the past decade, there have been a number of cases of people all over the world coming together to solve a problem when information went viral through social media. In his book, *Empathic Civilization*, Rifkin (2009) discusses how empathy has evolved from blood ties, to religious ties, to national ties, and he says it may not be such a stretch to think that technology will connect our empathy with all humanity and other species. He says in an interview by TVO, "Empathy is our invisible hand. It allows us to stretch our sensibility with another so we can cohere in larger social units" (2010). Philosopher Ervin Laszlo argues that our survival may require a concept of self that will be less ego centered and foster "greater empathy among people, and greater sensitivity to animals, plants, and the entire biosphere. It could create subtle contact with the rest of the cosmos" (Laszlo, 2007, p. 130). Otto Scharmer and Katrin Kaeufer's recent book (2013) outlines eight major systems, including capital, consumption, technology, and ownership that are transforming guided by subtle shifts from ego- to eco-system awareness.

Empathy as the Recognition That We Cocreate the World

We have created a society that is quick to find someone to blame for any problem. Finger pointing seems virtually ubiquitous and can be disheartening to watch, such as in political campaigns. But when we understand the interrelationships and complexities of a system, we can see that we are all trapped in structures—structures deeply embedded in our thinking. There isn't just one person to blame for most issues; typically, each one of us has contributed in some way or another. We may criticize the oil and gas companies, but we buy their products. We may dislike intrusive advertising but the messages conveyed are the ones we pay attention to.

Transcendent empathy starts here: knowing that we are all caught in systems which dictate how we think and behave and which we in turn reenforce by our ways of thinking and behaving. "First we shape the walls, and then the walls shape us", as Winston Churchill observed. The rules that govern life in every organization are rarely written down. Rather they are "enacted" by the organizations' members as they go about their day-to-day ways of solving problems and getting their work done—just like tacit structures of habitual thought and action that shape how a family works. It is humbling to recognize that we have cocreated the world in which we live, but it is also the source of systemic compassion. Although we in the United States tend to look for a leader who will magically transform the society, it is naïve to assume that one person can fundamentally change a system. It takes a reflective and caring community to create the conditions for systemic change.

Consider the problem of street dog fighting among inner city teenagers. Dog fighting is illegal in all states in the United States, and it is easy to be horrified by such a cruel "sport". Seeing bloody, badly injured dogs, most people understandably react with anger toward the boys and men involved. It is easy to point fingers at these people and call them criminals and think tougher laws or stronger enforcement is needed to solve the problem. There certainly are criminals who organize and profit from this practice and should be punished accordingly—but what is the core issue, and how are we all part of it? National Public Radio (NPR) had a powerful story of a former dog fighter who now helps these young men and guides them to live a life with more constructive and meaningful activities. He described these young men's lives as lives with no hope, lives consumed by crime and drugs. They have been told they are "nobody" and having a tough, mean dog is one of the only ways they know how to feel and show self-worth. Seeing this reality helps us realize that the real problem beneath street dog fighting is poverty, desperation, and lack of hope. We cannot save the dogs from the cruelty of fighting without saving these young men.

Dog fighting is a visible tip of a large iceberg most of us in America try to avoid. With less than 5% of the world population, the United States now has over 25% of the world's prison inmates (Kelley, 2012). With many aspects of prison operations privatized, incarceration has become big business today in America, and we are all part of this by our lack of societal commitment to a problem that has been growing for over a generation. The fact that some of our young are living in poverty and desperation with no hope for the future is a collective, not individual, problem. It connects to education, social services, criminal justice, business, and ultimately our models of economic development. Seeing these connections does not make it easier to solve, but more systemic solutions will never come if we fail to see more of the whole of the problem.

It takes courage and deep awareness to recognize the systems in which we are trapped. Once we learn to step back and observe the situation instead of immediately resorting to knee jerk reactions, we can begin to see the habits or the mental models that hold us back, like our fear of people who grow up in circumstances very different from our own. This seeing sits at the heart of genuine systemic change.

While many think of systemic change as something dramatic and often perceive it as a goal, we have come to see is as a slowly unfolding consequence of people gradually coming to think and act differently. We have come to this view with the help of masters in the craft, like Roca Inc., a nationally recognized community organization that recruits gang members to become "street workers", who in turn recruit other gang members. In the cities where they operate, the police work differently, as do the courts, parole boards, and a host of related social service agencies. Reflecting in their 25-year journey, Roca has developed an elegant definition of systemic change: "incremental shifts in habits" (see www.rocainc.com). While new acts of legislation or policy can be part of this process, a policy that does manage to tap (and perhaps shape) public support can always be repealed or simply ignored in practice. Only when we understand that all social systems are continually regenerating themselves based on our habits of thought and action, can we see that systemic change does not happen by one leader's massive intervention alone but by the actions of many guided by a shared understanding and sensibility about deep change itself. As founder Molly Baldwin says, "After many years of struggle, we have come to see that there is simply no way to get to a good place in a bad way"—wisdom captured in Roca's simple Ghandian motto, "Be the Change".

While recognizing our own "handprint" on our toughest problems can be difficult, it is the doorway to tapping human capacity to do extraordinary things. Only when we recognize each other as cocreators of the world, for good and ill, can genuine shared visions beyond "motherhood and apple pie" begin to form and we begin to mobilize collective power and wisdom, especially from people who don't normally cooperate with each other.

Empathy as the Ability to See Connections across Time

Dynamic complexity exists when cause and effect are distant in time and space: for example, when there is a temporal delay between cause and effect. Dynamic complexity is a defining feature of a complex system—one that, more than any other, bedevils efforts to address deep problems. For years, systems experts have argued against the irrationality of focusing on short-term benefits and ignoring longer-term costs, especially when the costs might greatly outweigh the benefits, as with climate change, destruction of ecosystems, and concentration of extreme poverty. But the experts are often their own worst enemies, relying totally on rational arguments often heard as abstract and theoretical, especially by those fearful of change or committed to the status quo. Because they rely on predictions or projections of possible future, they are always open to debate—but, often, the debate never really occurs seriously, victim of the overwhelming emotional salience of the short term. In effect, they are trying to fight a complex battle armed only with rational argument, a weak read where the future is concerned.

"The mark of every Golden Age is that the children are the most important members of society", goes an old Chinese adage. Embedded in this simple statement is a profound strategy for dealing with our societal denial of the long-term. IF we really thought about the children and the fact that they are the ones who bear the risks, might the risks become more emotionally salient? For example, the hidden cost of inexpensive, low-quality food loaded with sugars and salt will be borne by a generation of children who become addicted to these foods at an early age. The fact that the addiction concentrates among poorer communities where junk food is often all that the local convenience store carries and where healthier foods are economically inaccessible adds an additional ethical dimension. The consequences of this situation are already evident now. The incidence of childhood diabetes among inner city children today is already at epidemic proportions—over two million young people under the age of 20 (2010 National Diabetes Fact Sheet). But of course the real suffering will not come until years from now, when these children become adults with all the attendant health conditions that their diabetic condition presages.

So long as these children are "someone else's kids" and will only suffer in some indefinite future, it is easy to disregard this as just another of the difficult problems someone else will need to address. But if you spend time in one of the growing number of inner city schools that has an organic garden, you might then talk with a young person who tells you, "I never understood how what I eat made it impossible for me to concentrate and was a reason I failed in school—but now I DO; and I am helping my family learn also". Should you have this opportunity, the issue of the future well-being of *this* child will become real to *you* in a different way. You will see that not only is this problem your problem but you will see that the children, their teachers and their local community are deeply engaged in real solutions, in shifting the system of food that shapes their lives.

Empathy as the ability to make deep connections across time and space is essential if we are to become agents for creating healthier systems. As an everyday example, before we throw away a plastic bag, we might stop and put ourselves forward in time to imagine the bag joining an already huge plastic mass in the ocean and the possibility of a marine mammal being choked to death by it. Or as we take a walk, we might remove a piece of broken glass in the middle of the path so someone else walking the path later will be safe. Feeling connected to the next person, to the next generation, and to those who will live far way in a distant future is not foreign to us as humans. Indeed, it is a defining feature of civilization, as beautifully articulated a thousand years ago by "Peacemaker", the iconic law of the Iroquois: "Think not of yourself, or of your children. Think of those who are seven generations in the future and whose faces are still coming up from under the Earth".

Empathy as Organizational Culture

Empathy can also be present in every part of a value chain of any business or industry. When we see a product that has the highest quality, beauty, and elegance, we know that empathy was present in the minds of the individuals who helped create it. Empathy and care can be felt from a product that is made carefully and thoughtfully, with the enjoyment and safety of the consumer in mind. A 400 year-old restaurant in Kyoto, Japan, serves culinary masterpieces with a genuine heart of service and humility. This is empathy in practice. When they prepare the food, they are one with the guest and with the vision of the guest's appreciation of the food. The tea ceremony, which teaches ways of ultimate service to guests, influenced this culture of care, and such influence is found in the business practices of many long-lived Japanese companies in Kyoto.

The immaculate work of a Japanese moving company is another example of empathy. The movers cover all walls and furniture to prevent damage, take off their shoes every time they enter the house, and even change their socks when they enter a new house. They practice empathy by treating the customers and their belongings exactly as they would like to be treated—with care and respect. In this case, the movers pay attention to not only their customers, but also the neighbors of their customers. They apologize to the neighbors for any inconvenience they might cause by parking large trucks in narrow streets of Japan, and deliver small gifts to them. Paying attention to quality, precision, and utmost care in the work they do are manifestations of empathy.

The role of empathy can be seen in design thinking as well. A "human-centered design process" is one where good design is derived from empathizing with people and their needs and values (Plattner, 2012). Empathizing involves designers observing, engaging, and learning about users in their contexts, after which designers move to defining the challenge, and then onto idea generation and prototyping (Plattner, 2012). From this perspective, high-quality products cannot be designed without first knowing what it is like to be in the shoes of the user.

When empathy extends to relations with suppliers and shapes a business's choice of what material to purchase and where to purchase it, this expression of empathy can bridge broad concerns about sustainability with concrete business practices. Long-lived companies tend to treat suppliers as part of the extended "human community" that makes the company's mission possible (de Geus, 1997). Today, more and more leaders with a longer-term vision for their business are shaping supply chains that can assure quality and reliability, which often translates into internalizing investments in social and biological well-being. For example, like other leaders in its industry, Starbucks has developed its own measuring system for assessing the social and ecological sustainability of its coffee sourcing practices and is working to extend this to other key ingredients like cocoa. Nike rates all new products based on "embedded" energy, water, waste, and toxicity—which means assessing these factors across entire supply chains. This concern extends to commodity as well as specialty inputs. For example, large-scale palm oil plantations are replacing the forests of Indonesia and other tropical countries, killing endangered species and key "carbon sinks", as well as contributing directly to climate-warming gases when the forest are burned (World Watch). Along with other large buyers, Unilever has cocreated the Palm Oil Roundtable and is now a leader promoting GreenPalm Certificates. The company promises to use only sustainable palm oil by 2015, regardless of the cost.

Internal promoters of such practices do not see themselves as practicing philanthropy but good strategic business thinking. As a founder of one of the largest food retailers in America put it, "Once we remind ourselves that we buy food from farmers not 'suppliers', it becomes obvious that the health of these farming communities and their abilities to continually invest in their own future, is the key to our long-term quality supply".

RETHINKING HUMAN NATURE AND THE CONCEPT OF SELF

In the West, we value independence and individualism, which have historical roots in early Greek civilization. Capitalist economic models view humans as separate individuals and are based on the notion of an independent self. One of the fundamental propositions of free market economics is for all people at all times to seek maximization of self-interest and personal utility. Humans as "homo economicus" pursue their own interests in opportunistic, transactional ways. Independence inherently promotes competition, fighting for resources, and mistaken interpretation of Darwin's "survival of the fittest" (Pirson & Lawrence, 2010). Darwin's concept of natural selection has been taken to the extreme and become the idea that one should compete and win, not cooperate and help a rival—totally missing the cooperative dynamics build into nature, where often it is entire ecosystems that adapt and survive not just individual species (Nowak, 2012).

There are many examples of cooperative behavior in nature exhibited by nonhuman species. Vampire bats, for example, practice direct reciprocity by feeding a fellow bat who did not get a meal, and later receiving help when in need by the one it had helped earlier (Nowak, 2012). It is incredible that they know and remember who helped them earlier so they can reciprocate. Lionesses are known to care for cubs who are not their own, and dolphins who have learned how to catch fish using a conch shell teach others how to do it. Not only does cooperation, not just competition, shape animal behavior, Nowak (2012) is convinced that the humans are the most cooperative of all species based on our language abilities. When you think about it, we are not particularly fast or strong compared to our mammalian relatives; our ability to survive, grow and evolve depended a great deal on our ability to work together.

We tend to assume that morality and ethics are taught by cultures, but there is growing evidence that prosocial behavior is part of our genetic as well as cultural inheritance. For example, in a study done by Yale researchers, 16 10-month-old babies and 12 6-month -old babies were shown a puppet show in which a neutral figure is helped by another figure (helper) and hindered by the third figure (hinderer) (Gannon & Bryner, 2012). When presented with the helper and hinderer puppets after the show, 14 out of 16 10-month-olds and all 12 six-month-olds chose the helper figure (Gannon & Bryner, 2012).

These examples reveal our predisposition as a species to empathize, care, and to cooperate. But Nowak (2012) notes that there have been ups and downs in the cycle of cooperation and defection in our species' history, tensions that are front and center as we discover if we will be able to create a sustainable and healthy world.

Genetic predispositions can be nurtured or thwarted by culture. Those same babies in the Yale study, 8 to 10 years later, may exhibit very different choices based on the extent to which compassion and concern for others has been cultivated. The United States in particular presents a complex picture of competition and cooperation. According to Schor (2004), Americans are more materialistic than many other nations. American children consume 45% of all the toys produced in the world, and nearly half of fourth to eighth graders dream about becoming rich. Yet, as a culture we also love team sports and coaches who can develop effective teams; they are held in high esteem, just as are theatre directors and musicians who develop great ensembles. Although all too often it is supplanted by distrust today, historically we placed high value on cooperation at the level of community, and Benkler (2011, para. 7) points out that "75% of U.S. cities with populations of more than 50,000 have successfully adopted some version of community policing, which reduces crime not by imposing harsher penalties but by humanizing the interactions of the police with local communities".

Arguably, at no prior time in human history have we needed to recognize our capacity to cooperate as an expression of deep, innate motivations. But our frenetic "multitasking" ways of living not only keep us in a state of perpetual busyness and distractedness but pull us into a complex drama of ever-changing roles and ways of relating bound in those roles. While the multiple roles of work, family, and community are nothing new, communication technologies and globalization may be increasing the complexity of the relationships in which our roles are embedded. As we constantly shift from role to role, we may then fall into the trap of relativism, in which we have different faces depending on the context and the role we are playing. That would be tragic because, no matter the role we play in our complex, interconnected webs of relationships, the source of the goodness in everything we do is our authentic, immutable self, which must be actively cultivated.

CULTIVATING TRANSCENDENT EMPATHY

"To become a leader you must first become a human being", according to the Confucian philosophy of traditional Chinese culture. This simple statement expresses a timeless notion that developing as a leader is a lifetime journey of cultivating our capacity to see and sense what is needed for the whole. In *The Great Learning*, this cultivation is expressed in term of "seven meditative spaces of leadership cultivation", starting with learning how to stop and then actually stopping (the mind), so that one can begin to actually see what exists and what is needed. Two generations after Confucius, Mencius elaborated this understanding in terms of "the unmovable mind", meaning that his mind-heart no longer "was movable by any honor, glamour, insult, and hardship", saying that he had well learned this from Confucius, who, in the *Analects*, says: "at 40, I was unconfused".

In a world where things are happening with increasing speed, a different way of knowing is required based on slowing down in order to be able to see the larger system, to make connections, and to recognize real issues. We need to learn to quiet the chatter in our mind in order to stay connected to our deeper sense of self and place. "Mindful learning", based on Langer's research (1989), is characterized by the ability to "disentangle itself from premature conclusions, categorization and routinized ways of perceiving and thinking" (Siegel, 2007, p.7).

When we quiet our mind, we can more easily access information at a deep level where our ego interferes less. Emptying the mind and going to the place of less habitual thought allows ideas and information to emerge from a larger "field" where all possibilities reside (Laszlo, 2007). We may be more used to "knowing" as fast thinking ("hare brain"), such as when we search for information or an answer, and be less familiar with slow knowing ("tortoise mind") (Claxton, 1997), but most all of us also recognize this way of knowing, in which we let awareness unfold and let our ego and all its concerns step a bit out of the way. By letting go of the old and reaching the deepest part of who we are, we can connect to the source of authentic presence and creativity (Scharmer, 2007). Scharmer calls this presencing (present and sensing) in Theory U, which is a methodology to lead profound change by opening our minds, hearts, and will. In presencing, we can let the old go and let the new come from the deepest source. Reaching into the source is important because the source is "the place from where we operate" when we are at our best (Scharmer, 2007). We would want the place from where we operate to reflect what we would like to see in the outer world. If we wish to see peace, we first need to have peace in the very place from where we operate. One person may not be able to change the world, but change starts with each of us. Perhaps we should not underestimate the ability of the flutter of a little butterfly's wings to cause a tornado half way around the world.

"Profound challenges and opportunities for our emergent global civilization lie ahead" (Kelly, 2006, p. 14), and we are at a threshold. The verb "lead" has an Indo-European root *leith*, which means to cross a threshold, so a leader is someone who steps across the threshold. It takes courage to step into the unknown and explore new ways. It takes an open heart to give up old ways to which we may be attached. Crossing the threshold, every decision we make has consequences, and cultivating transcendent empathy could make all the difference in finding the wisdom to shape a future of well-being for the whole.

REFERENCES

A Quick Tour of Systems Thinking and Organizational Learning. (2012). Pegasus Communications. Retrieved January 2, 2013 from http://www.pegasuscom.com/lrnmore.html

Anderson, J. G., Wilmouth, D. M., Smith. J., & Sayers, D. S. (2012). UV dosage levels in summer: Increased risk of ozone loss from convectively injected water vapor. *Science*, 337(6096), 835–839.

Benkler, Y. (2011, July/August). The unselfish gene. *Harvard Business Review*, 89 (7/8), 76–85.

Bohm (1980). *Wholeness and the implicate order*. Boston: Routledge and Kegan Paul.

Claxton, G. (1997). *Hare brain, tortoise mind*. NY: Harper Collins.

de Geus, Arie (1997). *The living company*. Boston: Harvard Business School Press.

de Waal, F. (2006). *Primates and philosophers: How morality evolved*. Princeton, NJ: Princeton University Press.

Gannon, M., & Bryner, J. (2012, August). Do babies have a moral compass? Debate heats up. *LiveScience*. Retrieved October 30, 2012, from http://www.livescience.com/22399-babies-moral-compass.html

Gibran, K. (1923). *The Prophet*. NY: Alfred A. Knopf.

Global Palm Oil Demand Fueling Deforestation. (2012). *Worldwatch Institute*. Retrieved September 15, 2012, from http://www.worldwatch.org/node/6059

Greason, P., & Cashwell, G. (2009). Mindfulness and counseling self-efficacy: The mediating role of attention and empathy. *Counselor Education & Supervision*, 49, 2–19.

Hoffman, M. L. (1987). The consciousness of empathy to justice and moral judgment. In N. Eisenberg & J. Strayer (Eds.), *Empathy and its development* (pp. 47–80). Cambridge: Cambridge University Press, pp. 47–80.

IPCC (2012). Managing the risks of extreme events and disasters to advance climate change adaptation. Retrieved August 1, 2012, from http://www.ipcc-wg2.gov/SREX/images/uploads/SREX-All_FINAL.pdf

Kelley, M. (2012, April 12). 13 signs that America's prison system is out of control. *Business Insider.* Retrieved from http://www.businessinsider.com/americas-prison-system-is-out-of-control-2012-4?op=1.

Kelly, E. (2006). *Powerful times.* Upper Saddle River, NJ: Wharton School Publishing.

Kind, S., Irwin, R., Grauer, K., and De Cosson, A. (2005). Medicine wheel imag(in) ings: Exploring holistic curriculum perspectives. *Art Education, 58*(5), 33–38.

Langer, E. (1989). *Mindfulness.* Reading, MA: Addison Wesley.

Lappe, A. (2010). Diet for a hot planet. In D. Imhoff (Ed.), *CAFO.* Los Angeles: Watershed Media.

Laszlo, E. (2007). *Science and the Akashic field.* Rochester, VT: Inner Traditions.

Matuarana, H., & Varela, F. (1980). *Autopoiesis and cognition: The organization of the living.* Boston: Reidel.

Maturana, H., & Varela, F. (1987). *The tree of knowledge: The biological roots of human understanding.* Boston: Shambhala (revised edition 1998).

National Diabetes Fact Sheet. (2011). Center for Disease Controls and Prevention. Retrieved January 2, 2013, from http://www.cdc.gov/diabetes/pubs/pdf/ndfs_2011.pdf

Nowak, M. (2012). Why we help. What makes us human (Special Collector's Edition). *Scientific American,,* 22 (1), 92–97.Olfman, S. (2006). Self, identity, and generativity. In R. Cavoukian & S. Olfman (Eds.), *Child honoring.* Westport, CT: Praeger Publishers.

Parry, W. (2011). Overuse of antibiotics is seen behind many human ills. *Livescience.* Retrieved August 2, 2012, from http://www.livescience.com/15740-helpful-bacteria-antibiotics.html

Parry, W. (2012). Soil microbes harbor nasty antibiotic resistance genes. *LiveScience.* Retrieved September 26, 2012, from http://www.livescience.com/22835-soil-bacteria-antibiotic-resistance.html

Pavlovich, K., & Krahnke, K. (2012). Empathy, connectedness and organization. *Journal of Business Ethics, 105,* 131–137.

Pirson, M. A., & Lawrence, P. R. (2010). Humanism in business—Towards a paradigm shift? *Journal of Business Ethics, 93,* 553–565.

Plattner, H. (2012). Introduction to design thinking process guide. Stanford Humanities Lab and Metamedia. Retrieved November 25, 2012, from http://human itieslab.stanford.edu/admin/directory.html

Quinn, R. (2007). *Lift: Becoming a positive force in any situation.* San Francisco: Berrett-Koehler Publishers.

Rifkin, J. (2009). *Empathic civilization.* NY: Penguin Group.

Rifkin, J. (2010). Jeremy Rifkin: The empathic civilization [video file] Retrieved from http://www.youtube.com/watch?v = nQN_13KawUw

Scharmer, C. O. (2007). *Theory U.* Cambridge, MA: SoL.

Scharmer, C. O., and Kaeufer, K. (2013). *Leading from the emerging future.* San Francisco: Berrett-Koehler Publishers.

Schor, J. (2004). *Born to buy.* NY: Scribner.

Seitanidi, M., & Crane, A. (2009). Implementing CSR through partnerships: Understanding the selection, design and institutionalization of nonprofit-business partnerships. *Journal of BusinessEthics, 85*(2), 413–429. doi: 10.1007/s10551–008–9743-y

Senge, P. (1990). *The fifth discipline.* NY: Doubleday.

Senge, P., Smith, B., Krushwitz, N., Laur, J., & Schley, S. (2008). *The necessary revolution: Working together to create a sustainable world.* NY: Doubleday.

Senge, P., Kleiner, A., Roberts, C., Ross, R., & Smith, B. (1994). *The fifth discipline field book.* NY: Doubleday.

Shah, A. (2010). Poverty facts and stats. Global issues. Retrieved October 10, 2012, from http://www.globalissues.org/article/26/poverty-facts-and-stats

Siegel, D.J. (2007). *Mindful brain*. NY: W.W. Norton & Company, Inc.
Talbot, M. (1991). *Holographic universe*. NY: Harper Collins.
Waddock, S. (2009). Leading corporate citizens. NY: McGraw-Hill Irwin.
Wolpert, S. (2009, October 8). Last time carbon dioxide levels were this high: 15 million years ago, scientists report. UCLA Newsroom. Retrieved from http://newsroom.ucla.edu/portal/ucla/last-time-carbon-dioxide-levels-111074.aspx.
World Footprint. (2012). Global footprint network. Retrieved August 10, 2012, from http://www.footprintnetwork.org/en/index.php/GFN/page/world_footprint/

Bibliography

A quick tour of systems thinking and organizational learning (2012). Pegasus Communications. Retrieved from http://www.pegasuscom.com/lrnmore.html.

Adam, J., Bore, M., McKendree, J., Munro, D., & Powis, D. (2012). Can personal qualities of medical students predict in-course examination success and professional behavior? An exploratory prospective cohort study. *BMC Medical Education, 12,* 69–76.

Aiken, G. A. (2006). *The potential effect of mindfulness meditation on the cultivation of empathy in psychotherapy: A qualitative inquiry.* Ph.D. 3217528, Saybrook Graduate School and Research Center—California. OxResearch; ProQuest Central; ProQuest Dissertations & Theses A&I database.

Alexander, C. N., Cranson, R. W., Boyer, R., & Orme-Johnson, D. W. (1986). Transcendental consciousness: A fourth state of consciousness beyond sleep, dreaming and waking. In J. Gackenbach (Ed.), *Sourcebook on sleep and dreams* (pp. 282–315). NY: Garland.

Alexander, C. N., Davies, J. L., Dixon, C., Dillbeck, M. C., Druker, S. M., Oetzel, R., . . . Orme-Johnson, D. W. (1990). Growth of higher stages of consciousness: Maharishi's Vedic psychology of human development. In C. N. Alexander & E. J. Langer (Eds.), *Higher stages of human development: Perspectives on adult growth* (pp. 286–341). NY: Oxford University Press.

Alexander, C. N., DeArmond, D. L., Heaton, D. P., Stevens M. M., & Schmidt-Wilk, J. (2004). *Does spiritual practice reduce managerial stress? A prospective study of the Transcendental Meditation program in business.* Paper presented at the annual meeting of the Academy of Management, New Orleans.

Alexander, C. N., & Orme-Johnson, D. W. (2003). Walpole study of the Transcendental Meditation program in maximum security prisoners II: Longitudinal study of development and psychopathology. *Journal of Offender Rehabilitation, 36,* 127–160.

Alexander, C. N., Rainforth, M. V., & Gelderloos, P. (1991). Transcendental Meditation, self-actualization, and psychological health: A conceptual overview and statistical meta-analysis. *Journal of Social Behavior and Personality,* 6(5), 189–247.

Alexander, C., Rainforth, M., Frank, P., Grant, J., Von Stade, C., & Walton, K. (2003). Walpole study of the Transcendental Meditation program in maximum security prisoners III: Reduced recidivism. *Journal of Offender Rehabilitation, 36,* 161–180.

Alexander, C. N., Swanson, G. C., Rainforth, M. V., Carlisle, T. W., Todd, C. C., & Oates, R. (1993). Effects of the Transcendental Meditation program on stress-reduction, health, and employee development: A prospective study in two occupational settings. *Anxiety, Stress, and Coping, 6,* 245–262.

Alexander, C.N., Walton, K.G., & Goodman, R.S. (2003). Walpole study of the Transcendental Meditation program in maximum security prisoners I: Cross-sectional differences in development and psychopathology. *Journal of Offender Rehabilitation, 36*, 97–125.

Allessandri, G., & Vecchione, M. (2012). The higher-order factors of the Big Five as predictors of job performance. *Personality and Individual Differences, 53*, 779–784.

Alma, H.A. (2008). Self-development as a spiritual process: The role of empathy and imagination in finding spiritual orientation. *Pastoral Psychology, 57*, 59–63.

Amason, A.C. (1996). Distinguishing the effects of functional and dysfunctional conflict on strategic decision making: Resolving a paradox for top management teams. *Academy of Management Journal, 39*(1), 123–148.

American Psychiatric Association (1994).*Diagnostic and statistical manual of mental disorders* (4th ed.). Washington, DC: American Psychiatric Association.

Anderson, J.G., Wilmouth, D.M., Smith, J., & Sayers, D.S. (2012). UV dosage levels in summer: Increased risk of ozone loss from convectively injected water vapor. *Science, 337*(6096), 835–839.

Antonakis, J. (2004). On why 'EI' will not predict leadership effectiveness beyond IQ or the 'Big Five': An extension and rejoinder. *Organizational Analysis, 12*(2), 171–182.

Arora, S., Ashrafian, H., Davis, R., Athanasiou, T., Darzi, A., & Sevdalis, N. (2010). Emotional intelligence in medicine: A systematic review through the context of the ACGME competencies. *Medical Education, 44*, 749–764.

Ashkanasy, N.M., Dasborough, M.T., & Ascough, K.W. (2009). Developing leaders: Teaching about emotional intelligence and training in emotional skills. In S.J. Armstrong & C.V. Fukami (Eds.), *The SAGE handbook of management learning, education and development* (pp. 161–185). London: SAGE Publications Ltd.

Ashkanasy, N.M., Paulsen, N., & Tee, E.Y.J. (2012). Extending relational leadership theory: The role of affective process in shaping leader-follower relationships. In Mary Uhl-Bien & Sonia M. Ospina (Eds.), *Advancing relationship leadership research: A dialogue among perspectives* (pp. 335–359). Charlotte, NC: Information Age Publishing.

Atkins, P.W., & Parker, S.K. (2012). Understanding individual compassion in organizations: The role of appraisals and psychological flexibility. *Academy of Management Review, 37*(4), 524–546.

Austin, E.J., Evans, P., Goldwater, R., & Potter, V. (2005). A preliminary study of emotional intelligence, empathy and exam performance in first year medical students. *Personality and Individual Differences, 39*, 1395–1405.

Austin, E.J., Evans, P., Magnus, B., & O'Hanlon, K. (2007). A preliminary study of empathy, emotional intelligence and examination performance in MBChB students. *Medical Education, 41*, 684–689.Badger, K., Royse, D., & Craig, C. (2008). Hospital social workers and indirect trauma exposure: An exploratory study of contributing factors. *Health & Social Work, 33*(1), 63–71. doi: 10.1093/hsw/33.1.63

Badiou, A. (2003). *Saint Paul: The foundation of universalism*. Palo Alto, CA: Stanford University Press.

Baer, R., Carmody, J., & Hunsinger, M. (2012). Weekly change in mindfulness and perceived stress in a mindfulness-based stress reduction program. *Journal of Clinical Psychology, 68*(7), 755–765.

Baer, R.A., Smith, G.T., Hopkins, J., Krietemeyer, J., & Toney, L. (2006). Using self-report assessment methods to explore facets of mindfulness. *Assessment, 13*(1), 27–45.

Bandura, A., Barbaranelli, C., Caprara, G. V., & Pastorelli, C. (1996). Mechanisms of moral disengagement in the exercise of moral agency. *Journal of Personality and Social Psychology, 71*, 364–374. doi: 10.1037/0022-3514.71.2.364

Barnes-Holmes, D., Hayes, S. C., & Dymond, S. (2001). Self and self-directed rules. In S. C. Hayes, D. Barnes-Holmes, & B. Roche (Eds.), *Relational frame theory: A post-Skinnerian account of human language and cognition* (pp. 119–139). NY: Kluwer Academic/Plenum.

Baron-Cohen, S., & Wheelwright, S. (2004). The empathy quotient: An investigation of adults with Asperger syndrome or high functioning autism, and normal sex differences. *Journal of Autism and Developmental Disorders, 34*(2), 163–175. doi: 10.1023/B:JADD.0000022607.19833.00

Batson, C. D. (1990). How social an animal. The human capacity for caring. *American Psychologist, 45*, 336–346. doi: 10.1037/0003-066X.45.3.336

Batson, C. D. (2008). *Empathy-induced altruism motivation.* Paper presented at the Inaugural Herzliya Symposium on "Prosocial Motives, Emotions, and Behavior," Herzliya, Israel.

Batson, C. D. (2009). Two forms of perspective taking: Imagining how another feels and imagining how you would feel. In K. D. Markman, W.M.P. Klein, & J. A. Suhr (Eds.), *Handbook of imagination and mental simulation* (pp. 267–279). NY: Psychology Press.

Batson, C. D., & Ahmad, N. Y. (2009). Empathy-induced altruism: A threat to the collective good altruism and prosocial behavior in groups in Shane R. Thye, Edward J. Lawler (ed.) *Altruism and Prosocial Behavior in Groups* (Advances in Group Processes, Volume 26), Emerald Group Publishing Limited, pp.1–23.

Batson, C. D., Batson, J. G., Griffitt, C. A., Barrientos, S., Brandt, J. R., Sprengelmeyer, P. et al. (1989). Negative-state relief and the empathy altruism hypothesis. *Journal of Personality and Social Psychology, 56*, 922–933. doi: 10.1037/0022-3514.56.6.922

Batson, C. D., & Shaw, L. L. (1991). Evidence for altruism: Toward a pluralism of prosocial motives. *Psychological Inquiry, 2*, 107–122. doi: 10.1207/s15327965pli0202_1Batson, C. D., Batson, J. G., Slingsby, J. K., Harrell, K. L., Peekna, H. M., & Todd, R. M. (1991). Empathic joy and the empathy-altruism hypothesis. *Journal of Personality and Social Psychology, 61*, 413–426. doi: 10.1037/0022-3514.61.3.413

Batson, D., Batson, J., Todd, M., Brummett, B., Shaw, L., & Aldeguer, C. (1995). Empathy and the collective good: Caring for one of the others in a social dilemma. *Journal of Personality and Psychology, 68*(4), 619–631.

Batson, C. D., Bolen, M., Cross, J., & Heuringer-Benefiel, H. (1986). Where is the altruism in the altruistic personality? *Journal of Personality and Social Psychology, 50*, 212–220. doi: 10.1037/0022-3514.50.1.212

Batson, C. D., Duncan, B. D., Ackerman, P., Buckley, T., & Birch, K. (1981). Is empathic emotion a source of altruistic motivation? *Journal of Personality and Social Psychology, 40*, 290–302. doi: 10.1037//0022-3514.40.2.290

Batson, C. D., Klein, T. R., Highberger, L., & Shaw L. L. (1995). Immorality from empathy-induced altruism: When compassion and justice conflict. *Journal of Personality and Social Psychology, 68*, 1042–1054. doi: 10.1037/0022-3514.68.6.1042

Batson, C. D., Lishner, D. A., Cook, J., & Sawyer, S. (2005). Similarity and nurturance: Two possible sources of empathy for strangers. *Basic and Applied Social Psychology, 27*, 15–25. doi: 10.1207/s15324834basp2701_2

Battistich, V. (2008). Voices: A practitioner's perspective: Character education, prevention, and positive youth development. *Journal of Research in Character Education, 6*, 81–90.

Battistich, V., Solomon, D., Watson, M., & Schaps, E. (1997). Caring school communities. *Educational Psychologist, 32*, 137–151.

Battistich, V., Watson, M., Solomon, D., Lewis, C., & Schaps, E. (1999). Beyond the three R's: A broader agenda for school reform. *Elementary School Journal,* 99, 415–431.

Battistich, V., Watson, M., Solomon, D., Schaps, E., & Solomon, J. (1991). The Child Development Project: A comprehensive program for the development of prosocial character. In W. M. Kurtines & J. L. Gewirtz (Eds.), *Handbook of moral behavior and development: Vol 3. Application* (pp. 1–34). Hillsdale, NJ: Lawrence Erlbaum Associates.

Baudry, F. (1989). Character, character type, and character organization. *Journal of the American Psychoanalytic Association,* 37, 655–686.

Beddoe, A. E., & Murphy, S. O. (2004). Does mindfulness decrease stress and foster empathy among nursing students? *The Journal of Nursing Education,* 43(7), 305–312.

Benkler, Y. (2011, July). The unselfish gene. *Harvard Business Review.*

Bennet, J. M. (2001). *The empathic healer: An endangered species.* London: Academic Press.

Bennis, W., & Thomas, R. (2007). *Leading for a lifetime.* Boston: HBR.

Benson, P. L. (2006). *All kids are our kids: What communities must do to raise caring and responsible children and adolescents.* 2nd ed. San Francisco: Jossey-Bass.

Bethel, S. M. (2009). *A new breed of leader.* NY: Penguin.

Bishop, S. R., Lau, M., Shapiro, S., Carlson, L., Anderson, N. D., Carmody, J., . . . Devins, G. (2004). Mindfulness: A proposed operational definition. *Clinical Psychology: Science and Practice,* 11(3), 230–241.

Block-Lerner, J., Adair, C., Plumb, J. C., Rhatigan, D. L., & Orsillo, S. M. (2007). The case for mindfulness-based approaches in the cultivation of empathy: Does nonjudgmental, present-moment awareness increase capacity for perspective-taking and empathic concern? *Journal of Marital and Family Therapy,* 33(4), 501.

Bohm, D. (1980). *Wholeness and the implicate order.* London: Ark Paperbacks.

Bore, M. R., Munro, D., Kerridge, I., & Powis, D. A. (2005a). Not moral "reasoning": A Libertarian-Communitarian dimension of moral orientation and Schwartz's value types. *Australian Journal of Psychology,* 57, 38–48.

Bore, M. R., Munro, D., Kerridge, I., & Powis, D. A. (2005b). Selection of medical students according to their moral orientation. *Medical Education,* 39, 266–275.

Bore, M., Munro, D., & Powis, D. (2009). A comprehensive model for the selection of medical students. *Medical Teacher,* 31, 1066–1072.

Borges, N. J., Stratton, T. D., Wagner, P. J., & Elam, C. L. (2009). Emotional intelligence and medical specialty choice: Findings from three empirical studies. *Medical Education,* 43, 565–572.

Bossidy, L., & Charan, R. (2002). *Execution.* NY: Crown Business.

Bowlby, J. (1969). *Attachment and loss: Vol. 1. Attachment.* NY: Basic.

Boyatzis, R. E. (2006). An overview of intentional change from a complexity perspective. *Journal of Management Development,* 25(7), 607–623.

Boyatzis, R. E., & Akrivou, K. (2006). The ideal self as the driver of intentional change. *Journal of Management Development,* 25(7), 624–642.

Boyatzis, R. E., Passarelli, A. M., Koenig, K., Lowe, M., Mathew, B., Stoller, J. K., & Phillips, M. (2012). Examination of the neural substrates activated in memories of experiences with resonant and dissonant leaders. *Leadership Quarterly,* 23(2), 259–272.

Brief, A. P., Dietz, J., Cohen, R. R., Pugh, S. D., & Vaslow, J. B. (2000). Just doing business: Modern racism and obedience to authority as explanations for employment discrimination. *Organizational Behavior and Human Decision Processes,* 81, 72–97. doi:10.1006/obhd.1999.2867

Brothers, L. (1989). A biological perspective on empathy. *The American Journal of Psychiatry,* 146, 1.

Brown, C. L. (2005). Overcoming barriers to use of promising research among elite Middle East policy groups. *Journal of Social Behavior and Personality, 17*(1), 489–546.

Buckman, R. Tulsky, J., & Rodin, G. (2011). Empathic responses in clinical practice: Intuition or tuition? *Canadian Medical Association Journal, 183*(5), 569–571.

Capra, F. (1999). *The tao of physics: An exploration of the parallels between modern physics and eastern mysticism* (4th ed.). Boston: Shambhala.

Carmody, J., & Baer, R. (2008). Relationships between mindfulness practice and levels of mindfulness, medical and psychological symptoms and well-being in a mindfulness-based stress reduction program. *Journal of Behavioral Medicine, 31*(1), 23–33. doi: 10.1007/s10865-007-9130-7

Carr, S. E. (2009). Emotional intelligence in medical students: Does it correlate with selection measures? *Medical Education, 43*, 1069–1077.

Carrera, P., Oceja, L., Caballero, A., Munoz, D., Lopez-Pérez, B., & Ambrona, T. (2012). I feel so sorry! Tapping the joint influence of empathy and personal distress on helping behavior. *Motivation and Emotion*. Advance online publication. doi: 10.1007/s11031-012-9302-9

Carroll, P., & Roth, Y. (2010). *Win forever*. NY: Penguin.

Caruso, D. R., & Salovey, P. (2004). *The emotionally intelligent manager*. San Francisco: Jossey-Bass.

Chandler, H. M., Alexander, C. N., & Heaton, D. P. (2005). Transcendental Meditation and postconventional self development: A 10-year longitudinal study. *Journal of Social Behavior and Personality, 17*, 93–121.

Chen, D., Lew, R., Hershman, W., & Orlander, J. (2007). A cross-sectional measurement of medical student empathy. *Journal of General Internal Medicine, 22*, 1434–1438.

Chen, M. J. (2010). *West meets east: Enlightening, balancing and transcending*. In the Academy of Management Conference, San Antonio, August 8–12, 2011.

Chin-Fang Yang, & Chin-Yi Chen. (2012). The Impact of spiritual leadership on organizational behavior: A multi-sample analysis. *Journal of Business Ethics, 105*(1), 107–114.

Chlopan, B. E., McCain, M. L., Carbonell, J. L., & Hagen, R. L. (1985). Empathy: Review of available measures. *Journal of Personality and Social Psychology, 48*, 635–653.

Ciarrochi, J., & Mayer, J. D. (2007). *Applying emotional intelligence: A practitioner's guide. Applying emotional intelligence: A practitioner's guide xiv*, p.169. NY: Psychology Press.

Claxton, G. (1997). *Hare brain, tortoise mind*. NY: Harper Collins.

Cohen, A. (2008, January 25). [Web log message]. Retrieved from http://theboard. blogs.nytimes. com/2008/01/25/going-going-gone-meg-whitman-leaves-ebay/

Cohen, T. R. (2010). Moral emotions and unethical bargaining: The differential effects of empathy and perspective taking in deterring deceitful negotiation. *Journal of Business Ethics, 94*, 569–579. doi: 10.1007/s10551-009-0338-z

Collins, J. (2009). *How the mighty fall*. NY: Harper Collins.

Colliver, J. A., Conlee, M. J., Verhulst, S. J., & Dorsey, J. K. (2010). Reports of the decline of empathy during medical education are greatly exaggerated: A re-examination of the research. *Academic Medicine, 85*, 588–593.

Cook-Greuter, S. R. (2000). Mature ego development: A gateway to ego transcendence? *Journal of Adult Development, 7*, 227–240.

Coulehan, J. L., Platt, F. W., Egener, B., Frankel, R., Lin, C. T., Lown, B., & Salazar, W. H. (2001). "Let me see if i have this right . . ." Words that help build empathy. *Annals of Internal Medicine, 135*(3), 221–227.

Cox, C. L., Uddin, L. Q., Di Martino, A., Castellanos, F. X., Milham, M. P., & Kelly, C. (2012). The balance between feeling and knowing: Affective and cognitive empathy are reflected in the brain's intrinsic functional dynamics. *Social Cognitive and Affective Neuroscience, 7*(6), 727–737.

Cox, J. (2011). Empathy, identity and engagement in person-centred medicine: The sociocultural context. *Journal of Evaluation in Clinical Practice, 17*(2), 350–353.

CPXample. (2010, June 29). Procter & Gamble: Helping kids live, learn and thrive. Retrieved from http://www.cpxample.com/2010/06/procter-gamble-helping-kids-live-learn-and-thrive/

Cranson, R. W., Orme-Johnson, D. W., Gackenbach, J., Dillbeck, M. C., Jones, C. H., & Alexander, C. N. (1991). Transcendental Meditation and improved performance on intelligence-related measures: A longitudinal study. *Journal of Personality and Individual Differences, 12*, 1105–1116.

Cullen, W., Bury, G., & Leahy, M. (2003). What makes a good doctor? A cross sectional survey of public opinion. *Irish Medical Journal, 96*(2), 38–41.

Damasio, A. R. (1994). *Descartes' error: Emotion, reason, and the human brain.* NY: G. P. Putnam.

Daniels, R. (2003). Impact of tea cultivation on anurans in the Western Ghats. *Current Science, 85*(10), retrieved from http://www.iisc.ernet.in/currsci/nov252003/1415.pdf

Darwin, C. (1872). *The expression of emotions in man and animals.* London: Murray.

Davidson, R. J. (2002). Anxiety and affective style: Role of prefrontal cortex and amygdala. *Biological Psychiatry, 51*(1), 68–80.

Davies, J. L., & Alexander, C. N. (2005). Alleviating political violence through reducing collective tension: Impact assessment analysis of the Lebanon war. *Journal of Social Behavior and Personality, 17*, 285–338.

Davis, H. (ed. 1940). *Gulliver's travels. The prose works of Jonathan Swift, XI,* 267. London: Chatto & Winders.

Davis, M. H. (1980). A multidimensional approach to individual differences in empathy. *JSAS Catalog of Selected Documents in Psychology, 10*, 85.

Davis, M. H. (1983). Measuring individual-differences in empathy: Evidence for a multidimensional approach. *Journal of Personality and Social Psychology, 44*, 113–126.

de Geus, Arie (1997). *The living company.* Boston: Harvard Business School Press.

de Vignemont, F., & Singer, T. (2006). The empathic brain: How, when and why? *Trends in Cognitive Sciences, 10*(10), 435–441.

de Waal, F. (2009). *The age of empathy: Nature's lessons for a kinder society.* NY: Harmony Books/Random House.

Debold, E. (2002). Epistemology, fourth order consciousness, and the subject-object relationship, or . . . how the self evolves with Robert Kegan. *What Is Enlightenment, 22,* Fall-Winter. Retrieved March 12, 2008 from http://www.wie.org/j22/kegan.asp?page=2

Decety, J., & Michalska, K. J. (2010). Neurodevelopmental changes in the circuits underlying empathy and sympathy from childhood to adulthood. *Developmental Science, 13*(6), 886–899.

Decety, J., & Lamm, C. (2006). Human empathy through the lens of social neuroscience. *The Scientific World Journal, 6,* 1146–1163. doi: 10.1100/tsw.2006.221

Decety, J., & Lamm, C. (2007). The role of the right temporoparietal junction in social interaction: How low-level computational processes contribute to meta-cognition. *The Neuroscientist, 13*(6), 580–593. doi: 10.1177/1073858407304654

Dehler, G. E., & Welsh, M. A. (2003). The experience of work: Spirituality and the new workplace. In R. A. Giacalone & C. L. Jurkiewicz (Eds.), *Handbook of workplace spirituality and organizational performance* (pp. 108–122). NY: M. E. Sharpe.

Detert, J. R., Treviño, L. K., & Sweitzer, V. L. (2008). Moral disengagement in ethical decision making: A study of antecedents and outcomes. *Journal of Applied Psychology, 93*, 374–391. doi: 10.1037/0021-9010.93.2.374

Dietz, J., & Kleinlogel, E. P. (in press). Wage cuts and managers' empathy: How a positive emotion contributes to positive organizational ethics in difficult times. *Journal of Business Ethics.*

Dillbeck, M. C. (1988). The self-interacting dynamics of consciousness as the source of the creative process in nature and in human life: The mechanics of individual intelligence arising from the field of cosmic intelligence—the cosmic psyche. *Modern Science and Vedic Science, 2*(3), 245–278.

Dillbeck, M. C., & Orme-Johnson, D. W. (1987). Physiological differences between Transcendental Meditation and rest. *American Psychologist, 42*, 879–881.

Dilthey, W. (1976). *Selective writings.* Ed. H. P. Richman. England: Cambridge University.

Doidge, N. (2007). *The brain that changes itself.* NY: Viking.

Dominelli, L., & Gollins, T. (1997). Men, power, and caring relationships. *Sociological Review, 396*–415.

Dovidio, J. F., Allen, J. L., & Schroeder, D. A. (1990). Specificity of empathy-induced helping: Evidence for altruistic motivation. *Journal of Personality and Social Psychology, 59*, 249–260. doi: 10.1037//0022-3514.59.2.249

Driver, M. J., & Pate, L. E. (2002). Decision making. In F. Luthans (Ed.), *Virtual organizational behavior.* (pp. 1–26). NY: McGraw-Hill.

Duan, C. M., & Hill, C. E. (1996). The current state of empathy research. *Journal of Counseling Psychology, 43*, 261–274. doi: 10.1037/0022-0167.43.3.261

Duffy, D. J. (2009).Mirror neurons and the re-enchantment of bioethics. *The American Journal of Bioethics, 9*(9), 2–4.

Dutton, J. E., Worline, M. C., Frost, P. J., & Lilius, J. (2006). Explaining compassion organizing. *Administrative Science Quarterly, 51*, 59–96. doi: 10.2189/asqu.51.1.59

Dweck, C. S., Hong, Y.-Y., & Chiu, C.-Y. (1993). Implicit theories: Individual differences in the likelihood and meaning of dispositional inference. *Personality and Social Psychology Bulletin, 19*(5), 644–656. doi: 10.1177/0146167293195015

Eccles, J. S., & Gootman, J. A. (Eds.). (2002*). Community programs to promote youth development.* Washington, DC: National Academy Press.

Edelson, M. (1988). *Psychoanalysis: A theory in crisis.* Chicago: University of Chicago Press.

Ehrmann, J., Ehrmann, P., & Jordan, G. (2011). *InSideOut coaching: How sports can transform lives.* NY: Simon & Schuster.

Eisberg, N. (2007). Collaborate to innovate. *Chemistry & Industry, 12*, 25–26.

Eisenberg, N. (2005). Moral motivation through the lifespan, In *Current Theory and Research in Motivation.* Lincoln: University of Nebraska, 51.

Eisenberg, N. (2010). Empathy-related responding: Links with self-regulation, moral judgment, and moral behavior. In M. Mikulincer (Ed.), *Prosocial motives, emotions, and behavior: The better angels of our nature* (pp. 129–148). Washington, DC: American Psychological Association.

Eisenberg, N., Guthrie, I. K., Murphy, B. C., Shepard, S. A., Cumberland, A., & Carlo, G. (1999). Consistency and development of prosocial dispositions: A longitudinal study. *Child Development, 70*, 1360–1372. doi: 10.1111/1467-8624.00100

Eisenberg, N., & Miller, P. A. (1987). The relation of empathy to pro-social and related behaviors. *Psychological Bulletin, 101*, 91–119. doi: 10.1037/0033-2909.101.1.91

Eisenberg, N., & Strayer, J. (Eds.). (1987). *Empathy and its development.* Cambridge: Cambridge University Press.

Eisenberg, N., Valiente, C., & Champion, C. (2004). Empathy-related responding: Moral, social, and socialization correlates. In A. G. Miller (Ed.), *The social psychology of good and evil* (pp. 386–415). NY: Guilford.

Eisenhardt, K. M. (1989). Building theories from case study research. *Academy of Management Review, 14*(4), 532–550.

Eliot, T. S. (1952). *The rock: The complete poems and plays*. Orlando, FL: Harcourt Press.

Elizur, A., & Rosenheim, E. (1982). Empathy and attitudes among medical students: The effects of group experience. *Journal of Medical Education, 57*, 675–683.

Elzubeir, M. A., & Rizk, D. E. (2001). Identifying characteristics that students, interns and residents look for in their role models. *Medical Education, 35*, 272–277.

Eppley, K. R., Abrams, A. I., & Shear, J. (1989). Differential effects of relaxation techniques on trait anxiety: A meta-analysis. *Journal of Clinical Psychology, 45*, 957–974.

Erikson, E. H. (1985). *Childhood and society*. NY: Norton.

Evans, B. J., Stanley, R. O., & Burrows, G. D. (1993). Measuring medical students' empathy skills. *British Journal of Medical Psychology, 66*, 121–133.

Fales, E., & Markovsky, B. (1997). Evaluating heterodox theories. *Social Forces, 76*, 511–525.

Fernndez-Olano, C., Montoya-Fernndez, J., & Salinas-Sanchez, A. S. (2008). Impact of clinical interview training on the empathy level of medical students and medical residents. *Medical Teacher, 30*, 322–324.

Feshbach, N. D. (1997). Empathy: The formative years—Implications for clinical practice. In A. C. Bohart and L. S. Greenberg (Eds.), *Empathy reconsidered: New directions in psychotherapy*, (pp. 33–39). Washington, DC: American Psychological Association.

Figley, C. R. (2002). *Treating compassion fatigue* (pp. viii, 227), NY: Brunner-Routledge; US.

Fineman, S. (2003). *Understanding emotions at work*. Thousand Oaks, CA: SAGE.

Fineman, S. (2004). Getting the measure of emotion—and the cautionary tale of EI. *Human Relations, 57*(6), 719–740.

Fineman, S. (2006). On being positive: Concerns and counterpoints. *Academy of Management Review, 31*(2), 270–291.

Fiske, S. T., & Taylor, S. E. (1991). *Social cognition* (2nd ed.). NY: McGraw-Hill.

Fletcher, L., Schoendorff, B., & Hayes, S. (2010). Searching for mindfulness in the brain: A process-oriented approach to examining the neural correlates of mindfulness. *Mindfulness, 1*(1), 41–63. doi: 10.1007/s12671-010-0006-5

Flury, J., & Ickes, W. (2006). Emotional intelligence and empathic accuracy in friendships and dating relationships. In J. Ciarrochi, J. R. Forgas, & J. D. Mayer (Eds.), Emotional intelligence in everyday life (2nd ed.) (pp. 140–165). Hove, England: Taylor & Francis.

Foody, M., Barnes-Holmes, Y., & Barnes-Holmes, D. (2012). The role of self in acceptance and commitment therapy. In L. McHugh & I. Stewart (Eds.), *The self and perspective taking: Contributions and applications from modern behavioral science* (pp. 125–142). Oakland, CA: Context Press.

Forsyth, G. (1980). Analysis of the concept of empathy-illustrations of one approach. *Advances in Nursing Science, 2*, 33–42.

Fraser-Thomas, J. L., Côté, J., & Deakin, J. (2005). Youth sport programs: An avenue to foster positive youth development. *Physical Education and Sport Pedagogy, 10*, 19–40. doi: 10.1080=1740898042000334890

Freud, S. (1975). Beyond the pleasure principle. In I J. Strachey (Ed. & Trans.), *The standard edition of the complete psychological works of Sigmund Freud* (Vol. 18, pp. 7–64). London: Hogarth. (Original work published 1920.)

Frew, D. R. (1974). Transcendental Meditation and productivity. *Academy of Management Journal, 17*, 245–262.

Friedman, M. (1970, September 13). The social responsibility of business is to increase profits. *New York Times Magazine*, 32–33, 122–126.

Fromm, E. (1976). *To have or to be?* NY: Harper & Row.

Fry, M. D., & Gano-Overway, L. A. (2010). Exploring the contribution of the caring climate to the youth sport experience. *Journal of Applied Sport Psychology, 22*, 294–304.

Fultz, J., Batson, C. D., Fortenbach, V. A., McCarthy, P. M., & Varney, L. L. (1986). Social evaluation and the empathy-altruism hypothesis. *Journal of Personality and Social Psychology, 50*, 761–769. doi: 10.1037//0022-3514.50.4.761

Fuster, J. M. (2000). Executive frontal functions. *Experimental Brain Research, 133*(1), 66–70.

Galantino, M. L., Baime, M., Maguire, M., Szapary, P. O., & Farrar, J. T. (2005). Short communication: Association of psychological and physiological measures of stress in health-care professionals during an 8-week mindfulness meditation program: Mindfulness in practice. *Stress and Health, 21*(4), 255–261.

Gallese, V. (2007). Commentary on Toward a neuroscience of empathy: Integrating affective and cognitive perspectives. *Neuropsychoanalysis, 9*(1), 146–151.

Gallup, G. G., & Platek, S. M. (2002). Cognitive empathy presupposes self-awareness: Evidence from phylogeny, ontogeny, neuropsychology, and mental illness. *Behavioral and Brain Sciences, 25*, 36–37.

Gallwey, T. W. (1997). *The inner game of tennis: The classic guide to the mental side of peak performance.* NY: Random House Trade.

Gannon, M., & Bryner, J. (2012,August). Do babies have a moral compass? Debate heats up. *LiveScience.* Retrieved October 30, 2012 from http://www.livescience.com/22399-babies-moral-compass.html

Gano-Overway, L. A. (in press). Exploring the connections between caring and social behaviors in physical education research. *Quarterly for Exercise and Sport.*

Gano-Overway, L. A., Michelle Magyar, T., Kim, M. S., Newton, M., Fry, M. D., & Guivernau, M. R. (2009). Influence of caring youth sport contexts on efficacy—related beliefs and social behavior. *Developmental Psychology, 45*(2), 239–340.

Gano-Overway, L. A., Newton, M., Magyar, T. M., Fry, M., Kim, M., & Guivernau, M. (2009). Influence of caring youth sport contexts on efficacy-related beliefs and social behaviors. *Developmental Psychology, 45*(2), 329–340.

Garcia-Zamor, J. C. (2003). Workplace spirituality and organizational performance. *Public Administration Review, 63*, 355–363.

Gardner, H. (1993). *Frames of mind: The theory of multiple intelligences.* NY: Basic.

Gaudine, A., & Thorne, L. (2001). Emotion and ethical decision-making in organizations. *Journal of Business Ethics, 31*, 175–187. doi: 10.1023/A:1010711413444

Gauss, C. E. (1973–1974). Empathy. In P. P. Wiener (Ed.), *Dictionary of the history of ideas: Studies of selected pivotal ideas* (Vol. 2, pp.85–89). NY: Scribner.

Gaye, A. (n.d.) Retrieved from http://www.searchquotes.com/quotation/Power_comes_not_from_the_barrel_of_a_gun,_but_from_one's_awareness_of_his_or_her_own_cultural_streng/21398/

George, J. M. (2000). Emotions and leadership: The role of EI. *Human Relations, 53*(8), 1027–1055.

Gibbons, J., Bore, M., Munro, D., & Powis, D. (2007). Using Personal Quality Assessment for selection of social work students. *Australian Social Work, 60*, 210–221.

Gilligan, C. (1993). *In a different voice. Psychological theory and women's development.* Cambridge, MA: Harvard University Press. (Original work published in 1982.)

Global palm oil demand fueling deforestation (2012). *Worldwatch Institute.* Retrieved September 15, 2012 from http://www.worldwatch.org/node/6059

Glomb, T. M., Duffy, M. K., Bono, J. E., & Yang, T. (2011). Mindfulness at work. *Research in Personnel and Human Resources Management, 30,* 115–157. doi: 10.1108/S0742-7301(2011)0000030005

Goldberg, L. R., Johnson, J. A., Eber, H. W., Hogan, R., Ashton, M. C., Cloninger, C. R., & Gough, H. G. (2006). The international personality item pool and the future of public-domain personality measures. *Journal of Research in Personality, 40,* 84–96.

Goleman, D. (1995). *Emotional intelligence: Why it can matter more than IQ.* NY: Bantam.

Goleman, D. (1998). *Working with emotional intelligence.* NY: Bantam Dell.

Goleman, D. (2006a). *Emotional intelligence.* 10th Anniversary Edition. NY: Bantam.

Goleman, D. (2006b). *Social intelligence.* NY: Bantam.

Goleman, D. (2006c). *Working with emotional intelligence.* NY: Bantam Dell.

Goleman, D., & Boyatzis, R. (2008, September). Social intelligence and the biology of leadership. *Harvard Business Review,* 74–81.

Goleman, D., Boyatzis, R., & McKee, A. (2002). *Primal leadership: Realizing the power of emotional intelligence.* Boston: Harvard University Press.

Goman, C. K. (2011). *The silent language of leaders.* San Francisco: Jossey Bass.

Gould, D., Flett, R., & Lauer, L. (2012). The relationship between psychosocial developmental and the sports climate experienced by underserved youth. *Psychology of Sport and Exercise, 13,* 80–87. doi:10.1016/j.psychsport.2011.07.005

Greason, P. B., & Cashwell, C. S. (2009). Mindfulness and counseling self-efficacy: The mediating role of attention and empathy. *Counselor Education and Supervision, 49*(1), 2–19.

Gustavsson, B. (1992). *The transcendent organization.* Unpublished doctoral dissertation, University of Stockholm.

Hagelin, J. S. (1987). Is consciousness the unified field? A field theorist's perspective. *Modern Science and Vedic Science, 1*(1), 29–88.

Hagelin, J. S., Rainforth, M. V., Orme-Johnson, D. W., Cavanaugh, K. L., Alexander, C. N., Shatkin, S. F., . . . Ross, E. (1999). Effects of group practice of the Transcendental Meditation program on preventing violent crime in Washington D.C.: Results of the national demonstration project, June–July, 1993. *Social Indicators Research, 47,*153–201.

Haque, O. S., & Waytz, A. (2012) Dehumanization in medicine: Causes, solutions, and functions. *Perspectives on Psychological Science, 7,* 176–186.

Harmon, W. (1988). *Global mind change.* NY: Warner Books.

Harung, H. S., Heaton, D. P., & Alexander, C. N. (1999). Evolution of organizations in the new millennium. *Leadership and Organization Development Journal, 20*(3), 198–207.

Harung, H., Travis, F., Blank, W., & Heaton, D. (2009) Higher development, brain integration, and excellence in leadership. *Management Decision, 47*(6), 872–894.

Harung, H. S., Travis, F., Pensgaard, A .M., Boes, R., Cook-Greuter, S., & Daley, K. (2011). Higher psycho-physiological refinement in world-class Norwegian athletes: Brain measures of performance capacity. *Scandanavian Journal of Medicine and Science in Sports, 21*(1), 32–41.

Haslam, N. (2007). Humanising medical practice: The role of empathy. *Medical Journal of Australia, 187,* 381–382.

Hatfield, E., Rapson, R. L., & Le, Y. L. (2009). Emotional contagion and empathy. In J. Decety & W. Ickes (Eds.), *The social neuroscience of empathy.* Cambridge, MA: MIT.

Hayes, S. C. (1984). Making sense of spirituality. *Behaviorism, 12*(2), 99–110.
Hayes, S. C., Barnes-Holmes, D., & Roche, B. (2001). *Relational frame theory: A post-Skinnerian account of human language and cognition.* NY: Kluwer Academic/Plenum.
Hayes, S. C., Bissett, R., Roget, N., Padilla, M., Kohlenberg, B. S., Fisher, G., & Niccolls, R. (2004). The impact of acceptance and commitment training and multicultural training on the stigmatizing attitudes and professional turnout of substance abuse counselors. *Behavior Therapy, 35*(4), 821–835.
Hayes, S. C., & Plumb, J. C. (2007). Mindfulness from the bottom up: Providing an inductive framework for understanding mindfulness processes and their application to human suffering. *Psychological Inquiry, 18*(4), 242–248.
Hayes, S. C., & Shenk, C. (2004). Operationalizing mindfulness without unnecessary Attachments. *clinical psychology: Science and practice, 11*(3), 249.
Hayes, S. C., Strosahl, K. D., & Wilson, K. G. (2011). *Acceptance and commitment therapy: The process and practice of mindful change* (2nd ed.). NY: The Guilford Press.
Heaphy, E. (2007). Bodily insights: Three lenses on positive organizational relationships. In J. Dutton & B. Ragins (Eds.), *Exploring positive relationships at work* (pp. 47–71). Mahwah, NJ: Lawrence Earlbaum Associates.
Heaton, D. P. (2011). Transcendent experience and development of the post-representational Self. In A. Pfaffenberger, P. Marko, & Combs, A. (Eds.), *The postconventional personality: Perspectives on higher development* (pp. 175–188
Heaton, D. P., & Schmidt-Wilk, J. (2008). Leadership development through development of consciousness. In G. Biberman & L. Tischler (Eds.), *Spirituality in business: Current theory and practice and future directions* (pp. 125–140). London: Palgrave Macmillan.
Heaton, D. P., Travis, F., & Subramaniam, R. (2012). A consciousness-based approach to management education for integrity. In C. Wankel & A. Stachowicz-Stanusch (Eds.), *Handbook of research on teaching ethics in business and management education* (pp. 66–79). Hershey, PA: IGI Global.
Hellison, D. (2011). *Teaching personal and social responsibility through physical activity* (3rd ed.). Champaign, IL: Human Kinetics.
Hellison, D., Cutforth, N., Kallusky, J., Martinek, T., Parker, M., & Stiehl, J. (2000). *Youth development and physical activity: Linking universities and communities.* Champaign, IL: Human Kinetics.
Herriott, E. M. (2000). *Elements of entrepreneurial success: The links among inner competencies, inner development and success.* Unpublished doctoral dissertation, Maharishi University of Management, Fairfield, IA.
Herriott, E. M., Schmidt-Wilk, J., & Heaton, D. P. (2009). Spiritual dimensions of entrepreneurship in Transcendental Meditation and TM-Sidhi program practitioners. *Journal of Management, Spirituality and Religion, 6*(3), 195–208.
Herron, R. E., Hillis, S. L., Mandarino, J. V., Orme-Johnson, D. W., & Walton, K. G. (1996). Reducing medical costs: The impact of the Transcendental Meditation program on government payments to physicians in Quebec. *American Journal of Health Promotion, 10*(3), 206–216.
Hochschild, A. R. (1983). *The managed heart: The commercialization of human feeling.* Berkeley: University of California Press.
Hodges, S. D., & Biswas-Diener, R. (2007). Balancing the empathy expense account: Strategies for regulating empathic response. In T.F.D. Farrow & P.W.R. Woodruff (Eds.), *Empathy in mental illness* (pp. 389–405). Cambridge: Cambridge University Press.
Hoffman, M. (2000). *Empathy and moral development: Implications for caring and justice.* Cambridge: Cambridge University Press.

Hoffman, M. L. (2001). Toward a comprehensive empathy-based theory of pro social moral development. In A. C. Bohart & D. J. Stipeck (Eds.), *Constructive and destructive behavior: Implications for family, school, and society* (pp. 61–86). Washington, DC: American Psychological Association; Cambridge: Cambridge University Press.

Hogan, R. (1969). Development of an empathy scale. *Journal of Consulting and Clinical Psychology, 33,* 307–316.

Hogan, R., & Hogan, J. (2001). Assessing leadership: A view of the dark side. *International Journal of Selection and Assessment, 9,* 40–51.

Hogg, M. A. (2001). A social identity theory of leadership. *Personality and Social Psychology Review, 5*(3), 184–200. doi: 10.1207/s15327957pspr0503_1

Hogue, D. A. (2003).Sensing the other in worship: Mirror neurons and the empathizing brain. *Liturgy, 21*(3), 31–39.

Hojat, M. (2007). *Empathy in patient care: Antecedents, development, measurement, and outcomes.* NY: Springer.

Hojat, M., Gonnella, J. S., Mangione, S., Nasca, T., Nasca, T. J., Veloski, . . . Magee, M. (2002). Empathy in medical students as related to academic performance, clinical competence and gender. *Medical Education, 36,* 1–6.

Hojat, M., Louis, D., Markham, F., Wender, R., Rabinowitz, C., & Gonnella, J. (2011). Physicians' empathy and clinical outcomes for diabetic patients. *Academic Medicine, 86*(3), 359–364.

Hojat, M., Mangione S., & Nasca T. J. (2001). The Jefferson Scale of Empathy: development and preliminary psychometric data. *Educational and Psychological Measurement, 61,* 349–365.

Hojat, M., Vengare M . J., & Maxwell K. (2009). The devil is in the third year: A longitudinal study of erosion of empathy in medical school. *Academic Medicine, 84,* 1182–1191.

Hojat, M., Zuckerman, M., Magee, M., Mangione, S., Nasca, T., Vergare, M., & Gonnella, J. S. (2005). Empathy in medical students as related to specialty interest, personality, and perceptions of father and mother. *Personality and Individual Differences, 39,* 1205–1215.

Hollingsworth, A. (2008). Neuroscience and spirituality: Implications of interpersonal neurobiology for a spirituality of compassion. *Zygon, 43* (4), 837–860.

Hölzel, B. K., Lazar, S. W., Gard, T., Schuman-Olivier, Z., Vago, D. R., Ott, U., & Schuman-Olivier, Z. (2012). Perspectives on psychological science: Conceptual and neural Perspective. *Perspectives on Psychological Science.* doi:10.1177/1745691611419671

Hölzel, B. Lazar, S. Gard, T. Schuman-Olivier, Z. Vago, D. & Ulrich, O. (2011). How does mindfulness meditationwork? Proposing mechanisms of action from a conceptual and neural perspective. *Perspectives on Psychological Science, 6*(6), 537–559.

Hornblow, A. R., Kidson, M. A., & Jones, K. V. (1977). Measuring medical students' empathy: A validation study. *Medical Education, 11,* 7–12.

Horowitz, J. (2008, December 26). *The Pete Carroll effect.* Retrieved from www. petecarroll.com /2008/12/26/the-pete-carroll-effect/

Houlcroft, L., Bore, M., & Munro, D. (2012). Three faces of narcissism. *Personality and Individual Differences, 53,* 274–278.

Humphrey, R. H. (2006). Promising research opportunities in emotions and coping with conflict. *Journal of Management and Organization, 12*(2), 179–186.

Huxley, A. (1945). *The perennial philosophy.* NY: Harper and Row.

Iacoboni, M. (2009). *Mirroring people: The science of empathy and how we connect with others.* NY: Picador.

IPCC (2012). Managing the risks of extreme events and disasters to advance climate change adaptation. Retrieved August 1, 2012 from http://www.ipcc-wg2.gov/ SREX/images/uploads/SREX-All_FINAL.pdf

Isaacs, W. (1999). *Dialogue and the art of thinking together.* NY: Doubleday.

Isen, A. M. & Daubman, K. A. (1984). The influence of affect on categorization. *Journal of Character and Social Psychology, 47*(6), 1206–1217.

Izard, C. E. (1991). *The psychology of emotions.* NY: Plenum.

Jack, A. I., Dawson, A., Begany, K., Leckie, R., Barry, K., Ciccia, K., & Snyder, A. (2012). fMRI reveals reciprocal inhibition between social and physical cognitive domains. Retrieved from NeuroImagehttp://dx.doi.org/10.1016/j.neuroimage.2012.10.

Jantsch, E. (1980). *The self-organizing universe.* Oxford: Pergamon Press.

Jardim, A. (1970). *The first Henry Ford: A study in personality.* Cambridge: MIT.

Jarski, R. W., Gjerde, C. L., Bratton, B. D., Brown, D. D,. & Matthes, S. S. (1985). A comparison of four empathy instruments in simulated patient-medical student interactions. *Journal of Medical Education, 60,* 545–551.

Jentz, B. (2007). *Talk sense: Communicating to lead and learn.* Acton, MA: Research for better teaching.

Johnson, C. E. (2012*). Meeting the ethical challenges of leadership.* Thousand Oaks, CA: SAGE.

Johnson, S. M. (1994). *Character styles.* NY: W. W. Norton.

Joubert, P. M., Kruger, C., Bergh, A.–M., Pickworth, G. E., Van Staden, C. W., Roos, J. L., . . . Lindeque, B. G. (2006). Medical students on the value of role models for developing 'soft skills'—"That's the way you do it." *South African Psychiatry Review, 9,* 28–32.

Kabat-Zinn, J. (2003). Mindfulness-based interventions in context: Past, present, and future. Clinical psychology: *Science and Practice, 10*(2), 144.

Kahneman, D., & Riis, J. (2005). Living, and thinking about it: Two perspectives on life. In F.A. Huppert, N. Baylis & B. Keverne (Eds.), *The science of well-being* (pp. 285–304). Oxford: Oxford University Press.

Kail, E. (2011, October 28). Leadership character: The role of empathy. *Washington Post.* Retrieved from http://www.washingtonpost.com/blogs/guestinsights/post/ leadershipcharacte r-the-role-of-empathy/2011/04/04/gIQAQXVGQM_blog.html

Kegan, R. (1994). *In over our heads: The mental demands of modern life.* Cambridge, MA: Harvard University Press.

Kelly, E. (2006). *Powerful times.* Upper Saddle River, NJ: Wharton School Publishing.

Kelley, M. (April 12, 2012). 13 signs that America's prison system is out of control. *Business Insider.*

Kenny, N. P., Mann, K. V., & MacLeod, H. (2003). Role modeling in physicians' professional formation: Reconsidering an essential but untapped educational strategy. *Academic Medicine, 78,* 1203–1210.

Kets de Vries, M. F.R., Carlock, R. S. & Florent-Treacy, E. (2007). *Family business on the couch: A psychological perspective.* Chichester: John Wiley.

Kets de Vries, M. F.R., & Miller, D. (1984). *The neurotic organization.* San Francisco: Jossey-Bass.

Keysers, C., & Fadiga, L. (2008). The mirror neuron system: New frontiers. *Social Neuroscience, 3*(3–4), 193–198.

Kimes, M. (2009). P&G's leadership machine. *Fortune, 159*(7), 22.

Kind, S., Irwin, R., Grauer, K., & De Cosson, A. (2005). Medicine wheel imag(in) ings: Exploring holistic curriculum perspectives. *Art Education, 58*(5), 33–38.

Kisfalvi, V. (1995). Laisser nos émotions à la porte? *Gestion, 20*(3), 110–113.

Kisfalvi, V. (2000). The threat of failure, the perils of success and CEO character: Sources of strategic persistence. *Organization Studies, 21*(3), 611–639.

Kisfalvi, V. (2002). The entrepreneur's character, life issues, and strategy making: A field study. *Journal of Business Venturing, 7*(5), 489–518.

Kisfalvi, V., & Maguire, S. (2011). The nature of institutional entrepreneurs: Lessons from Rachel Carson. *Journal of Management Inquiry, 20*(2), 152–177.

Kisfalvi, V., & Pitcher, P. (2003). Doing what feels right: The influence of CEO character and emotions on top management team dynamics. *Journal of Management Inquiry, 12,* 42–66.

Klein, M. (1948). *Contributions to psychoanalysis, 1921–1945.* London: Hogarth.

Klemp, G. (2005). Emotional intelligence and leadership: What really matters. *Cambria Consulting,* 1–4.

Knights, J. A., & Kennedy, B. J. (2006). Medical school selection: Screening for dysfunctional tendencies. *Medical Education, 40,* 1058–1064.

Kohlberg, L. (1981). *The philosophy of moral development: Moral stages and the idea of justice: Vol. I: Essays on moral development.* San Francisco: Harper and Row.

Kohlberg, L. (1984). *Essays on moral development, Vol. II: The psychology of moral development.* NY: Harper and Row.

Kohut, H. (1971). *The analysis of the self.* NY: International Universities Press.

Kong-Hee, K. (2012). Emotion and strategic decision-making behavior: Developing a theoretical model. *International Journal of Business and Social Science, 3*(1), 105–113.

Kouzes, J. M., & Posner, B. Z. (2007). *The leadership challenge* (4th ed.). San Francisco: Jossey-Bass.

Krasner, M. S., Epstein, R. M., Beckman, H., Suchman, A. L., Chapman, B., Mooney, C. J., & Quill, T. E. (2009). Association of an educational program in mindful communication with burnout, empathy, and attitudes among primary care physicians. *Journal of the American Medical Association, 302*(12), 1284–1293.

Kristeller, L. J., & Johnson, T. (2005). Science looks at spirituality. Cultivating loving kindness of meditation on empathy, compassion, and altruism. *Zygon, 40*(2), 391–407.

Kube, S., Maréchal, M. A., & Puppe, C. (2006). Putting reciprocity to work: Positive versus negative responses in the field (Working Paper No.2006–27). Retrieved from the Social Science Research Network website: http://ssrn.com/abstract=944393

Lafley, A. G., & Charan, R. (2008). *The game-changer: How you can drive revenue and profit growth with innovation.* NY: Crowne Business.

Lamm, C., Batson, C. D., & Decety, J. (2007). The neural substrate of human empathy: Effects of perspective taking and cognitive appraisal. *Journal of Cognitive Neuroscience, 19*(1), 42–58.

Lamm, C., Meltzoff, A. N., & Decety, J. (2010). How do we empathize with someone who is not like us? A functional magnetic resonance imaging study. *Journal of Cognitive Neuroscience, 22*(2), 362–376.

Langer, E. (1989). *Mindfulness.* Reading, MA: Addison Wesley.

Lappe, A. (2010). Diet for a hot planet. In D. Imhoff (Ed.), *CAFO.* Los Angeles: Watershed Media.

Larsson, I. E., Sahlsten, M.J.M., Segesten, K., & Plos, K. A. (2011). E. Patients' perceptions of barriers for participation in nursing care. *Scandinavian Journal of Caring Sciences, 25,* 575–582.

Laszlo, E. (1995). *The interconnected universe: Conceptual foundations of a transdisciplinary unified theory.* Singapore: World Scientific.

Laszlo, E. (2007). *Science and the Akashic field.* Rochester, VT: Inner Traditions.

Layton, J. M., & Wykle, M. H. (1990). A validity study of four empathy instruments. *Research in Nursing and Health, 13,* 319–325.

Lazar, S., Kerr, C., Wasserman, R., Gray, J., Greve, D., & Treadway, M. (2005). Meditation experience is associated with increased cortical thickness. *NeuroReport, 16*(17), 1893–1897.

Lazarus, R. S. (1982). Thoughts on the relations between emotion and cognition. *American Psychologist, 37*(9), 1019–1024.

Lazarus, R. S. (1984). On the primacy of cognition. *American Psychologist, 39*(2), 124–129.

LeDoux, J. E. (1996). *The emotional brain: The mysterious underpinnings of emotional life.* NY: Simon & Schuster.

Lee, J. A., & Murnighan, J. K. (2001). The empathy-prospect model and the choice to help. *Journal of Applied Social Psychology, 31*, 816–839. doi: 10.1111/j.1559-1816.2001.tb01415.x

LenkaBula, P. (2008). Beyond anthropocentricity—Botho/*Ubuntu* and the quest for economic and ecological justice in Africa.*Religion & Theology, 15*, 375–394. doi: 10.1163/157430108X376591

Lennick, D., Kile, F., & Jordan, K. (2011). *Moral intelligence 2.0.* NY: Prentice Hall.

Lerner, R. M., Fisher, C. M., & Weinberg, R. A. (2000). Toward a science for and of the people: Promoting civil society through the application of developmental science. *Child Development, 71*, 11–20.

Lesh, T. V. (1970). Zen meditation and the development of empathy in counselors. *Journal of Humanistic Psychology, 10*(1), 39–74. doi: 10.1177/002216787001000105

Leung, M.-K. K., Chan, C. C. H., Yin, J., Lee, C.-F. F., So, K.-F. F., & Lee, T.M.C. (2012). Increased gray-matter volume in the right angular and posterior parahippocampal gyri in loving-kindness meditators. Social cognitive and affective neuroscience. doi: 10.1093/scan/nss076

Lewicki, R. J., Saunders, D. M., & Barry, B. (2007). *Negotiation: Readings, exercises, and cases* (5th ed.). Boston: McGraw-Hill/Irwin.

Liggan, D. Y., & Kay, J. (1999). Some neurobiological aspects of psychotherapy: A review. *Journal of Psychotherapy Practice and Research, 8,*103–114.

Lilius, J., Worline, M., Dutton, J., Kanov, J., Frost, P., & Maitlis, S. (2008). Contours of compassion at work. *Journal of Organizational Behavior, 29*(2), 193–218.

Locke, E. A. (2005). Why emotional intelligence is an invalid concept. *Journal of Organizational Behavior, 26*, 425–431.

Loevinger, J. (1976). *Ego development: Conceptions and theories.* San Francisco: Jossey-Bass.

Lombardo, M. V., Barnes, J. L., Wheelwright, S. J., & Baron-Cohen S. (2007). Self-referential cognition and empathy in autism. *PLoS ONE 2*(9), e883.doi:10.1371/journal.pone.0000883

Lord, R. G., & Hall, R. J. (2005). Identity, deep structure and the development of leadership skill. *The Leadership Quarterly, 16*(4), 591–615.

Lowe, M., Kerridge, I., Bore, M., Munro, D., & Powis, D. A. (2001). Is it possible to assess the "ethics" of medical school applicants? *Journal of Medical Ethics, 27*, 404–408.

Lown, B. A., Chou, C. L., Clark, W. D., Haidet, P., White, M. K., Krupat, E., . . . Anderson, M. B. (2007). Caring attitudes in medical education: Perceptions of deans and curriculum leaders. *Journal of General Internal Medicine, 22*, 1514–1522.

Lutz, A., Brefczynski-Lewis, J., Johnstone, T., & Davidson, R. J. (2008). Regulation of the neural circuitry of emotion by compassion meditation: Effects of meditative expertise. *PLoS ONE, 3*(3), e1897.

Lynoe, N., Lofmark, R., & Thulesius, H. O. (2008). Teaching medical ethics: What is the impact of role models? Some experiences from Swedish medical schools. *Journal of Medical Ethics, 34*, 315–316.

Macnaughton, J. (2009). The dangerous practice of empathy. *The Lancet, 373*(9679), 1940–1941.

Maharishi Mahesh Yogi (1963). *Science of being and art of living.* NY: Signet.

Maharishi Mahesh Yogi (1969). *On the Bhagavad-Gita: A new translation and commentary with Sanskrit text—Chapters 1 to 6.* Baltimore, MD: Penguin/Arkana.

Maharishi Mahesh Yogi (1972). *The science of creative intelligence.* Videotaped course manual. Fairfield, IA: Maharishi International University Press.

Maharishi Mahesh Yogi (1976). *Creating an ideal society: A global undertaking.* Rheinweiler, Germany: MERU Press.

Maharishi Mahesh Yogi (1985). Inaugural address of His Holiness Maharishi Mahesh Yogi. In *Maharishi Vedic University Inauguration* (pp. 56–78). Washington, DC: Age of Enlightenment Press.

Maharishi Mahesh Yogi (1986). *Life supported by natural law.* Fairfield, IA: Maharishi International University Press.

Maharishi Mahesh Yogi (1994). *Vedic knowledge for everyone.* India: Age of Enlightenment Publications.

Maharishi Mahesh Yogi (1995). *Maharishi University of Management: Wholeness on the move.* Vlodrop, Holland: Maharishi Vedic University Press.

Malcomson, B. (2007, August 13). *Making a better L.A.* Retrieved from www.petecarroll.com /2007/08/13/making-a-better-l-a/

Mann, K. V., Ruedy, J., Millar, N., & Andreou, P. (2005). Achievement of non-cognitive goals of undergraduate medical education: perceptions of medical students, residents, faculty and other health professionals. *Medical Education, 39*, 40–48.

Mano, H. (1994). Risk-taking, framing effects, and affect. *Organizational Behavior & Human Decision Processes, 57*, 38–58.

Martinek, T., Schilling, T., & Hellison, D. (2006). The development of compassionate and caring leadership among adolescents. *Physical Education and Sport Pedagogy, 11*, 141–157.

Mascaro, J. S., Rilling, J. K., Tenzin Negi L., Raison, C. L. (2012). Compassion meditation enhances empathic accuracy and related neural activity. *Social Cognitive and Affective Neuroscience, On-line first 29 September* doi:10.1093/scan/nss095

Maslow, A. (1962/1968). *Toward a psychology of being.* Princeton, NJ: Van Nostrand.

Maslow, A. H. (1943). A theory of human motivation. *Psychological Review 50*(4), 370–396.

Maslow, A. H. (1998). *Maslow on management.* NY: John Wiley & Sons.

Mast, M. S., & Ickes, W. (2007). Empathic accuracy: Measurement and potential clinical applications. InT. Farrow & P. Woodruff (Eds.). *Empathy in mental illness* (pp. 408–427). NY: Cambridge University Press.

Masuda, A., Hayes, S. C., Fletcher, L. B., Seignourel, P. J., Bunting, K., Herbst, S. A., . . . Lillis, J. (2007). Impact of acceptance and commitment therapy versus education on stigma toward people with psychological disorders. *Behavior Research and Therapy, 45*(11), 2764–2772.

Matsumo, D., & Williamson, B. (2009). Spontaneous facial expressions of emotion in congenitally and non-congenitally blind individuals. *Journal of Personality and Social Psychology, 96*(1), 1–10.

Matthews, C. (2000). Role modelling: How does it influence teaching in family medicine? *Medical Education, 34*, 443–448.

Matthews, G., Zeidner, M., & Roberts, R. D. (Eds.). (2007). *The science of emotional intelligence: Knowns and unknowns.* NY: Oxford University Press.

Maturana, H., & Varela, F. (1980). *Autopoiesis and cognition: The organization of the living.* Boston: Reidel.

Maturana, H., & Varela, F. (1987). *The tree of knowledge: The biological roots of human understanding.* Boston: Shambhala. (Revised edition 1998.)

Mayer, J.D., Salovey, P., & Caruso, D. (2002). *The Mayer-Salovey-Caruso emotional intelligence test (MSCEIT)*. Toronto: The Multi-Health Systems.

Mayer, J.D., & Salovey, P. (1997). What is emotional intelligence? In P. Salovey & D. Sluyter (Eds.), *Emotional development and emotional intelligence: Implications for educators* (pp. 3–31). NY: Basic Books.

Mazutis, D., & Slawinski, N. (2008). Leading organizational learning through authentic dialogue. *Management Learning, 39*(4), 437–456.

McBane, D. (1995). Empathy and the salesperson: A multidimensional perspective. *Psychology and Marketing, 12*(4), 349–370.

McCollum, B. (1999). Leadership development and self-development: An empirical study. *Career Development International, 4*, 149–154.

McCollum, E.E., & Gehart, D.R. (2010). Using mindfulness meditation to teach beginning therapists therapeutic presence: A qualitative study. *Journal of Marital and Family Therapy, 36*(3), 347–360.

McConnell, B., & Huba, J. (2003). *Meg Whitman: How eBay rules*. Retrieved from http://www. creatingcustomerevangelists.com/resources/evangelists/meg_whitman.asp

McCracken, L.M., & Yang, S.-Y. (2008). A contextual cognitive-behavioral analysis of rehabilitation workers' health and well-being: Influences of acceptance, mindfulness, and values-based action. [Journal; Peer Reviewed Journal]. *Rehabilitation Psychology, 53*(4), 479–485.

McCuan, J. (2005, April 1). *26 most fascinating entrepreneurs*: Jack Mitchell. Retrieved from http://www.inc.com/magazine/20050401/26-mitchell.html

McDaniel, J. (2006). All animals matter: Marc Bekoff's contribution to constructive Christian theology. *Journal of Religion and Spirituality, 41*(1), 32–52.

McHugh, L., Barnes-Holmes, Y., & Barnes-Holmes, D. (2004). Perspective-taking as relational responding: A developmental profile. *Psychological Record, 54*(1), 115–144.

McHugh, L., Stewart, I., & Hooper, N. (2012). A contemporary functional analytic account of perspective taking. In L. McHugh & I. Stewart (Eds.), *The self and perspective taking: Contributions and applications from modern behavioral science* (pp. 55–72). Oakland, CA: Context Press.

McIntosh, F. (2011). *The relational leader*. Boston: Course Technology.

McMillan, D.W., & Chavis, D.M. (1986). Sense of community: A definition and theory. *Journal of Community Psychology, 14*, 6–23.

Mehrabian, A., & Epstein, N.A. (1972). A measure of emotional empathy. *Journal of Personality, 40*, 525–543.

Mencl, J., & May, D.R. (2009). The effects of proximity and empathy on ethical decision-making: An exploratory investigation. *Journal of Business Ethics, 85*, 201–226. doi: 10.1007/s10551-008-9765-5

Mercado, C.I. (1993). Caring as empowerment. School collaboration and community agency. *The Urban Review, 25*, 79–104.

Mesquita, B. (2003). Emotions as dynamic cultural phenomena. In R.J. Davidson, K.R. Scherer, & G.H. Hill (Eds.), *Handbook of affective sciences. Series in affective science* (pp. 871–890). NY: Oxford University Press.

Metz, T., & Gaie, J.B.R. (2010). The African ethic of *Ubuntu*/Botho: Implications for research on morality. *Journal of Moral Education, 39*, 273–290.

Misra-Hebert, A D., Isaacson, J.H., Kohn, M., Hull, A.L., Hojat, M., Papp, K.K., & Calabrese, L. (2012). Improving empathy of physicians through guided reflective writing. *International Journal of Medical Education, 3*, 71–77.

Mitchell, J. (2003). *Hug your customers: The proven way to personalize sales and achieve astounding results*. Hyperion Books.

Mitroff, I., & Denton, E. (1999). *A spiritual audit of corporate America: A hard look at spirituality, religion, and values in the workplace*. San Francisco: Jossey-Bass.

Mitroff, I.I., & Denton, E.A. (1999). A study of spirituality in the workplace. Sloan *Management Review* (Summer), 83–92.

Molisa, P. (2011). A spiritual reflection on emancipation and accounting. *Critical Perspectives on Accounting, 22,* 453–484.

Moll, J., de Oliveira-Souza, R., Eslinger, P.J., Bramati, I.E., Mouräao-Miranda, J., Andreiuolo, P.A., & Pessoa, L. (2002). The neural correlates of moral sensitivity: A functional magnetic resonance imaging investigation of basic and moral emotions. The *Journal of Neuroscience: The Official Journal of the Society for Neuroscience, 22*(7), 2730–2736.

Monica, E.L.L. (1981). Construct validity of an empathy instrument. *Research in Nursing & Health, 4*(4), 389–400. doi: 10.1002/nur.4770040406

Moore, B.E., & Fine, B. D (1990). Psychoanalytic terms and concepts. NY: *The American Psychoanalytic Association,* 123.

Morrison, M., & Borgen, W.A. (2010). How christian spiritual and religious beliefs help and hinder counselors' empathy toward clients. *Counseling and Values 55,* 25–45.

Munro, D., Bore, M., & Powis, D. (2005). Personality factors in professional ethical behavior: Studies of empathy and narcissism. *Australian Journal of Psychology, 57,* 49–60.

Munro, D., Bore, M., & Powis, D. (2008). Personality determinants of success in medical school and beyond: "Steady, sane and nice." In S. Boag (Ed.), *Personality down under: Perspectives from Australia, Chapter 9* (pp. 103–111). NY: Nova Science Publishers.

Murinson, B.B., Klick, B., Haythornthwaite, J.A., Shochet, R., Levine, R.B., & Wright, S.M. (2010). Formative experiences of emerging physicians: Gauging the impact of events that occur during medical school. *Academic Medicine, 85,* 1331–1337.

Muyia, H.M. (2009). Approaches to and instruments for measuring emotional intelligence: A review of selected literature. *Advances in Developing Human Resources, 11*(6), 690.

Natale, S. (1972). *An experiment in empathy.* Slough, England: National Foundation for Educational Research.

Natale, S., & Sora, S. (2010). Ethics in strategic thinking: Business processes and the global market collapse. *Journal of Business Ethics, 94*(3), 309–316.

National Diabetes Fact Sheet (2011). Center for Disease Controls and Prevention. Retrieved January 2, 2013 from http://www.cdc.gov/diabetes/pubs/pdf/ndfs_2011.pdf

Newton, M., Watson, D.L., Gano-Overway, L., Fry, M., Kim, M., & Magyar, M. (2007). The role of a caring-based intervention in a physical domain. *The Urban Review, 39,* 281–299.

Nidich, S.I., Rainforth, M.V., Haaga, D.A., Travis, F., King, C, Salerno, S., Schneider, R. (2010). A randomized controlled trial on effects of the Transcendental Meditation program on blood pressure, psychological distress, and coping in young adults. *American Journal of Hypertension, 22,* 1326–31.

Nkondo, G.M. (2007). *Ubuntu* as public policy in South Africa: A conceptual framework.International *Journal of African Renaissance Studies, 2,* 88–100. doi: 10.1080/18186870701384202

Noddings, N. (1992). *The challenge to care in schools: An alternative approach to education.* NY: Teacher College Press.

Noddings, N. (2002*). Educating moral people: A caring alternative to character education.* NY: Teacher College Press.

Noddings, N. (2003). *Caring: A feminine approach to ethics and moral education.* Berkeley: University of California Press. (Original work published in 1984.)

Noddings, N. (2010). *The maternal factor: Two paths to morality*. Berkeley: University of California Press.

Nowak, M. (2012). Why we help. What makes us human (special collector's edition). *Scientific American*. NY: Nature Publishing Group.

Noy, I. (2011).The macroeconomic aftermath of the earthquake/tsunami in Japan. *Econbrowser, March 15*. Retrieved from http://www.econbrowser.com/archives/2011/03/guest_contribut_8.html

Obama, B. (2010). *Empathy and literacy speech*. Retrieved from http://www.youtube.com/watch?v=LGHbbJ5xz3g

Oberman, L., & Ramachandran, V. (2007). The simulating social mind: The role of the mirror neuron system and simulation in the social and communicative deficits of autism spectrum disorders. *Psychological Bulletin, 133*(2), 310–327.

Oceja,L.V.(2008).Overcoming empathy-induced partiality:Two rules of thumb. *Basic and Applied Social Psychology, 30*, 176–182. doi: 10.1080/01973530802209236

Olfman, S. (2006). Self, identity, and generativity. In R. Cavoukian & S. Olfman (Eds.), *Child honoring*. Westport, CT: Praeger Publishers.

Orme-Johnson, D.W. (1987). Medical care utilization and the Transcendental Meditation program. *Psychosomatic Medicine, 49*, 493–507.

Orme-Johnson, D.W. (2000). An overview of Charles Alexander's contribution to psychology: Developing higher states of consciousness in the individual and society. *Journal of Adult Development, 7*, 199–216.

Orme-Johnson, D.W., Alexander, C.N., Davies, J.L., Chandler, H.M., & Larimore,W.E. (1988). Peace project in the Middle East: Effects of the Maharishi technology of the unified field. *Journal of Conflict Resolution, 32*, 776–812.

Orme-Johnson, D.W., & Oates, R.M. (2009). A field-theoretic view of consciousness: Reply to critics. *Journal of Scientific Exploration, 23*(2), 139–166.

Parry, W. (2011). Overuse of antibiotics is seen behind many human ills. *Livescience*. Retrieved August 2, 2012 from http://www.livescience.com/15740-helpful-bacteria-antibiotics.html

Parry, W. (2012). Soil microbes harbor nasty antibiotic resistance genes. *LiveScience*. Retrieved September 26, 2012 from http://www.livescience.com/22835-soil-bacteria-antibiotic-resistance.html

Patanjali (1978). *Yoga sutras*. Prasada (Trans.). New Delhi: Oriental Books Reprint Corp. (Original work published 1912.)

Pate, L.E. (1987). Improving managerial decision making. *Journal of Managerial Psychology, 2*(2), 9–15.

Pate, L.E. (1988). Using the Four ACES decision-making technique in the classroom. *Organizational Behavior Teaching Review (now Journal of Management Education), 12*(4), 155–158.

Pate, L.E., & Chesteen, S.A. (2000). Decision-making and work motivation: reframing the role of the pharmacist from intervention to direct patient care. In C. Nimmo (Ed.), *Staff Development for Pharmacy Practice*. Bethesda, MD: American Society of Health-System Pharmacists.

Pate, L.E., & Filley, A.C. (2002). Leadership and decision-making in medicine. In D. Albert (Ed.), *A Physician's Guide to Healthcare Management*. Malden, MA: Blackwell Science.

Pate, L.E., & Greiner, L.E. (1989). Resolving dilemmas in power and OD with the Four ACES technique. *Consultation: An International Journal, 8*(1), 58–67.

Pate, L.E., & Heiman, D.C. (1987). Organizational schematas: Beyond behavioristic and phenomenological approaches to learning and decision making. *Journal of Human Behavior and Learning, 4*(3), 26–32.

Pate, L.E., & Nielson, T.R. (1996). Empirical findings on the ACES Decision-Making Technique. *Psychological Reports, 78*, 1049–1050.

Pate, L. E. & Ryder, P. A. (1987). Effective decision making and the HRM professional. *Human Resource Management Australia (now Asia Pacific Journal of Human Resources), 25*(2), 72–76.

Pate, L. E., Young, J. E., & Swinth, R. L. (1988). Group processes in solving complex novel problems: Implications for executives' decision making. *Psychological Reports, 62,* 23–29.

Patnaik, D. (2009). Widespread empathy: Rewiring your corporation for intuition. Fast Company. Retrieved from http://www/fastcompany.com/blog/dev-patnaik/innovation/ widespread-empathy

Patnaik, D., & Mortensen, P. (2009). *Wired to care.* Upper Saddle River NJ: FT Press.

Paulhus, D. L., & Williams, K. M. (2002). The dark triad of personality: Narcissism, Machiavellianism, and psychopathy. *Journal of Research in Personality, 36,* 556–563.

Pavlovich, K. (2012). Faith, hope and care: Integrity and poverty alleviation through enterprise. In A. Wolfgang & A. Stachowicz-Stanusch (Eds.), *Business integrity in practice—insights from international case studies* (pp. 79–84). NY: Business Expert Press, in the first PRME Book Collection.

Pavlovich, K., & Krahnke, K. (2012). Empathy, connectedness, and organisation. *Journal of Business Ethics, 105,* 131–137. doi: 10.1007/s10551-011-0961-3

Pearl, J. H., & Carlozzi, A. F. (1994). Effect of meditation on empathy and anxiety. *Perceptual and Motor Skills, 78*(1), 297–298.

Pennebaker, J. W., Booth, R. J., & Francis, M. E. (2007). Operator's manual linguistic inquiry and word count: LIWC2007. Retrieved from http://homepage.psy.utexas.edu/homepage/faculty/pennebaker/reprints/LIWC2007_OperatorManual.pdf

Pete Carroll USC Head Football Coach. Retrieved from http://www.usctrojans.com/sports/m-footbl/mtt/carroll_pete00.html

Petersen, L.-E., & Dietz, J. (2008). Employment discrimination: Authority figures' demographic preferences and followers' affective organizational commitment. *Journal of Applied Psychology, 93,* 1287–1300. doi: 10.1037/a0012867

Petitpas, A. J., Cornelius, A. E., Van Raalte, J. L., & Jones, T.(2005). A framework for planning youth sport programs that foster psychosocial development. *The Sport Psychologist, 19,* 63–80.

Piaget, J. (1969). *The psychology of the child.* NY: Harper Torch books.

Pincus, A. L., Ansell, E. B., Pimentel, C. A., Cain, N. M., Wright, A.G.C., & Levy, K. N. (2009). Initial construction and validation of the pathological narcissism inventory. *Psychological Assessment, 21,* 365–379.

Pink, D. H. (2005). *A whole new mind.* NY: Penguin.

Pirson, M. A., & Lawrence, P. R. (2010). Humanism in business—towards a paradigm shift? *Journal of Business Ethics, 93,* 553–565.

Platek, S. M., Critton, S. R., Myers, T. E., & Gallup, G. G. (2003). Contagious yawning: The role of self-awareness and mental state attribution. *Cognitive Brain Research, 17*(2), 223–227.

Plattner, H. (2012). Introduction to design thinking process guide. Stanford Humanities Lab and Metamedia. Retrieved November 25, 2012 from http://humanitieslab.stanford.edu/admin/directory.html

Plummer, M. P. (2008). *The impact of therapists' personal practice of mindfulness meditation on clients' experience of received empathy.* Psychology dissertation, Massachusetts School of Professional Psychology, United States—Massachusetts. ProQuest Dissertations & Theses A&I database.

Polychroniou, P. V. (2009). Relationship between emotional intelligence and transformational leadership of supervisors. *Team Performance Management, 15*(7), 343–356.

Powis, D., Bore, M., Munro, D., & Lumsden, M.A. (2005). Development of the Personal Qualities Assessment as a tool for selecting medical students. *Journal of Adult and Continuing Education, 11*, 3–14.

Preston, S.D. (2007). A perception-action model for empathy. In T. Farrow & P. Woodruff (Eds.), *Empathy in Mental Illness* (pp. 428–447). Cambridge: Cambridge University Press.

Preston, S.D., & de Waal, F.B.M. (2002). Empathy: Its ultimate and proximate bases. *Behavioral and Brain Sciences, 25*(1), 1–71.

Price, P.B., Lewis, E.G., Loughmiller, G.C., Nelson, D.E., Murray, S.L. & Taylor, C.W. (1971). Attributes of a good practicing physician. *Journal of Medical Education, 46*, 229–237.

Probst T.M., & Strand P. (2010). Perceiving and responding to job insecurity: A workplace spirituality perspective. *Journal of Management, Spirituality & Religion, 7*(2), 135–156.

Procter & Gamble. (2008). *2008 annual report.* Retrieved from http://annualreport.pg.com/ annualreport2008/

Procter & Gamble (2012). *Heritage.* Retrieved from http://www.pg.com/en_US/ company/ heritage.shtml

Quinn, R. (2007). *Lift: Becoming a positive force in any situation.* San Francisco: Berrett-Koehler Publishers.

Rameson, L.T., Morelli, S.A., & Lieberman, M.D. (2012). The neural correlates of empathy: Experience, automacity and prosocial behavior. *Journal of Cognitive Neuroscience, 24*(1), 235–245.

Raskin, R., & Hall, C.S. (1981). The Narcissistic Personality Inventory: Alternative form reliability and further evidence of construct validity. *Journal of Personality Assessment, 45*, 159–162.

Raskin, R.N., & Hall, C.S. (1979). A narcissistic personality inventory. *Psychological Reports, 45*, 590.

Ray, M.L. (1993). Introduction. In M.L. Ray & A. Renzler (Eds.), *The new paradigm in business: Emerging strategies for leadership and organizational change* (pp. 1–15). Los Angeles: Jeremy P. Tarcher/Perigee.

Reese, F.R., & Myers, E.J. (2012). EcoWellness: The missing factor in holistic wellness models. *Journaling of Counseling & Development, 90*, 400–407.

Reich, Wilhelm (1933). *Character analysis.* NY: Orgone Institute Press.

Retailer of the year Mitchells/Richards. (2001, November).*?What are you doing, Dave?"The computers at Mitchells and Richards know what you did last summer, 56.* Retrieved from http://www.mitchellstores.com/site/wp-content/themes/ cadc/images/pr_mitchells_mr1.pdf

Riess, H. (2010). Empathy in medicine—A neurobiological perspective. *Journal of the American Medical Association, 304*, 1604–1605.

Rifkin, J. (2009). *Empathic civilization.* NY: Penguin Group.

Rifkin, J. (2010). Jeremy Rifkin: The empathic civilization [video file] Retrieved from http://www.youtube.com/watch?v=nQN_13KawUw

Rig Veda (1896). Translated by Ralph T. Griffith.

Riggio, R.E., & Reichard, R.J. (2008). The emotional and social intelligences of effective leadership: An emotional and social skill approach. *Journal of Managerial Psychology, 23*(2), 69–185.

Rogers, C.R. (1992). The necessary and sufficient conditions of therapeutic personality change. *Journal of Consulting and Clinical Psychology, 60*(6), 827–832. doi: 10.1037/0022-006x.60.6.827

Rosenthal, N. (2011), *Transcendence: Healing and transformation through transcendental meditation.* NY: Tarcher.

Russett, B. (1988). Editor's comment. *Journal of Conflict Resolution, 32,* 773–775.

Sahdra, B. K., MacLean, K. A., Ferrer, E., Shaver, P. R., Rosenberg, E. L., Jacobs, T. L., . . . Saron, C. D. (2011). Enhanced response inhibition during intensive meditation training predicts improvements in self-reported adaptive socioemotional functioning. *Emotion, 11*(2), 299–312.

Sanders, E. J., Hopkins, E. W., & Geroy, D. G. (2003). From transactional to transcendental: Towards an integrated theory of leadership. *Journal of Leadership & Organizational Studies, 9*(4), 21–31.

Sanson-Fisher, R. W., & Poole, A. D. (1978). Training medical students to empathize: An experimental study. *Medical Journal of Australia, 1,* 473–476.

Sawhney, S. (2012). *Effects of the TM technique on anxiety, emotional intelligence and trust: Implications for supply chain management.* Unpublished doctoral dissertation. Maharishi University of Management, Fairfield, IA.

Schaps, E. (March/April 2009). Creating caring school communities. *Leadership,* 8–11.

Scharmer, C. O., & Kaeufer, K. (2013). *Leading from the emerging future.* San Francisco: Berrett-Koehler Publishers.

Scharmer, O. (2007). *Theory U.* Cambridge, MA: SoL.

Schmidt-Wilk, J. (2000). Consciousness-based management development: Case studies of international top management teams. *Journal of Transnational Management Development, 5,* 61–85.

Schmidt-Wilk, J. 2003. TQM and the Transcendental Meditation program in a Swedish top management team. *The TQM Magazine, 15,* 219–229.

Schmidt-Wilk, J., Alexander, C. N., & Swanson, G. C. (1996). Developing consciousness in organizations: The Transcendental Meditation program in business. *Journal of Business and Psychology, 10,* 429–444.

Schmidt-Wilk, J., Heaton, D. P., & Steingard, D. (2000). Higher education for higher consciousness. *Journal of Management Education, 24,* 580–611.

Schnabl, G. K., Hassard, T. H. & Kopelow, M. L. (1991). The assessment of interpersonal skills using standardized patients. *Academic Medicine, 66*(9, Supplement), 34–36.

Schneider, R. H., Staggers, F., Alexander, C. N., Sheppard, W., Rainforth, M., & Kondwani, K. (1995). A randomized controlled trial of stress reduction for hypertension in older African Americans. *Hypertension, 26*(5), 820–827.

Schneider, S. C., & Shrivastava, P. (1988). Basic assumptions themes in organizations. *Human Relations, 41*(7), 493–516.

Schor, J. (2004). *Born to buy.* NY: Scibner.

Schwartz, D. & Malach-Pines, A. (2007). High technology entrepreneurs versus small business owners in Israel. *The Journal of Entrepreneurship, 16*(1), 1–17.

Schwartz, J., Stapp, H., & Beauregard, M. (2005). Quantum physics in neuroscience and psychology: A neurophysical model of mind–brain interaction. *Philosophical Transactions of the Royal Society, 360*(1458), 1309–1327.

Segal, H. (1981). *The work of Hanna Segal. A Kleinian approach to clinical practice.* NY: Jason Aronson.

Seitanidi, M., & Crane, A. (2009). Implementing CSR through partnerships: Understanding the selection, design and institutionalization of nonprofit-business partnerships. *Journal of Business Ethics, 85*(2), 413–429. doi:10.1007/s10551-008-9743-y.

Senge, P. M. (1990). *The Fifth Discipline.* NY: Doubleday/Currency.

Senge, P., Kleiner, A., Roberts, C., Ross, R., & Smith, B. (1994). *The fifth discipline field book.* NY: Doubleday.

Senge, P., Smith, B., Krushwitz, N., Laur, J., & Schley, S. (2008). *The necessary revolution: Working together to create a sustainable world.* NY: Doubleday

Shah, A. (2010). Poverty facts and stats. Global issues. Retrieved October 10, 2012 from http://www.globalissues.org/article/26/poverty-facts-and-stats

Shamay-Tsoory, S. (2011). The neural bases for empathy. *Neuroscientist, 17*(1), 18–24.

Shamay-Tsoory, S. G., Aharon-Peretz, J., & Perry, D. (2009). Two systems for empathy: A double dissociation between emotional and cognitive empathy in inferior frontal gyrus versus ventromedial prefrontal lesions. *Brain, 132*(3), 617–627.

Shamay-Tsoory, S. G., Tomer, R., Goldsher, D., Berger, B. D., & Aharon-Peretz, J. (2004). Impairment in cognitive and affective empathy in patients with brain lesions: Anatomical and cognitive correlates. *Journal of Clinical and Experimental Neuropsychology, 28*(8), 1113–1127.

Shapiro, J. (2002). How do physicians teach empathy in the primary care setting? *Academic Medicine, 77*(4), 323–328.

Shapiro, S. L., Brown, K. W., Thoresen, C., & Plante, T. G. (2011). The moderation of mindfulness-based stress reduction effects by trait mindfulness: Results from a randomized controlled trial. *Journal of Clinical Psychology, 67*(3), 267–277. doi: 10.1002/jclp.20761

Shapiro, S. L., Schwartz, G. E., & Bonner, G. (1998). Effects of mindfulness-based stress reduction on medical and premedical students. *Journal of Behavioral Medicine, 21*(6), 581–599.

Shear, J. (2006). Transcendental Meditation. In J. Shear (Ed.), *The Experience of meditation: Experts introduce the major traditions* (pp. 23–48). St. Paul, MN: Paragon House.

Shutte, A. (1993). *Philosophy for Africa.* Milwaukee, WI: Marquette University Press.

Shutte, A. (2001). *Ubuntu: An ethic for a new South Africa.* Republic of South Africa: Cluster.

Siegel, D. J. (2007). *Mindful Brain.* NY: W.W. Norton & Company, Inc.

Siegler, M., Reaven, N., Lipinski, R., & Stocking, C. (1987). Effect of role-model clinicians on students' attitudes in a second-year course on introduction to the patient. *Journal of Medical Education, 62*, 935–937.

Silvia, P. J., & Duval, T. S. (2001). Objective self-awareness theory: Recent progress and enduring problems. *Personality and Social Psychology Review, 5*, 230–241.

Simons, T., Pelled, L. H., & Smith, K. A. (1999). Making use of difference: Diversity, debate, and decision comprehensiveness in top management teams. *Academy of Management Journal, 42*(6), 662–673.

Singer, T., & Lamm, C. (2009). The social neuroscience of empathy. *Annals of The New York Academy of Sciences, 1156*(1), 81–96.

Skinner, B. F. (1974). *About behaviorism.* NY: Knopft

Skinner, C., & Spurgeon, P. (2005). Valuing empathy and emotional intelligence in health leadership: A study of empathy, leadership behavior and outcome effectiveness. *Health Services Management Research, 18*(1), 1–12.

So, K. T., & Orme-Johnson, D. W. (2001). Three randomized experiments on the longitudinal effects of the transcendental meditation technique on cognition. *Intelligence, 29*, 419–440.

Solms, M. (2000). Preliminaries for an integration of psychoanalysis and neuroscience. In J. A. Winer (Ed.), *The annual of psychoanalysis* (pp. 179–200). 28. Hillsdale, NJ: The Analytic Press.

Spencer, J. (2004). Decline in empathy in medical education: How can we stop the rot? *Medical Education, 38*, 916–918.

Stansbury, J., & Sonenshein, S. (2012). Positive business ethics: Grounding and elaborating a theory. In K. S. Cameron & G. M. Spreitzer (Eds.), *The Oxford handbook of positive organizational scholarship* (pp. 340–352). Oxford:: Oxford University Press.

Stein, S.J., Papadogiannis, P., Yip, J.A., & Sitarenios, G. (2009). Emotional intelligence of leaders: A profile of top executives. *Leadership & Organization Development Journal, 30*(1), 87–101.

Stepien, K.A., & Baernstein, A. (2006). Educating for empathy: A review. *Journal of General Internal Medicine, 21*, 524–530.

Stocks, E.L., Lishner, D.A., & Decker, S.K. (2009). Altruism or psychological escape: Why does empathy promote prosocial behavior? *European Journal of Social Psychology, 39*, 649–665. doi: 10.1002/ejsp.561

Stratton, T.D., Saunders, J.A., & Elam, C.L. (2008). Changes in medical students' emotional intelligence: An exploratory study. *Teaching and Learning in Medicine, 20*, 279–284.

Talbot, M. (1991). *Holographic Universe*. NY: Harper Collins.

Tangney, J.P., Stuewig, J., & Mashek, D.J. (2007). Moral emotions and moral behavior. *Annual Review of Psychology, 58*, 345–372. doi: 10.1146/annurev. psych.56.091103.070145

Tappin, S., & Cave, A. (2010). *The new secrets of CEO's*. Boston: Nicholas Brealey.

ten Cate, T.J., & De Haes, J.C.J.M. (2000). Summative assessment of medical students in the affective domain. *Medical Teacher, 22*, 40–43.

Tenbrunsel, A.E., & Smith-Crowe, K. (2008). Ethical decision making: Where we've been and where we're going. *The Academy of Management Annals, 2*, 545–607. doi: 10.1080/19416520802211677

Thatcher, R. W, Krause, P., & Hrybyk, M. (1986). Cortico-cortical associations and EEG coherence: A two-compartmental model. *Electroencephalography Clinical Neurophysiology, 64*(2):123–143.

Thatcher, R.W., North, D.M., & Biver, C.J. (2008). Development of cortical connections as measured by EEG coherence and phase delays. *Human Brain Mapping, 29*(12), 1400–1415.

Thomas, J.T., & Otis, M.D. (2010). Intrapsychic predictors of professional quality of life: Mindfulness, empathy, and emotional separation. *Journal of the Society for Social Work and Research, 1*(2), 83–98.

Tichy, N. (2009). Lafley's legacy: From crisis to consumer-driven. Businessweek Online, 14. Retrieved from http://www.businessweek.com/managing/content/jun2009/ca20090610_248094.htm

Tipsord, J.M. (2009). *The effects of mindfulness training and individual differences in mindfulness on social perception and empathy*. Dissertation, Dissertation Abstracts International: Section B: *The Sciences and Engineering, 70*(11-B), 7273.

Tolle, E. (2004). *The power of now*. Adelaide, Australia: Hachette.

Tolle, E. (2005). *A new earth: Create a better life*. London: Penguin.

Torneke, N. (2010). *Learning RFT*. Oakland, CA: New Harbinger Publications.

Travis, F. (1979). The TM technique and creativity: A longitudinal study of Cornell University undergraduates. *The Journal of Creative Behavior, 13*, 169–180.

Travis, F.T., Arenander, A., & DuBois, D. (2004) Psychological and physiological characteristics of a proposed object-referral/self-referral continuum of self-awareness. *Consciousness and Cognition, 13*(2), 401–420.

Travis, F., Haaga, D., Hagelin, J., Arenander, A., Tanner, M., & Schneider, R. (2010). A self-referential default brain state: Patterns of coherence, power, and eLORETA sources during eyes-closed rest and Transcendental Meditation practice. *Cognitive Processing, 11*(1), 21–30.

Travis, F., Harung, H.S., & Lagrosen, Y. (2011). Moral development, executive functioning, peak experiences and brain patterns in professional and amateur classical musicians: Interpreted in light of a Unified Theory of Performance. *Consciousness and Cognition, 20*(4), 1256–1264.

Travis, F., & Pearson, C. (2000). Pure consciousness: distinct phenomenological and physiological correlates of "consciousness itself." *The International Journal of Neuroscience, 100*, 1–4.

Travis, F., & Shear, J. (2010). Focused attention, open monitoring and automatic self-transcending: Categories to organize meditations from Vedic, Buddhist and Chinese traditions. *Consciousness and Cognition, 19*, 1110–1119.

Travis, F. T., Tecce, J., Arenander, A., &Wallace, R. K. (2002). Patterns of EEG coherence, power, and contingent negative variation characterize the integration of transcendental and waking states. *Biological Psychology, 61*, 293–319.

Travis, F., & Wallace, R.K. (1999). Autonomic and EEG patterns during eyes-closed rest and Transcendental Meditation (TM) practice: The basis for a neural model of TM practice. *Consciousness and Cognition, 8*(3), 302–318.

Trope, Y., & Liberman, N. (2010). Construal-level theory of psychological distance. *Psychological Review, 117*(2), 440–463.

Trout, J. (2009).*Why empathy matters*. NY: Penguin.

Turnbull, O.H., & Solms, M. (2007). Awareness, desire, and false beliefs: Freud in the light of modern neuropsychology. *Cortex, 43*(8), 1083–1090.

Tutu, D.M. (1999).*No future without forgiveness*. NY: Doubleday.

Van Lange, P. (2008). Does empathy trigger only altruistic motivation? How about selflessness or justice? *Emotions, 8*(6), 766–774.

Venter, E. (2004). The notion of *Ubuntu* and communalism in African educational discourse. *Studies in Philosophy and Education, 23*, 149–160.

Verhaert, G.A., & Van den Poel, D. (2010). Empathy as added value in predicting donation behavior. *Journal of Business Research, 64*, 1288–1295. doi: 10.1016/j.jbusres.2010.12.024

Vilardaga, R. Estévez, A., Levin, M.E., & Hayes, S.C. (2012). Deictic relational Responding, empathy and experiential avoidance as predictors of social anhedonia: Further contributions from relational frame theory. *The Psychological Record, 62*(3), 409–432.

Waddock, S. (2009). Leading corporate citizens. NY: McGraw-Hill Irwin.

Wai, M., & Tiliopoulos, N. (2012). The affective and cognitive empathic nature of the dark triad of personality. *Personality and Individual Differences, 52*, 794–799.

Wälder, R. (1936). The principle of multiple function: Observations on over-determination. *Psychoanalytic Quarterly, 5*,45–62.

Walter, F., Cole, M.S., & Humphrey, R.H. (2011). Emotional intelligence: Sine qua non of leadership or folderol? *The Academy of Management Perspectives, 25*(1), 45.

Wear, D. (2002). "Face-to-face with it": Medical students' narratives about their end-of-life education. *Academic Medicine, 77*, 271–277.

Weng, H.-C., Steed, J.F., Yu, S.-W., Liu, Y.-T., Hsu, C.-C. Yu, T.-J., & Chen, W. (2011). The effect of surgeon empathy and emotional intelligence on patient satisfaction. *Advances in Health Sciences Education, 16*, 591–600.

Westen, Drew (1990). Psychoanalytic approaches to personality. In L.A. Pervin (Ed.), *A handbook of personality: Theory and research* (pp. 21–65). NY: Guilford Press.

Westley, F., & Mintzberg, H. (1989). Visionary leadership and strategic management. *Strategic Management Journal, 10*, 17–32.

Wheatley, M.J. (1992). *Leadership and the new science: Learning about organization from an orderly universe*. San Francisco: Berrett-Koehler.

Whitman, M., & Hamilton, J.O. (2010). *The power of many*. NY: Three Rivers.

Wilson C.B. (2011). Mirroring processes, religious perception and ecological adaptation: Toward an empathic theory of religion. *Journal for the Study of Religion, Nature & Culture, 5*(3), 307–326.

Wimmer, H., & Perner, J. (1983). Beliefs about beliefs: Representation and constraining function of wrong beliefs in young children's understanding of deception. *Cognition, 13*(1), 103–128. doi: 10.1016/0010-0277(83)90004-5

Winnicott, D. W. (1953). Transitional objects and transitional phenomena—A study of the first not-me possession. *International Journal of Psycho-Analysis, 34,* 89–97.

Winnicott, D. W. (1965). *The maturational processes and the facilitating environment: Studies in the theory of emotional development.* NY: International Universities Press.

Wolpert, S. (2009, October 8). Last time carbon dioxide levels were this high: 15 million years ago, scientists report. UCLA Newsroom.

Woltin, K. A., Corneille, O., Yzerbyt, V. Y., & Förster, J. (2011). Narrowing down to open up for other people's concerns: Empathic concern can be enhanced by inducing detailed processing. *Journal of Experimental Social Psychology, 47,* 418–425.

World Footprint (2012). Global Footprint Network. Retrieved August 10, 2012 from http://www.footprintnetwork.org/en/index.php/GFN/page/world_footprint/

Wright, W. F., & Bower, G. H. (1992). Mood effects on subjective probability assessment. *Organizational Behavior & Human Decision Processes, 52,* 276–291.

Zajonc, R. B. (1980). Feeling and thinking: Preferences need no inferences. *American Psychologist, 35*(2): 151–175.

Zajonc, R. B. (1984). On the primacy if affect. *American Psychologist, 39*(2), 117–123.

Zaleznik, A. (1977). Managers and leaders—are they different? *Harvard Business Review, 55*(3), 67–78.

Zaleznik, A., & Kets de Vries, M. (1975). *Power and the corporate mind.* Boston: Houghton-Mifflin.

Contributors

Paul Atkins, is an Associate Professor in Organisational Behaviour at the Crawford School of Public Policy, Australian National University (ANU). He holds degrees in Psychology and Cognitive Science and his PhD was conducted at the Applied Psychology Unit, University of Cambridge. His research on mindfulness draws upon both traditional and modern scientific understandings, particularly Relational Frame Theory. His research focuses on better understanding the effects of mindfulness and psychological flexibility on identity, work attitudes, communication and relationships. He teaches courses in organisational behaviour, leadership and mindfulness. He has recently published an article in Academy of Management Review exploring the effects of Acceptance and Commitment Training upon compassionate behaviour in organisations.

Dunia Harajli Berry, is a lecturer of Management and Communications Skills at the Lebanese American University (LAU). She is a Doctoral Candidate at Grenoble École de Management. She is vice president of an NGO that works on alleviating human suffering. As a volunteer for the UNDP, she researched CSR/ Business Community Relations in Lebanon extensively. She is a certified Emotional Intelligence trainer (MSCEIT certificate) and her teaching and research explore the realms of corporate social responsibility, workplace spirituality, empathy, Islamic business ethics, emotional/ spiritual intelligence and education.

Miles Bore, gained his PhD in Psychology in 2001 and is currently a Senior Lecturer and Head of the School of Psychology at the University of Newcastle Australia. Miles' research interests are in the areas of personality, moral decision making and psychometrics. He has worked with Don Munro and David Powis since 1996 on developing a model of medical student selection and the Personal Quality Assessment (PQA) measures of moral orientation, mental agility and relevant health professional personality traits.

Joerg Dietz, is a Full Professor Organizational Behavior and Associate Dean of Faculty and Research in the Faculty of Business and Economics at the University of Lausanne, Switzerland. He has also held long-term academic positions in the United States and Canada and has taught in several other European and Asian countries. Prior to his academic career, he worked in the investment banking department of a German bank. Joerg earned his Ph.D. in Organizational Behavior from Tulane University. His research interests include cross-cultural management, workplace diversity and contextual antecedents of organizational behavior, and his research has been published in journals such as the *Academy of Management Journal*, the *Journal of Applied Psychology*, and *Organizational Behavior and Human Decision Processes*. He has won numerous research awards including most recently the 2010 Carolyn Dexter Award for best international research paper at the Academy of Management Conference and the 2009 Saroj Parasuraman Award for the outstanding publication of the year in the area of gender and diversity from the GDO division of the Academy of Management.

Caroline Doran, has a PhD in Organization and Management. She began her management career in Brittany France as a management intern in 1988 and left industry in 2004 to pursue a career in teaching. During that time she worked in London, Corsica, Alaska, New York, and San Francisco in various management positions in the hospitality sector. Caroline currently teaches Business Ethics and Social Responsibility in addition to Global Perspectives in Business and Society at Saint Mary's College of California.

Lori Gano-Overway (PhD), is an associate professor at Bridgewater College where she teaches sport and exercise psychology, organization and administration of physical activity programs, and research methods. Her research focuses on how the climate created by coaches and physical educators can positively influence youth development, achievement motivation, and good sport conduct. She has served on the executive board member for the National Council for the Accreditation of Coaching Education (NCACE) and as the social psychology section chair for the Association of Applied Sport Psychology. She is a former intercollegiate swimmer and currently enjoys hiking and biking for leisure.

Dennis Heaton (PhD), is Professor of Management and Director of the Ph.D. Program in Management at Maharishi University of Management in Fairfield, Iowa, USA. His work focuses on ethical business practice in light of the full range of human development as understood within Western psychology and the Eastern Vedic tradition. Dr. Heaton's articles about spirituality in management have been published in numerous journals including *Journal of Management, Spirituality and Religion; the Journal of Organizational Change Management; the Journal of Management Education;* and *the*

Journal of Human Values. He has contributed chapters in nine prior books and is the volume editor of *Consciousness-Based Education and Management.* Fairfield, IA: Maharishi University of Management Press.

Veronika Kisfalvi (MBA, HEC Montréal; Ph.D., McGill University), is professor of Management at HEC Montréal, where she teaches courses on leadership, management skills and managerial decision making. Her current research interests focus on leaders and their development, the relationships between personality, emotions and strategic decision making, top management team dynamics and reflexivity in qualitative research. Her work has appeared in *Journal of Business Venturing, Journal of Management Inquiry, Organization Studies* and *Management,* among others. Prior to her academic career, Prof. Kisfalvi held management positions in both private sector and not-for-profit organizations.

Emmanuelle P. Kleinlogel, (Faculty of Business and Economics, University of Lausanne, Switzerland) is PhD candidate in Management with a specialization in Organizational Behavior. Her main research interest includes the expression of prejudice, employment discrimination, moral disengagement, and compliant behavior.

Keiko Krahnke, is Associate Professor of Management at the University of Northern Colorado. She has research interest in empathy, systems thinking, ethics, and spirituality. Her recent publications include an article in Journal of Business Ethics and Best Paper Proceedings of the Academy of Management. She has served as Chair of Management, Spirituality and Religion at the Academy of Management.

Vassili Joannidès, is a professor of management at Grenoble École de Management and Queensland University of Technology School of Accountancy and the founding partner of De Burg & Associés. His research investigates the religious foundations of accountability, finance and management as well as hetereodox practices within ethnic communities. He is an associate editor of the *Journal of Accounting & Organizational Change.*

Anthony F. Libertella, is a Professor of Management and Law at Adelphi University, School of Business. Dr. Libertella formerly served as the Dean of the Adelphi University School of Business for eight years. He has served as the editor and co-editor of two academic business journals and recently served as the Section Editor (business law) of the *Journal of Business Ethics* (Netherlands). His current research focuses on leadership, strategy, and the legal environment of business. He received his B.A. from Iona College and his M.A. and Ph.D. degrees from The Ohio State University. In addition, he received his J.D. degree from St. John's University School of Law.

Don Munro, received his degrees in psychology from Manchester and London Universities in UK. He spent the first part of his career at the Universities of Zambia and Rhodesia/Zimbabwe, where he developed interests in cross-cultural and applied psychology and in personality and psychometrics. The latter part of his career has been at the university of Newcastle, Australia. Now retired from full-time academic teaching, he has worked since the late 1990s with colleagues Miles Bore and David Powis on a research and development program for improving selection for medical schools, and particularly on developing selection tests in the non-cognitive area.

Samuel Natale (PhD), is a graduate of the University of Oxford. He is Professor of Strategy and Ethics, at the Willumstadt School of Business, Adelphi University, N.Y. as well as Senior Research Associate, Department of Educational Studies, University of Oxford, England and Associate Fellow of SKOPE, University of Oxford. Concomitantly, he is Visiting Scholar, Blackfriars Hall, Oxford. Previously, he has been visiting fellow of Kellogg College as well as Mansfield College within the university. He is an has authored/edited over 28 books and hundreds of professional and academic articles. He is the Editor in Chief of the *International Journal of Decision Ethics* as well as Section editor of *The Journal of Business Ethics*. Dr. Natale serves on many other journal boards.

Larry E. Pate (Ph.D., University of Illinois), is Senior Partner and Chief Learning Officer of Decision Systems International, an education, training, and consulting firm dedicated to helping individuals make better decisions in their professional and personal lives. Previously, he taught at the University of Southern California, University of Wisconsin-Madison, and most recently held the Burwell Endowed Chair at the University of North Dakota, USA. He was the Inaugural Visiting Fellow of the Australia and New Zealand Academy of Management

David Powis (PhD), has been a university teacher of, and researcher in, physiology and medical education since 1972. At the University of Newcastle, Australia he has developed a professional interest and worked extensively in the area of medical student selection with the aim of establishing fair principles and appropriate strategy for selecting students for health professional courses. Since 1997 he has worked with Miles Bore and Don Munro to develop and evaluate the Personal Qualities Assessment (www.pqa.net.au) as an instrument for this strategy.

Peter Senge, is a senior lecturer at the Massachusetts Institute of Technology and founding chair of the SoL (Society for Organizational Learning) Council. He is the author of The Fifth Discipline: The Art and Practice of the Learning Organization, co-author of the three related fieldbooks,

Presence: An Exploration of Profound Change in People, Society, and Organizations and most recently, The Necessary Revolution: How Individuals and Organizations are Working Together to Create a Sustainable World. Peter lectures throughout the world about decentralizing the role of leadership in organizations to enhance the capacity of all people to work toward healthier human systems.

Traci Shoblom, is Senior Partner and Chief Marketing Officer of Decision Systems International, an education, training, and consulting firm dedicated to helping individuals make better decisions in their professional and personal lives. Previously, she worked with several management thought-leaders, such as Marshall Goldsmith and Ken Blanchard, and conducted more than 7,500 executive coaching sessions around the world.

Fred Travis (PhD), is Director of the Center for Brain, Consciousness and Cognition at Maharishi University of Management where he is also Dean of the Graduate School. The purpose of the Brain Center is to delineate brain and physiological functioning during higher stages of human development. His research has developed and applied a Brain Integration Scale to measure integrated brain functioning. He has numerous publications in journals such as *Managerial Decision, International Journal of Psychophysiology, International Journal of Neuroscience,* and *Biological Psychology.*

Joanna Beth Tweedy, is the founding editor and host of *Quiddity* International Literary Journal and Public-Radio Program, housed at Benedictine University and distributed by NPR-member WUIS. She is the author of *The Yonder Side of Sass and Texas* (Southeast Missouri University Press, 2009), and her poetry and fiction have been published in journals and anthologies and have received honors from *Glimmer Train,* the Southern Women Writers Conference, and the Ray Bradbury Creative Writing Contest, among others. An ardent foreign-adventurist with chronic and gravitational homesoil leanings, Tweedy is a native of Little Egypt in the Shawnee Hills of southernmost Illinois.